remove this checkout from your record.
re date due.

THE WALLED TOWNS OF IRELAND: 1

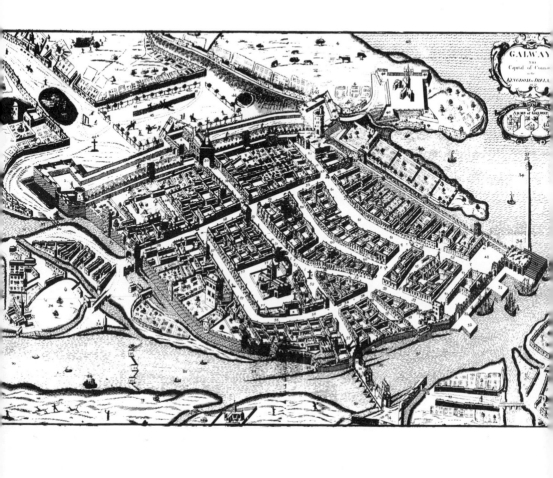

The Walled Towns of Ireland

Volume 1

AVRIL THOMAS

IRISH ACADEMIC PRESS

This book was typeset by
Seton Music Graphics Ltd, Bantry,
for Irish Academic Press, Kill Lane,
Blackrock, Co. Dublin.

British Library Cataloguing in Publication Data
A catalogue record for this book
is available from the British Library

ISBN 0–7165–2474–0 Volume 1
ISBN 0–7165–2475–9 Volume 2
Set ISBN 0–7165–2481–3

ACKNOWLEDGEMENTS

All the illustrations listed on p. viii were provided by the author,
with the exception of the following, for which due acknowl-
edgment is made: nos. 2 and 5, to The National Library of Ireland;
no. 3 to the Ordnance Survey; frontispiece and nos. 6 and 11 to
Trinity College Library; no. 7 to His Grace the Archbishop of
Canterbury and the Trustees of Lambeth Palace Library; no. 8 to
the Marquess of Salisbury; no. 10 to the Public Record Office,
Kew; no. 21 to National Maritime Museum, Greenwich; nos. 14
and 25 to Duffner Brothers of Drogheda.

Printed and bound by Billings & Sons, Worcestershire

Contents

For my family

List of Tables, Figures, Maps and Illustrations

Preface

The research for this book involved contact with many individuals and institutions, and much delving in published works. I am happy to record my indebtedness to those whose ideas have been influential and to those who have given practical help—teachers, former academic colleagues, librarians and their assistants, family and friends. While it would be nice to be able to express one's gratitude simply but sincerely in this way, there are some individuals whose contribution cannot thus be acknowledged adequately.

I am particularly grateful for the assistance afforded me over many years in the Manuscript Room of Trinity College, Dublin, and in the Irish Library at Coleraine, and for the privileged access that I was allowed with regard to the historical collections of the Royal Dublin Society and the University of Ulster. Like many others, I have benefitted greatly from the generous assistance that was so characteristic of Professor J.H. Andrews, until recently at Trinity College, Dublin. His expertise, especially in the field of Irish cartography, has been of much value and I owe the idea for this book to a lecture from his undergraduate course in Irish historical geography. I am happy to record, too, my gratitude to a number of academics associated with the University of Ulster at Coleraine—Dr K.L. Wallwork, Dr D. McCourt, Dr B.J. Graham and Dr M. Poole—and to Dr R.E. Glasscock of Cambridge University, all of whom have helped with comments on the text. Nonetheless, the views expressed there are my responsibility alone, as are the errors that may have eluded careful scrutiny.

The research was begun at the University of Leicester and continued at Dublin and Coleraine, and I am grateful to those institutions for financial and technical support. Photographic reproduction was carried out principally by Mr N. McDowell of the Geography Department at Coleraine. I appreciate very much the careful attention he gave to matters of detail, particularly with regard to the maps. Equally, I am grateful to Mr Michael Adams and his colleagues at Irish Academic Press for the care they have taken and for their advice over matters of detail in the final stages.

Thanks are also due to my husband for his constant encouragement and to our children for their tolerance. My sister, Dorothy Elliott, undertook the considerable burden of typing the various stages of the text with expertise and good humour. I thank her and her husband, who organised the computer processing, and also their sons who were very competent assistants. I am very happy, too, to be able to express my gratitude to my parents, without whose support for my education no research would have been possible.

Finally, I have pleasure in recording my gratitude to those with whom I stayed on visits throughout Ireland. These often took me, armed with camera and map, into the back streets and hidden places of Irish towns, sometimes to the amazement of the residents. Such areas usually proved much more interesting and memorable than the better known thoroughfares. I hope that this book will encourage others to explore Irish towns, especially those which were, or may have been, walled, and will be useful to some who may be inspired to study their own towns in greater depth.

Note: The sources for the evidence used in the following chapters are cited in detail in the gazetteer entries for individual walled towns in volume 2.

CHAPTER 1

Introduction

IRISH WALLED TOWNS

The research on which this book is based had two main objects. The first was the identification of walled towns in Ireland.[1] In the context of Irish historical documents this often required the approach of a detective, involving as it did the piecing together of apparently unconnected and often meagre shreds of evidence. The second object, to consider comparatively the towns that had been identified, required a much broader scale of activity. This was because it involved the possible impact of the walled circuit on the development of the town, both as a morphological entity and as a centre of population.

For some towns the first object presents no problems in so far as parts of the curtain wall, gates or towers survive. The best known is Londonderry, largely because of the famous siege which took place eighty years after the town wall was built. Also, despite this event, the walled circuit there remains today not only almost completely intact but visibly so, due to its location along the upper edges of the hill site. Indeed, Derry is so obviously Ireland's 'premier' walled town that its place as a comparatively recent example of a not-uncommon breed is easily overlooked. This is, perhaps, inevitable as so much of the fabric of Irish towns has been destroyed in the course of a long and frequently turbulent history. Even so, remnants of the town defences can still be seen at a number of other places. Amongst the best are Dublin, Drogheda, Kilkenny, Clonmel, Waterford, Youghal, Limerick and Athenry. In addition, increasingly in recent years, archaeological investigations have started to reveal structures long buried. Notable examples here are the successive Hiberno-Norse defences of the original waterfront at Dublin, short stretches of the later medieval town wall with its towers at Cork, and the foundations of large and elaborate Norman gatehouses at Limerick and Waterford. For other towns there is the evidence of early maps, a graphic and valuable source but, at its earliest, one which refers to the immediate post-medieval period, by which time many walled circuits were centuries old. Purely written forms of documentary evidence may also be available which relate to the formative or early phases of their development. These include eye-witness descriptions made by citizens or visitors, property deeds of burgesses or other landowners, town records which may recite regulations for the use of the defensive system, and charters from the king or the local lord. The last may be general or specific to defence when the term 'murage' is used. The prime purpose of such grants was the financing of town wall construction and maintenance. They were granted from the early thirteenth century in Ireland, as in England, often at increasingly frequent intervals. Similar provisions were included in many seventeenth century charters of incorporation and indeed, in some cases, the customs allowed in them were still being collected in the early nineteenth century. By then, of course, the proceeds were not being used for the original purpose, nor could have been so used, because at most towns the walls had long ceased to exist as an effective system. For yet other towns, however, the evidence is less than satisfactory in quantity, being limited to a single document such as a murage grant. Sometimes the evidence is limited in quality too. Then it may be equivocal or, at worst, secondary and uncorroborated. Problems of evidence are inevitable in any historical research in Ireland because of the chequered fate suffered by many of its documents, both state and private. These, and the problems, are discussed in detail in chapter 2. Nonetheless, given the resulting residual nature of the documentary evidence, coupled with the high rate of destruction of field evidence, it is, perhaps, surprising that so many Irish towns can be proved to have been walled. There are more than fifty, for most of which the details of the walled circuit are either known or can be partially reconstructed (Table 1.1, list A). To these may be added over thirty where the 'intention to wall' can be demonstrated, an intention which for some may well have become a reality (Table 1.1, list B). There is a further small group for which the evidence is as yet very slight, those appended to list B as 'doubtful'. Further work in the archives may result in the discovery of previously unknown documents and, potentially now more rewarding although expensive, increased archaeological investigation may enhance our knowledge considerably. As a result the discovery of new sites and the 'upgrading' of some currently on list B remains a possibility. Mullingar is a case in point following very recent research (Andrews forthcoming). Another possibility is the 'downgrading' of a few sites on list A, the evidence for which is not as fully corroborated as that for the majority. Therefore, neither of these lists should be regarded as 'set in stone' but merely as a basis for study. They are a convenient means of dealing with a range of evidence and, to a considerable degree, they are also a reflection of the extent of sources currently available for any particular site.

Not all the settlements concerned are towns today, and some may never have so functioned, although most had the legal status of chartered borough. But, all the largest towns and cities of present-day Ireland are included, except for those which have developed in the last century as industrial or dormitory towns. Also, over half of the present medium sized towns (populations in the range of 10,000–20,000) and half of the small towns (5000–10,000) were once walled towns too.[2] Looking back to earlier periods, the prominence of walled towns within the urban system is very clear. In a set of *Plans Of The Principal Towns, Forts And Harbours In Ireland*, published in 1744 and 1751,[3] thirteen towns were included, all walled. Indeed, the dominant feature of most of these plans is the wall surrounding almost the entire town. This is particularly so in the case of the four Ulster towns illustrated—Belfast, Carrickfergus, Coleraine and Londonderry— but is likewise true of Galway, Athlone, Limerick and Waterford. Only Dublin and Cork were by then spreading out beyond their medieval walled circuits but Drogheda, on a map of the Boyne valley, is depicted just by the outline of its walls. In this case the walled circuit was used as a short-hand device to represent the town itself. Clearly, these towns were not just relics of the Middle Ages

Table 1.1: Identification

LIST A: WALLED TOWNS

1 Adare
2 Ardee
3 Athboy
4 Athenry
5 Athlone
6 Athy
7 Bandon
8 Belfast
9 Buttevant
10 Callan
11 Carlingford
12 Carlow
13 Carrickfergus
14 Carrick-on-Suir
15 Cashel
16 Castledermot
17 Clonmel
18 Clonmines
19 Coleraine

20 Cork
21 Dingle
22 Downpatrick
23 Drogheda
24 Dublin
25 Dundalk
26 Dungarvan
27 Fethard
28 Fore
29 Galway
30 Gowran
31 Inistioge
32 Jamestown
33 Kells(Meath)
34 Kildare
35 Kilkenny
36 Kilmallock
37 Kinsale
38 Limerick

39 Londonderry
40 Loughrea
41 Maryborough (Port Laoise)
42 Naas
43 Navan (An Uaimh)
44 Nenagh
45 New Ross
46 Newry
47 Philipstown (Daingean)
48 Rindown
49 Roscommon
50 Thomastown
51 Thurles
52 Tipperary
53 Trim
54 Waterford
55 Wexford
56 Youghal

CRITERIA: *Physical remains of town wall or towers,* and/or *a range of documentary evidence comprising maps, verbal descriptions, land deeds, murage and other town records.*

LIST B: UNPROVEN—SOME EVIDENCE FOR WALLING

1 Ardfert
2 Arklow
3 Armagh
4 Askeaton
5 Burris
6 Caherconlish
7 Calverstown
8 Castleroche
9 Croom
10 Crumlin
11 Dalkey
12 Dunmore

13 Emly
14 Ferns
15 Garth
16 Kilcullen
17 Leighlin
18 Lifford
19 Mallow
20 Monaghan
21 Mullingar
22 Mourne/Mora
23 Mulsoecourt
24 Newcastle Mackinegan

25 Newtown Blathewyc
26 Portarlington
27 Rathkeale
28 Rosscarbery
29 Siddan
30 Sligo
31 Tallaght
32 Timolin
33 Tralee
34 Tullow
35 Wicklow

CRITERIA: *single medieval murage record, later walled town proposal or contemporary description.*

APPENDIX TO LIST B

Evidence doubtful because: (a) secondary only; or (b) murage applied to another feature or town; or (c) equivocal field/map or other written documents.

Antrim
Ardglass
Aughrim
Birr
Bunratty
Carrick-on-Shannon
Cavan

Charlemont
Clane
Dublin area towns
Enniscorthy
Gorey
Inishannon
Jerpoint

Kells-in-Ossory
Letteragh
Louth
Newcastle
Omagh
Tallow

Map 5.g shows location of lists A and B sites.

3

because they included some walled within the previous century, as well as some where the medieval defences had been upgraded or modernised. A century earlier, in the almost complete *Census of 1659* (ed. Pender 1939), all the top twenty towns listed were walled towns, as were most of the next twenty. For Elizabethan Ireland, some commentators have given a total of forty-three walled towns.[4] This figure is based, apparently, on a study of contemporary maps (MacCurtain 1972, 1). It is quite feasible when compared with those in Table 1.1, list A, due allowance having been made for the demise of some medieval settlements like Rindown and the development, later, of others such as Bandon. Indeed, the significance of walled towns was often emphasised in reports and accounts of both the Tudor and Stuart periods. In them 'walled town' was used as a category, distinct from and superior to 'town' or 'market town'. In a 1598 work,[5] for example, which covered much of the island on a county basis but not always in a consistent manner, twenty-six 'walled towns' were noted, all in Table 1.1, list A.

The second object, the comparative study of walled towns, is carried out here, whenever possible, chiefly in terms of the date or period of walling; the type of settlement when the town wall was built and now; the size and shape of the walled area; the structural form of the circuit and the nature of the site. The manner in which each of these aspects is distributed throughout Ireland is also considered. Such bases for comparison involve in themselves considerable variety; for example, the dates of walling range from the medieval to the early modern, that is from the earliest, the Hiberno-Norse, through the long Anglo-Norman period to the time of the sixteenth and seventeenth century Tudor and Stuart Plantations. Today, these settlements encompass villages like Jamestown and Adare and most types of Irish towns, including the capitals and largest cities of Dublin and Belfast.

Inevitably, some towns can be studied more intensively than others and so they will be basic to the general conclusions that are be drawn. Each site is dealt with as fully as possible in the gazetteer where a common format is used, with an abbreviated version for those in Table 1.1, list B, about which little is yet known. The entries start with a brief background, both historical and geographical, and the site is described. All surviving sections of the walled circuit, or related but now isolated structures, are listed under the heading of 'physical remains', including those structures that survived into into this century or have been revealed briefly in archaeological or other excavations. Where appropriate, features such as gates, which are still recorded in place names, are noted too. The next section is concerned with the available documentary evidence, or a relevant selection of it where the store is rich. The details of the circuit thus revealed are then displayed and analysed in relation to the site, other defensive elements such as castles, and the town plan, as it has evolved. Each entry ends with a review of the literature, where necessary, and a list of references specific to the site. Other sources of a more general nature that are used in each entry are detailed fully in the main bibliography. A map accompanies each entry for list A. It shows the known or presumed outline of the town wall in relation to castles or forts and the basic street system, dominant topographic features and focal points, such as churches and market areas. The gazetteer is structured, therefore, to stand on its own as a work of reference. At the same time it is the repository on which the chapters of this study are based, the source of the details from which the broader picture is drawn and comparisons made. Consequently, references which are detailed in the gazetteer are not repeated here in the text except when it is essential for reasons of clarity or convenience.

Problems of definition, both general and specific, inevitably arise in such a study. 'What is a town?' is a problem common to both historians and geographers, and it obviously has a relevance here, particularly for the more distant, medieval period. It will be discussed in the section below along with a consideration of the nature of a town wall. At this stage it may be useful to indicate that 'wall' is a deceptively simple term. It should not be read as meaning necessarily, or only, 'of stone', although most Irish walled towns had a stone curtain wall. In addition, a series of non-stone features were often associated with it; for example an earthen rampart, wooden buildings such as small towers, a water-filled fosse without, and an access space within. Moreover, the circuit might change with time, for instance a wooden stockade might be replaced *in situ* by a stone wall or a medieval stone circuit might be strengthened later by the addition of earthen structures more suited to the use of cannon. The disposition of key features such as gates might also change considerably through the centuries. Furthermore, there was not necessarily one town wall, simple or splendid, at any one site. It is known, for example, that there were probably three major extensions to the original circuit at Dublin and two at Waterford. The internal walls, which were thus produced, were not necessarily removed, but could, and did in these cases, result in visual, if not administrative, 'double walled towns'. At river-crossings opposite, rather than adjacent, double walled towns were possible too. Some of these were both separate and, indeed, rival walled administrations for much of their history. In yet other cases, suburban developments had prominent gates, and this adds further to the variety.

Therefore, in Ireland, walled towns were not uncommon and could vary considerably, from the simple to the complex, both in structure and outline. Comparisons with other countries would obviously be useful but, with so many sites in Ireland alone, this is not an area that can be pursued in any depth here. Looking briefly at the British scene, with which the Irish was closely connected at many levels, it is clear that much is known concerning the details of individual walled towns there.[6] Yet, as a topic dealt with comparatively, walled towns in the British Isles feature in only three books. Harvey's *The Castles and Walled Towns of England* (1911) actually includes Wales and takes a comprehensive, historical and topographic approach to 85 sites. The same ground has been covered from a more specialist viewpoint, that of murage grants, by Turner in *Town Defences in England and Wales* (1970) which includes 132 sites. At the most superficial level these numbers give a measure to those dealt with here, a maximum for Ireland of more than 80 and a minimum of about 50. However, regrettably, Fleming's *The Town-Wall Fortifications of Ireland* (1914) deals with a mere 19 sites. This number is particularly low because the author was concerned chiefly with the surviving fabric from the point of view of an architectural historian. The text is brief and occasionally inaccurate but there are illustrations of structures at each site. These are valuable in themselves and especially so if further degradation, or even loss, has occurred more recently.

In contrast, the approach taken in the present study is that of the geographer, interested essentially in spatial relationships. These will be considered within individual settlements and between settlements, both within the context of Ireland and over a considerable period of time. The topic is clearly essentially cross-disciplinary and so it is heavily dependent on the work of historians, both present and past. The latter are particularly important in Ireland because the earliest of them often recorded both structures and documents which have since disappeared. In this context the writings of early travellers have also been valuable and the products of eighteenth and nineteenth century landscape artists. A considerable debt must, therefore, be acknowledged to a range of individuals who might be covered by the term 'topographer'. Amongst these, and fortunately becoming increasingly active in Ireland, are urban archaeologists. Their work, it must be hoped, will provide answers to some at least of the problems which remain and are high-lighted here.

TOWNS AND TOWN WALLS

The term 'town' has been used so far without definition because, as a settlement form, its general features of agglomeration of people and buildings, and its emphasis on activities concerned with services, trade and manufacturing industry, as opposed to but not entirely excluding agriculture, are well established. However, the concept of town has been the subject of much debate since the end of the last century. This has been, principally, between those favouring a legalistic definition based on borough status, and those preferring a more functional or morphological approach implying clearly visible distinctions in land use or buildings. By now, a concensus has largely been achieved and the argument has moved on to the subject of urban origins, with attention focussing on the range of possible urban nuclei and the development of proto-towns as an initial stage. These earlier and later areas of debate, which also to some extent involve the relative importance of trade and defence, are reviewed in Tait (1936), Benton (1968), Barley (1977), Clarke and Simms (1985), amongst others. They are relevant to this study for three reasons—firstly, the geographical and historical position of Ireland with regard to Europe; secondly, the use of the town as a colonising agent in Ireland; and thirdly, the role of the town wall in some of the definitions and its use as an indicator of a particularly urban function.

Ireland's position in Europe is peripheral geographically in that it is offset to the west of the continental landmass. Sometimes it has been peripheral historically too; for example, it did not share in the experience of being a part of the Roman empire and thus lacked the associated urbanisation. Similarly, it was outside the main area where medieval feudalism developed at the end of the Dark Ages. This is not to deny that it had periods of strong contact with mainland

Europe, or a useful centrality with regard to the western fringes—the high period of the Celtic Church and the later Hiberno-Norse period were two such. Nor is it to suggest that Ireland was necessarily unique; much of northern and eastern Europe likewise lay beyond the *imperium* of Rome. Indeed, eastern Europe was, like Ireland, an area of in-migration during the thirteenth century peak of medieval population expansion because it, too, was still then thinly populated and consequently relatively undeveloped (Richter 1985, 291). Nonetheless, the successive nature of colonisation in Ireland—the areally limited Norse, followed by the vastly more expansive but ultimately incomplete Anglo-Norman, and later the essentially more localised but still extensive re-colonisations of the Tudor and Stuart governments—has been claimed to be unique (Quinn 1958, 20) and was certainly unusually prolonged, stretching over a period of nearly eight centuries. Furthermore, because of such contrasting experiences within Europe generally, the development of settlement forms is of particular interest in a peripheral area like Ireland, where the scope for modification would have been greater than might often have been possible elsewhere.

The second reason follows on from this because towns featured strongly in all the colonisations of Ireland, as they did in the German medieval expansion eastwards into the Slav lands. Consequently, not only is the concept of town itself important but the existence of antecedents—urban nuclei and proto-towns—is also relevant. The urban structure of many of the Scandinavian-founded settlements in Ireland has never been in doubt, but the recent excavations at Dublin have displayed its considerable sophistication (*National Museum, excavations* 1962–73). The possible role of the contemporary, indigenous, major monastic centres was recognised by Curtis (1938, 408). Recent writers have been able to substantiate this by—firstly, increasing the number of case studies; secondly, utilising new techniques such as aerial photography; and thirdly making comparisons with eastern Europe where archaeological work post-1945 has achieved significant advances in the study of town evolution (Doherty, Swan, Leciejewicz *et al.* in Clarke and Simms 1985). To summarise very briefly, Ireland may have had a rather thin veneer of settlement nuclei before the arrival of the Hiberno-Norse and later the Anglo-Normans, but it was neither empty nor was it totally uninfluenced by general European trends. In the present context, the most important of these was the increasing urbanisation which developed from *c*.1000 AD, largely as a result of growing prosperity. It was, in turn, based on the development of long-distance trade, but this occurred during a period in which political instability remained an inherent problem, a source of danger to people and goods alike, and thus to their settlements.

The proto-town has been defined by Ennen (1977, 10), in a 'retrospective view', as a form without not only town law and constitution but all-round economic direction, and the close association of a central market, craft-working and long-distance trade—'what they lacked most of all was a stable and external settlement fabric and a town wall that would guarantee them protection'. This is the view of a prominent scholar from one of the main core areas of European urbanism, the Franco-German lands. Her concept of the role of the town wall will be considered later but, disregarding the negatives, her concept may otherwise be taken as a definition of 'town'. To a large extent it combines the views of Graham and Bradley, two of the most active writers in recent years in Ireland on the medieval town. The results of their research set a framework for the present study. Graham (1977 app. I and 1985, 27) has identified between 200 and 300 medieval 'boroughs', using that term rather than 'town' because the evidence refers specifically to the legal status. Included, therefore, are both functioning towns, which he describes (1979, 113) as 'morphologically distinctive settlements' involving 'a concentration of population' set in a specialised economic and administrative framework, and prospective towns. Some of the latter may never have gone beyond the paper stage, while others, experiencing an apparently meagre development, have been called 'rural-boroughs' by Glasscock, in his earlier work on deserted medieval settlements in Ireland (1971, 288).

Similar problems of definition were encountered by Beresford (1967, 273) in his study of medieval town plantation in England, Wales and Gascony. Bradley (1985, 418–20), reviewing the same process in Ireland, favoured a more practical definition, in line with that of archaeologists such as Heighway and Biddle who were working in England from the late 1960s. The basic assumption is that 'material culture' (in the broadest sense) reflects an 'urban milieu which is distinct from a rural one'. This, Bradley maintained, requires specifically a street pattern set centrally in a communications network, and a density of population clearly greater than that of other settlements nearby. In addition, a market and church are regarded as essential and at least three of the following—town walls, castle, bridge, specialised religious establishments, 'an area of specialised technological activity', quays, administrative buildings and suburbs. Unfortunately, while being comprehensive this approach will suffer for some time from the same problem as a documentary based one—'the random and incomplete' nature of its record base (Graham 1979, 113). This is inevitable until a great deal more archaeological work is carried out in Ireland. The loss of town wall structures, which will become clear later in this study, on its own highlights this problem.

For Ireland, Bradley (1985, 425, fig.17.7) suggested that not more than 'one out of every four boroughs developed into a town' and, consequently, that the majority were but 'speculative foundations'. Certainly borough status, because of the greater freedom implicit in it, was used as a 'bait' to draw settlers to Ireland, as to other undeveloped parts of medieval Europe (Otway-Ruthven 1968, 116). Yet, safety in sheer numbers, which a nucleated form of settlement such as a town implies, and a town's economic functions of providing a market facility for local produce and a convenient source of imported goods, were also important factors behind borough creation. Indeed, they were possibly of more lasting significance (Graham, 1985, 26–9). Bradley's view of town development can only really be justified on a long-term basis because it omits the possibility that the development of a settlement could be considerable, before being drastically reduced. Certainly, to look briefly at just two walled towns—New Ross and Mallow—is to recognise variable reduction as a strong possibility. New Ross, dating from *c.*1210, was one of the most successful of the purely Anglo-Norman creations. In fact, it was so successful that, while still relatively new, it became a serious rival to the nearby, but older and very prominent, port of Waterford. Naturally, such competition by an 'upstart' was much resented. It was resisted vigorously by a variety of means; the legal wrangling alone produced much documentary material which, today, provides a valuable insight into urban affairs in thirteenth century Ireland (McEneaney 1979). In the later Middle Ages the development of New Ross was seriously undermined by attacks mounted every so often by the Irish of north Wexford and it never really recovered, at least to the extent of continuing to compete seriously with Waterford. Mallow, on the other hand, was probably only a 'proposed' walled town (Table 1.1, list B), the murage evidence being a grant acquired for it and two other 'vills' in 1286. This was broadly contemporary with the building of the town wall at New Ross which is said to have started in 1265, but Mallow's origin as an Anglo-Norman settlement was the older. A castle was built there in 1185, while the comparable Marshall castle was at 'Old' Ross, some distance from the riverside site of the future 'New' Ross. There is a reference to burgesses at Mallow in 1299, but the settlement, new 'walled town' or continuing 'castle hamlet', largely fades from the record until the Elizabethan wars in Munster and the subsequent plantation. The important points are, firstly, that it did not disappear altogether, and secondly, that the reality of its thirteenth to fifteenth century settlement form is simply not known. Indeed, it would have been surprising if Mallow had disappeared completely, given its location in the rich Blackwater valley at the point where the route from Cork to Limerick crossed this major river. However, the surrounding hills made this area increasingly a 'march' one and this development, which was far from unique in Anglo-Norman Ireland, may well have been the background to the murage grant. It would be wrong, therefore, to regard Mallow merely as a speculative development, and other 'towns', that might be so viewed, may have been simply even less fortunate than it in the long term.

Thus it is arguable that the intensity, as well as the extent, of urban development in mid or late thirteenth century Ireland may have been considerable before it suffered a profound decline in the subsequent centuries. Consequently, Bradley's (1985 app.) identification on a morphological basis of only 56 Anglo-Norman towns looks much too limited, while Graham's figures of 200–300 obviously relate to potential town development. In view of these parameters, a range of between 50 and 80 medieval walled towns, based on the evidence presently available, indicates that a substantial number of Irish towns were walled. Bradley, in fact, notes extant fragments of town walls at 29 towns. This figure could be raised to give possibly as many as 45 if documentary evidence was included too. In addition, there are other sites for which there is similar evidence but which do not feature at all in Bradley's list, despite their having, in common with those that do, medieval-based structures such as a castle, church and/or street pattern.

The third point, at which a general discussion of definitions bears on this study, is the use of the town wall as an indicator of urban settlement. Some writers have emphasised defence as crucial to early town development, especially at the beginning of the Middle Ages. One of the most notable was Pirenne (1925, 105–7). He saw the change from simple earthen bank-and-ditch style defences in the ninth century to stone walls by the twelfth century as being the result of the growing prosperity produced by the development of increasingly active trading links, which in turn was made possible by the defence available at certain sites. This is the context of the Norse colonisation of Ireland. Tait (1936, 26–8), in contrast, emphasised to a greater extent the importance of the prevailing political scene. He envisaged town walls as a necessary condition of urban growth during times of constant warfare, such as the Danish period of Anglo-Saxon England. Other writers, including Mumford (1961, 206 and 241), have pointed in similar vein to the widespread building of town walls during the declining, rather than the peak, years of the Roman Empire. Yet, the view of the town wall as an essential, rather than a possible, element which survives in Ennen's definition, quoted earlier, is the product of generalising from a particular area of Europe, the centre. The evidence from the western periphery appears to be more mixed, in Britain as well as in Ireland. This is not to deny the significance of walling, quite the opposite. As Smith (1967, 303) suggests, it can be used as an important indicator of town growth, in particular this can be the case with the building of a new town wall or the extension of an existing one. Likewise, the upgrading from earth to stone, which had a parallel in structural changes in castle building, may be viewed as significant. Any of these developments may, of course, have been influenced by fashion but the sheer cost involved, to judge from the extent of murage measures requested and granted, would have tended to limit such a factor. Therefore, where town walls were not the absolute norm, there is the possibility that they can be used to distinguish levels within a settlement hierarchy. In addition, Andrews (*NHI* III 1984, 472) in the context of Ireland *c*.1685 has used them in a diagnostic sense. At that time most Irish town walls were still standing, more or less complete, and so he envisaged them as distinguishing visibly urban from rural settlements, while accepting that there were legal and administrative differences too. The urbanisation of Ireland by successive colonisers had by then reached its peak, and those towns that had been walled substantially may well have survived best, given the many centuries of periodic warfare. Indeed, Ireland had possibly at last reached a stage found in central Europe some centuries earlier.

To some extent the distinction of 'walled' or 'not walled' rests on the structural nature of the wall or, perhaps more especially, on its complexity. Enclosures of stone, wood or earth were not peculiar only to towns, although one derivation of the word 'town' is 'enclosure' (Pirenne 1925, 40). 'Borough' too appeared in Anglo-Saxon times with the meaning of both 'stronghold' and 'palisade' (Maitland 1897, 224). Besides, at the simplest level, enclosures are omnipresent even in modern times—garden fence, field hedge, factory wall and countless others. Likewise, the earthen bank-and-ditch enclosures of Irish raths, or the stone walls of the cores of Celtic monastic centres, display the same desire to aid the preservation of property. This is true whether it be for for reasons of convenience in the sense of keeping animals from straying, or for those of security in preventing loss through attack from outside. In the monastic example, as at the personal level, there may also be an element of demarcation in the sense of defining certain rights or ownership over the enclosed area, as opposed to that beyond (Doherty 1985, 48; Swan 1985, 78). The degree to which town walls define towns in Ireland will be discussed later, but the presence of early extra-mural suburbs, at Dublin *c*.1200 and elsewhere, indicates the pressures against a town wall actually defining, or even confining, a town for any length of time.

It should be noted, however, that such definition could be more psychological than actual or legalistic. Mumford (1961, 45 and 66) pointed to both the 'aesthetically' clear line of the town wall and the sense of protection it gave, describing the latter as 'worth a whole army in defence'. Indeed, the 'ideal' medieval town of artistic works was usually depicted as walled, often splendidly so (Platt 1979, figs. 18–20). In this sense the town wall tended to symbolise, as it defined, the special freedoms peculiar to medieval towns (Stenton 1967, 172), just as later it came to represent by its very nature the limitations of medieval life. Parts of the wall, particularly a fine gate, often appeared on town seals, including those for Dublin, Athenry and Kilmallock, while many English and Welsh examples enhance the county maps in Speed's 1610 atlas. When attached as seals to documents sent far and wide, these tiny pictures of parts of the town defences advertised both the wealth of the town and the degree of protection available there to citizens and foreign traders alike. Of course, in the nature of advertising they might have given a partially, or even a wholly, inaccurate impression of the complete circuit for, like an army subjected to testing pressure, a town wall was only as good as its weakest point. Nonetheless, a fine gate house or a stretch of curtain wall, enhanced by a number of strong towers, might well inspire a sense of urban pride, particularly if it pointed favourably to a contrast with rival towns. In this sense the walled circuit was a very special element in the town, comparable with its churches and more truly belonging to it than a castle.

The protective value of a town wall, both as a convincing deterrent and as a serious physical barrier, and its aesthetic quality derived from demarcating the settlement, were dependent on its being visible, for the most part. Yet its very success in these respects, which could enable a town to prosper, might result in a diminution of these roles. Indeed, despite the uncertainties of medieval life, periods of peace were more usual than periods of war, and so an interest in defence was probably often difficult to sustain, especially if it cost money. Suburbs might develop without a walled town and street intensity might increase within so that, in time, much of the town wall might be obscured from view and its defensive capability might be seriously compromised. This could happen either in the short term, through rapid growth, or in the long term, through the survival of the circuit without alteration for many centuries. Apart from enforcing strict building regulations, a common solution operated in Ireland was the creation of extensions to the system. Thus, although potentially the most restrictive urban facility, even a stone town wall was not necessarily totally inflexible. The varied response at different Irish sites to such an expensive, but sometimes desirable, undertaking provides one of the main interests of the subject.

Clearly, recognising a well-developed town wall is not a problem, whether it be that of seventeenth century Londonderry where the wall still stands almost completely intact, or pre-historic Jericho. There, because of the sheer scale of its construction, the discovery of the wall was regarded as indicative of an urban, as opposed to a rural, economy (Kenyon 1957, 66–7). It is, however, rather more difficult to decide the point at which a poorly developed town wall, such as that at sixteenth century Carrickfergus, is significantly different from a village stockade. Indeed, the antecedents of a town wall may well lie in the latter (Mumford 1961, 5). There is, therefore, the possibility that town walling may essentially be an exercise in upgrading existing defences or, at the simplest level, uniting individual property boundaries to achieve a cohesive enclosure system that could provide security for the whole settlement.

This problem, as regards Ireland, may be illustrated by looking at some of the maps in the Hardiman Atlas (TCD MS 1209). The apparently hedge-and-ditch type enclosure, with two gates, around the small single-street settlement of Omagh, *c*.1610 (map 33), is not apparently very different from the unimproved earthen bank-and-ditch enclosure at Carrickfergus in 1567 (map 26). Yet, there are no documentary references to Omagh even being intended as the site of a walled town, as there are about the 'inadequacy' of the sixteenth century Carrickfergus wall. The defensive line shown on the early maps has been traced back to the thirteenth century there in recent excavations (Simpson and Dickson 1981). It was found to comprise an earthen bank supporting a wooden palisade, in conjunction with a ditch of considerable proportions—*c*.4m. Such a transformation, from a substantial but rudimentary medieval earthen structure to a sophisticated modern stone wall by the seventeenth century, may be taken as illustrative of a process which took place at least in part, quickly or slowly, at numerous other settlements throughout Ireland, as elsewhere. To some extent, the scale of the structure may be the most relevant distinguishing factor; for example, a ditch-and-gate enclosure, intended to serve both as a demarcation of a settlement's extent and as a means of keeping animals safely coralled, need be a much slighter and more easily altered structure than one intended for a minimum defensive purpose, like that of discouraging nocturnal raiders. On a map such a distinction is not always easily discerned, or even indicated if a small scale is used. Moreover, its insertion may be intended purely for reasons of pictorial quality rather that landscape reality. Such cartographic evidence, therefore, needs corroboration by excavation in the zone indicated. Unfortunately this is both an expensive activity and one so far only carried out at a few towns in Ireland. In addition, apart from surviving structures, which again are limited in number and to some extent in quality due to prolonged weathering, frequent repair or lack of care, the most graphic evidence is often to be found in the earliest map-views or written surveys, all of which are post-medieval. However, the evidence is rather better for the later Irish walled towns, especially those of the seventeenth century. This is fortunate because they have a wider importance in that it is they that make Irish walled towns both unique within the British Isles and more typical of the general European experience.

To a certain extent, therefore, when walled towns are listed they may actually be the 'successes' of the time, unless they are known to have been created as such, for example Conway and Caernarvon in North Wales during the 1280s and Londonderry and Bandon in Ireland *c*.1620.[7] That is, they may be those sites where upgrading from the simplest, and possibly universal, type of enclosure was sufficiently formidable, in terms of scale and/or material, to survive until modern times. The process by which this was achieved may also have warranted such a level of investment and direction, either locally or ultimately from the Crown, that documentation of it in the state records was inevitable. Indeed, it is because such investment of resources was possible, or deemed necessary, at such sites that the town wall may be regarded as significant, either in terms of the contemporary status of the settlement itself, or its prospective development as perceived at the time. The extent to which the walled circuit might subsequently influence the layout of the town, both in terms of the intensity of its buildings and the complexity of its street pattern, provides a further point of interest, as do the non-defensive uses to which the different parts of the circuit might be put. In these respects the impact of a town wall may even long outlast its fabric and so it must be considered to what extent walled circuits still exist as an active or passive legacy in Irish towns.

1. The terms 'Irish', 'Ireland' or 'the country' refer to the whole island of which the Republic of Ireland and Northern Ireland are the 20th century political constituents.
2. 1981 Census of Population for N. Ireland and Rep. of Ireland.
3. Tindal/Rapin, reproduced in Camblin 1951, pl.18
4. Maxwell 1940, 226; Hinton 1935, 6; O'Connor 1906, 80.
5. Anon., *A Description of Ireland*, 1598, ed. Hogan 1878.
6. Collectively, some British walled towns appear in the atlas, *Historic Towns*, ed. Lobel 1969, and in the earlier Victoria County History series. Current excavations at particular towns are summarised on an annual basis in the volumes of *Medieval Archaeology*, as are those at Irish walled towns. Otherwise, British examples appear in local or national journals.
7. Londonderry and Bandon are illustrated by maps in the Hardiman collection, TCD MS 1209, 22 and 42 resp., and may be compared with map 27 for contemporary Carrickfergus.

CHAPTER 2

Evidence

The evidence for each site is displayed in the gazetteer under the headings—(1) field evidence in the form of the physical remains of the town walls and related structures; and (2) documentary evidence provided by (a) maps and plans, (b) written descriptions and illustrations, (c) town records and property documents, and (d) murage grants and other charters. Each will be discussed here in turn and drawn together at the end in an explanation of the basis of Table 1.1, lists A+B.

PHYSICAL REMAINS

The field evidence provided by the physical remains of walls, gates, towers and other structures is, of course, the most satisfactory but unfortunately, with the exception of a few examples such as Londonderry and Athenry, it is essentially fragmentary—a stretch of wall here, rarely surviving to its full height; an isolated gate or tower there, often also imperfectly preserved or much altered. Many towns have several such survivals but the range is considerable. An example of the best is Youghal with its almost complete stretch of west wall, 450m long and strengthened still by two or three mural towers, as well as its two isolated gates, the formidable but restored Clock Gate and the more modest Water Gate. Perhaps the least well endowed is Athboy where there is just the base of a possible mural tower. There are many variations between these; for example, Kells in Meath has a single fine mural tower while Kilkenny in contrast has a number of structures—short stretches of degraded wall, a small gateway, a substantial tower and the partial remains of others. Such material evidence is not without problems of interpretation, as these examples suggest, both as a result of the extent of decay and/or obliteration of original features through 'restoration'. Decay is inevitable given the troubled history and the long time span. The latter also allows for much alteration due to changes in use. For example, parts of a town's defences may have additional, subsidiary and even opposing roles such as a boundary to property or a barrier to its expansion; a convenient point for collecting tolls or a hold-up to traffic flow; a guard house that could also be let in order to increase town finances, either temporarily to groups as a meeting hall or, more permanently, as a dwelling. In all these ways the fabric was liable to be altered with or without permission. The records of Cork and Dublin list many instances of gates or doors being cut in the wall, buildings being constructed against it preventing access, and towers or gatehouses being rented to guilds or individuals. Even some of the large bastions at Londonderry were fenced off for private use in the nineteenth century. A town fosse seems to have often been the local tip or rubbish dump and the rampart proved a tempting source of garden soil. Much has, therefore, been altered and even more lost. These range from piecemeal but continuous losses, due to weathering, to the more spectacular removal of a whole gateway, as happened at Jamestown in 1973. Then, a lorry damaged a side wall and the authorities rapidly completed the demolition in the interests of modern traffic.

Field evidence, however, is now capable of at least preservation, and even of expansion, due to two new factors. These are, firstly, the increased public awareness of what may broadly be termed 'landscape heritage'. This is an extension of a long but previously more narrowly based tradition of interest in old buildings. Secondly, there is the relatively recent spread of archaeological investigation both to urban areas and to medieval remains, as is evidenced, for example, by recent work in Downpatrick (Jope 1966; Brannon 1982). Again, the revelation of successive waterfront walls at Dublin and their subsequent, much-contested removal, albeit after careful documentation and study, has done a great deal both to extend our knowledge of that site and to increase more generally the level of awareness and appreciation. A real debt is owed to two earlier groups. These were the more instinctively aware citizens who, in a few areas in recent centuries fought to retain the fabric of their town walls against the plans of 'progressive' forces— Londonderry is case in point; and the historians who, at the same time but over a wider area, recorded individual structures that were under threat either from the ravages of man or time. This is not to suggest that all town walls ought to have been preserved, an impossible and truly confining view, but simply to recognise the extent to which our knowledge of the past and, through it, our understanding of the present landscape, is dependent on residual evidence, now often widely and unevenly distributed due to this degree of loss.

The field evidence provided by physical remains still standing, recorded or revealed, can be enhanced by other topographic evidence such as field boundaries; the side or end boundaries of properties which may, in some cases, date back to the original burgage plots; and changes in the street pattern. These are more suggestive features in this context and are dealt with in the final analytical section of the gazetteer where the evidence is discussed as a whole for each site. The evidence provided by place names is also noted here, if it is still in use, or elsewhere as appropriate to its derivation. The contribution is relatively small but, occasionally, it is of interest. The term 'town wall' occurs occasionally as a street name but gates are the most important, providing street or area names long after they have been removed. Essex Gate in Dublin is an example and curious in that, as a gate, it had a very short life although also a comparatively recent one. It was created in 1673–5 and removed before the end of that century. A possibly unique case is that of Northgate Street in Dundalk, which has been made recently as a new street and named after the gate which once stood in that area. Thus, it makes an appropriate link with the distant medieval past, while emphasising Dundalk's continuing role as the 'gate to the North'.

MAPS

Maps combine most fruitfully with field evidence but, again, the quantity available varies from place to place, through time and type. On their own the earliest may actually serve to identify walled towns but they are a post-medieval source. This is not as serious a problem as it might appear because it is arguable that features of the Middle Ages were to a large extent in Ireland, one of the least developed parts of Western Europe, still dominant into the middle and even the late sixteenth century, when maps or plans first appeared. It does mean, however, that we have no direct cartographic picture of an Irish medieval town in the late thirteenth century when the Anglo-Norman settlement had reached its peak. In fact, the walled circuits of the earliest could have been as much as three centuries old by the time they were first recorded on maps and, consequently, it would be wrong to expect that they would have been still in their original form exactly or even generally.

The maps range in type from the most useful, the large-scale plans, down to small-scale maps of large areas such as counties. Some are composites, for example the complete provincial series by Speed (1610) in which there are insets of towns on three sheets—Dublin, Cork and Limerick, and Galway. The Ulster sheet has, curiously, Enniskillen fort rather than the surviving chief medieval port town of Carrickfergus—the new plantation towns were only being built then. This is a particularly useful series because it is similar in date and style to Speed's English and Welsh maps. They are on the slightly larger scale of a county basis, with the county and, occasionally, other towns as insets. Many of these are also shown as walled towns.

Without comparable insets most of the sixteenth to eighteenth century maps of large areas in Ireland are often difficult to interpret, not least when they seem to give tiny pictures of the main towns. Three examples from the Irish midlands will serve to illustrate the problems. Firstly, the map of county Kildare from the 1685 Petty atlas, based on the earlier Down Survey (*c*.1657) but with some additions, shows Naas with a circular wall; an apparently formidable settlement, but not walled, at Kildare; and none of the other 'walled town' sites as anything other than named loose collections of buildings, including Castledermot whose wall still survives in part. Secondly, Blaeu's *c*.1662 map of the Barony of Idrone in Co. Carlow (reproduced in Smith 1982), which was based on the earlier work of Lythe (1568–71), shows both Carlow and Leighlinbridge as comparable major riverside towns, apparently walled. However, the tiny pictures are so highly stylised as to raise doubts regarding their accuracy and so it does not help to resolve their relative positions in Table 1.1 where Carlow is in list A and Leighlinbridge in list B. Thirdly, the rather more primitive map of Leix/Offaly, *c*.1563, (also in Smyth 1982) seems to be more realistic in its depiction of the new plantation fort-towns of Maryborough and Philipstown and the older, apparently walled, towns of Athy and Carlow. Clearly, the purpose of a map needs to be elucidated wherever possible in order to evaluate its reliability. One measure can be the accuracy with which well known features are shown. There is, for example, a rather sketchy map of Waterford Harbour (frontispiece in Hore III 1900–11), probably transcribed from one in Pynnar's 1624 survey of forts which, while adding little to our knowledge of Waterford or New Ross but not contradicting it

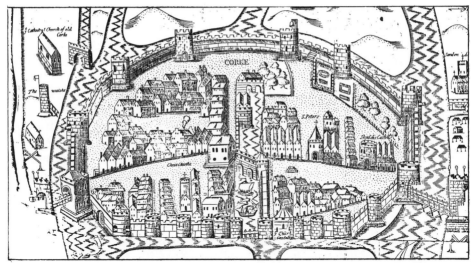

1 Cork, *c.*1587, from Stafford's *Pacata Hibernia*

either, shows Carrick-on-Suir and Thomastown as clearly and distinctively walled. As such it provides our only early pictures of these towns, and may be presumed to be reasonably accurate judging by its depictions of both Waterford and New Ross. On the other hand Inistioge is completely omitted. It was a medieval monastic settlement and apparently a walled town. It is situated between Thomastown and New Ross but Dunbrody, also a religious site, is marked further south. Possibly, the chief interest of the map maker was the estuary area up to Waterford and New Ross, and the rivers beyond with their towns were merely included as an abbreviated, and so selective, back-drop. Alternatively, as this is a redrawing, the problem may lie in the quality of the original map. This may have been poor in certain areas such as that of Inistioge.

A small number of towns have early or pre-seventeenth century maps or plans. Dublin is not amongst them, its earliest is the Speed (1610), but there is a very detailed written survey for 1585 from which it is possible to reconstruct a map (fig. 3.d). The main towns of Munster, some in Connacht and a few others are more fortunate. This may be seen as one of the few benefits arising from the prolonged wars of the late Elizabethan period. Map-making was actively encouraged by the government in London led by Lord Burghley, principally for use with military and settlement planning at a distance, but perhaps also out of a more broad-based interest in landscape and discovery that was especially characteristic of the Renaissance period. Waterford, Cork, Limerick and Galway each have two to four plans, some of which give a perspective view. While there are many cartographic disadvantages to this technique, not the least of which is that the foreground can obliterate much of the background, it is particularly useful for this study in that it shows much of the town wall in elevation. Consequently, it often provides the only source of details regarding its structure and associated features. Even better, there is a series of such 'picture maps' or 'map-views', which allows comparison between three walled towns—Cork (ill.1), Limerick and Youghal.

They have been dated to *c*.1587 but were published in 1633 in *Pacata Hibernia*, a history of the Munster war. They are rather stylised, and so not necessarily entirely accurate, but still are sufficiently different for each town to suggest that an element of local survey was involved. In addition, each of these towns has other, near contemporary, maps as well as good sources of evidence generally, so that specific features can be checked and the accuracy of the maps assessed. The most intensively covered town cartographically is Kinsale with no less than five maps or views dated to the year of the siege, which brought the Elizabethan wars to an end in 1601. From them a detailed picture of the town at that time can be constructed. In contrast, the many long-established towns of the Pale are not well endowed with maps for this early period although there are a couple—for Drogheda and Dundalk. They are less elaborate, being essentially quick perspective sketches which were enclosed originally in official or semi-official reports sent to the government in London, and so have survived in the state records. The rather idealised sketch of Drogheda in 1574 seems to have been intended for background information. It allows comparison with a Galway map of 1583 because they were both produced by the same government correspondent, Barnaby Gooche. The sketch of Dundalk, dated 1594, is rather more realistic but only covers part of the town where a particular defensive problem existed.

All these examples are representations of towns as they were seen at the time, either to the eye or from memory. It is impossible to judge now how many have been lost but the absence of one for Dublin must be significant. There are others, such as those for Maryborough, *c*.1560, and Roscommon, *c*.1581, whose value may be more limited. It is possible that they should be seen as planning models in that they were related to plantation schemes. They are therefore interesting at the conceptual level but they may not necessarily depict reality on the ground.

Maps related to plantation schemes are also a feature of the seventeenth century and, towards the end of it, there appeared military style plans of towns involved in the Jacobite/Williamite war. Generally, more towns are covered for this period with increasing cartographic accuracy. Of course, many of the most prominent already had pre-1610 plans, so that the study of changes at these sites and the evaluation of the map evidence, both of which are very important, is possible.

The major cartographic project of the mid-seventeenth century, the Down Survey, does not contribute as much as might be hoped, given its wide areal spread. This is because its interest was chiefly in rural land-holdings. Towns are shown in a variable but often stylised form, which is sometimes so meagre as to seem a short-hand. Nonetheless, a walled circuit is clearly indicated for Clonmel (ill.2), and the fairly detailed picture given of Kells is particularly useful because it is the only one available. On the other hand, the picture provided for Adare raises more problems than it solves. This is not necessarily a criticism of the style, it may be the result of major changes there in the late or post-medieval period. The plan of Drogheda is detailed and allows that town to have a cartographic representation for each of the three centuries preceding the modern period covered by the work of the Ordnance Survey.

The plantation-inspired maps relate mostly to Ulster towns and isolated sites

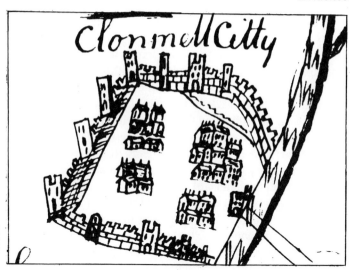

2 Clonmel, 1657, from the Down Survey

elsewhere, such as Bandon and Portarlington. For the latter there is just one plan which, like the *c*.1560 example for nearby Maryborough, may not represent reality. Bandon is supplied with three through which changes in the planning of the town's defences can be traced. The same is true for Londonderry and a series of maps shows how Carrickfergus, a poorly walled medieval town was finally brought up to date, defensively speaking. By the end of the century, when even more elaborate schemes were considered essential at least at a few key sites, yet another plan was made for Carrickfergus but it was probably not acted upon. In a similar way medieval Athlone gained a new lease of life both early and late in the seventeenth century. Maps survive for it as they do for other major centres such as Galway, Limerick, Cork, Waterford and Dublin, at all of which new style defences were proposed, and often built, some related to the medieval walls, some beyond. These are valuable both for the details of the new schemes and for the increasingly accurate depictions that they provide of the older circuits.

The seventeenth century town plans include the work of famous cartographers such as Raven, during the Ulster plantation, and Phillips and Goubet, at the end of the period. The expertise of the latter as military surveyors shows in their products. These also had a long life in the civil sphere, appearing in later atlases, sometimes in thin disguise, as in the Tindal/Rapin series of 1744/1751 (Camblin 1951, pl.18). Likewise, well-known surveyors dominated in the eighteenth century, particularly Scalé and Rocque. The former concentrated to some extent in the south and produced fine plans of the Devonshire, formerly Boyle, towns of Bandon and Youghal, as well as Waterford. The latter operated over a wider area producing fine plans of a number of towns including Cork, Kildare, Kilkenny and Dublin. Maps commissioned by the estate interest at many smaller towns, like Ardee and Loughrea, still survive and were the work of many different surveyors. They are more variable in their usefulness and sometimes only covered part of the town. Unlike the early work of the military surveyors, the defences of a town were no longer a priority and so the value of these maps is further limited. For the larger towns, maps were also made for the use of the general public as guides, either as single sheets or incorporated in books on the town or the county. Amongst the best are those made for Smith's histories of Cork, Waterford (1745) and Kerry (1756). The later edition of Cork city, 1774, being a revision of the original, 1750, is very useful for studying a city that was then developing fast but mostly in the areas beyond the walled circuit. Such history or guide-book maps continued to be produced into the early nineteenth century, until the six-inch series of the Ordnance Survey was ready to take over from them post-1833. Their use for this study decreases with the gradual disappearance of the town walls themselves but they can still be useful for displaying earlier street patterns which may have been related to features of the circuit originally.

Estate plans, in the limited sense of individual or group land-holdings in large urban areas, are another valuable source because the boundaries of such lands may include parts of the town wall. Waterford and Dublin both have fine col-lections of such plans and there may be many attached to land deeds still in private hands throughout the country. These could prove a useful source in the future and so it must be hoped that the efforts of Irish archivists to develop this source in recent years will be productive. Their use to elucidate a corner of the town wall at Dublin, where other cartographic evidence was contradictory largely due to problems of scale or technique, has been strikingly successful (Burke 1974). On a similar, localised scale there are the plans derived from new town developments, particularly those to do with harbour improvements close to town walls. This is true for the West Water Gate area of Limerick Irishtown. There, the wall and nearby gate disappeared during and after quay development and related street changes, but their foundations were recently revealed in excavation (Lynch 1984).

There are also a few historical or reconstruction maps, notably those for Limerick, 1761–8, and possibly Sligo, 1689. They are directly relevant in that they were attempts to trace the town walls and related features from surviving remnants or knowledge of them, but they need to be carefully assessed. The first large-scale plans of the Ordnance Survey, the six-inch series, also note 'historical' features such as the sites of town walls, gates or towers but, of course these have the advantage of an original survey base (ill. 3). This approach to historical sites does tend to be a little doubtful in terms of accuracy and haphazard in cover, in that it was dependent on local information, sometimes of variable quality. It can, however, be valuable because so many structures had disappeared by then. In certain places the surveyors were able to map sections of surviving town wall and in a few cases, such as Cashel, Dingle and Trim, these are the only known maps of the walled circuits. For others the OS maps serve to confirm or amplify the work of earlier surveyors. Much of this information was incorporated in the later twenty-five inch OS series and, recently, urban geographers and historians have found the areally more limited five-foot OS series a useful source for historical microfeatures, including the defences—for example, Andrews 1974 for Fethard and Carroll 1986 for Waterford.

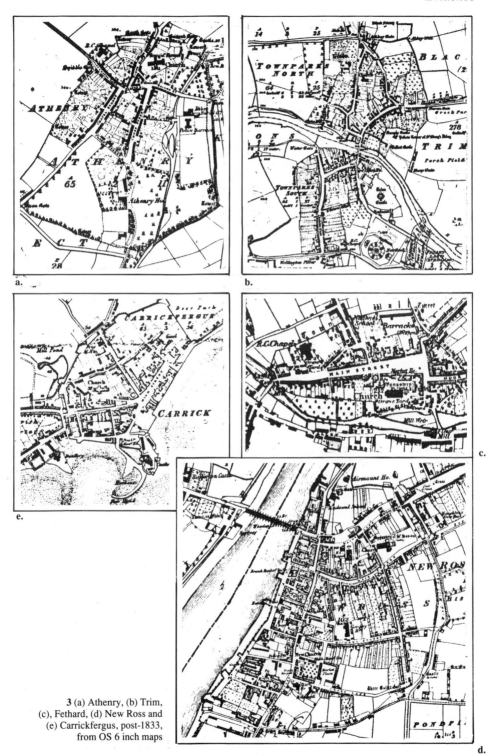

3 (a) Athenry, (b) Trim, (c), Fethard, (d) New Ross and (e) Carrickfergus, post-1833, from OS 6 inch maps

The collection of maps presently available, or particularly useful, for each site is listed in the gazetteer. For some towns there is no known positive map evidence, the towns walls having disappeared from the ground and from memory or tradition by the time the Ordnance surveyors were at work. This is true for most of the towns in Table 1.1, list B and for a few in list A as well. Tipperary is a case in point. It was probably a medieval walled town but it was not revived as such in the plantation period and no maps are known that show it in detail. At the other end of the scale, the best endowed are very well covered. Limerick is a good example. For it there are five pre-Speed maps, dating from *c*.1587 to *c*.1600, but it is not alone because for Cork, similarly, there are five, some of which are earlier, while for Galway and Waterford there are three each. Post-Speed Limerick is covered by a series of maps spread throughout the seventeenth century. There is one from each of the major sources—the Down Survey, 1657; Phillips, 1685; and Goubet, 1691—as well as additional maps inspired by the two Williamite sieges at the end of the century. There are also early, specialised maps of the castle which is situated on the walled circuit of the Englishtown. There are comparable collections of five maps each for Cork, Waterford and Galway and Londonderry joins the list as particularly well supplied, but for Dublin only three seventeenth century maps are known. From the early eighteenth century up to the OS period, post-1833, there is, again, for Limerick a range of different types of map—early, re-issued Phillips; plans of small town 'estates' and of new developments; new surveys *c*.1750–61 and 1769, the latter reproduced in Ferrar's history of the city (1787); and the 'historical' map. The position for the other major towns is comparable, if less rich, while the cartographic representation of Dublin is a considerable, if belated, improvement in the eighteeenth century.

Unfortunately, for many smaller towns, decay of the defences often preceded cartographic activity. In such cases, each map has to be carefully assessed for failure to mark the town wall need not necessarily indicate its actual disappearance. The surveyor might have been interested only in particular areas or aspects of the local topography, such as land holdings away from the wall or the essential elements of the street pattern. In fact, if a strong historic sense was not involved, relic features such as a town wall might actually be ignored. Being regarded as old-fashioned at best, they might be left out because they would be unlikely to show the town in a good light. On the other hand, when a competent surveyor such as Rocque marks the town wall on his Kilkenny map, 1758, but not on his Kildare, 1757, it seems reasonable to assume that this is significant. In such a case the map has a negative value in that it indicates that by then the town wall no longer existed. At the same time, such an apparently useless map may also show elements of the street pattern and boundary lines which are suggestive and do not appear on later maps because they, too, soon ceased to exist. Thus the most disappointing of maps may play a part in the general jigsaw that is the nature of historical evidence, especially in Ireland.

The non-cartographic documentary evidence is displayed in the gazetteer under three headings—firstly, written descriptions and pictorial illustrations, unless the latter refer to features which survive when they are listed at the relevant point in the previous section; secondly, town records and property deeds; and thirdly, murage grants and other charters. There is some overlap and so general comments will be made here before a discussion of each group in turn.

As is usual, a distinction can be made between primary and secondary material, the latter being based to some degree on the former. But, given the extent of loss in Irish records generally, some primary material is now only available in secondary works and so the distinction becomes rather blurred. This is particularly so in the case of early historians or compilers of reference works, such as Charles Smith and Samuel Lewis. Some of them used material that was then easily available but is now possibly lost, and others, like H.F. Hore and J.T. Gilbert, sought out original documents. Such writers, whose works range from books in a number of volumes to single brief articles in the early journals, especially the journal of the Royal Society of Antiquarians of Ireland, provide evidence for town wall structures which disappeared before the time of the Ordnance Survey, or were briefly revealed during periods of urban renewal as at Cork (Woods 1882–3). They are equally important for preserving in print early, eye-witness accounts of urban scenes and a range of documentary evidence related to land transactions and legal rights, as well as occasional state papers. It is well known, of course, that much Irish documentary evidence has been lost and doubtless some may have been missed here but certain local histories have proved to be either of little use topographically or plainly fanciful. They do not appear in the bibliography but occasionally one, such as Archdall's 1786 work, is tantalising in that it suggests that a previously unsuspected settlement, in this case Old Kilcullen, was a walled town but fails to produce convincing evidence.

Primary sources in the form of manuscript material, written as well as cartographic, have been consulted on a necessarily limited scale given the wide ranging nature of this study. Fortunately much of it exists in calendared form but further work on specific town or document collections might well be productive, both as regards new evidence and the re-evaluation of existing sources.

There are no contemporary records for the Hiberno-Norse period, except occasional references in the Irish annals, most of which were compiled much later. The Anglo-Norman records are found in six major collections mostly edited in the nineteenth and early twentieth centuries. Details of these are given in the bibliography; they are cited usually by initials which are indicated there too—the *Calendar of Documents relating to Ireland*, 1171–1307; *Chartae, Privilegia et Immunitates*, 1171–1395; *Rotulorum Patentium et Clausorum Cancellariae Hiberniae Calendarium*, 1171–1509; the *State Rolls of the Parliament of Ireland*, originally *the Statutes and Ordinances and Acts . . .* 1199–1483; the *Calendar of Charter Rolls*, 1226–1516; and the *Calendar of Justiciary Rolls* 1275–1314. There is some overlap of documents between these series, largely because the first two range widely and the others are more specialist. Some of the documents appear too in other collections confined to towns, for example in *Liber Munerum Publicorum Hiberniae* and the more recent *Na Buirgeísí* (ed. MacNiocaill 1964).

The number of documents recorded in these collections gains momentum with the firm establishment of the colony, especially from the early years of the thirteenth century. Two of the series end a century later and from then until the Irish parliament took a strong interest in towns in the fifteenth century there is a reduction in the amount of evidence available. Medieval documents also occur in reports of the *Deputy Keeper of Public Records*. Those of particularly interest are the financial ones, such as the surviving parts of the *Pipe Roll* series because they include records of murage payments. Murage documents are listed also with incorporation and other charters in the report of the major inquiry into *Municipal Corporations in Ireland*, ordered by parliament and published in 1835–6. This is a most useful source because it deals with corporate towns individually, often in considerable detail. Its commissioners frequently sought out documents both locally and in London.

For the later, Tudor/Stuart, period, the Charter and the Patent and Close Roll series continue. The calendar for the latter seems to be rather inaccurate in places, but it is also useful for the medieval period because its entries often contain recitals of foregoing charters and similar documents. The major series for this period is the *Calendar of State Papers, Ireland*. It contains a wide range of documents of direct relevance, including papers relating to the wars and subsequent plantations and assessements by civil and military officials. These are especially useful because they are concerned with the suitability of towns as garrison points and of landscapes for resettlement, either of which could involve the creation of defended towns. Associated with such projects are the maps, either thumbnail sketches or more sophisticated plans, already mentioned. There is, therefore, more overtly geographical material in these later state papers than in the medieval series, as befits the 'age of discovery'. Also available are eye-witness accounts of actual town wall building, for example at Carrickfergus and some of the Plantations towns. A parallel and comparable series is the *Calendar of Carew Papers* and there are other smaller collections relative to particular administrations in Ireland which are of occasional interest, as well as material in the *State Papers Domestic*.

There is some documentary material for individual towns in reports of the *Historic Manuscripts Commission*, in particular for Waterford and Galway. More has been published since *c*.1930 by the Irish successor, again for seventeenth century Waterford and for Kilkenny. The *Liber Primus Kilkenniensis* is especially good for the later medieval period and allows Kilkenny to act as an exemplar for Irish medieval towns generally. Most of the relevant material for Dublin has been published, chiefly under the editorship of Gilbert, and there is some for Drogheda too included in the earliest collection, the *Historic and Municipal Documents of Ireland*, 1172–1320. The more comprehensive *Calendar of the Ancient Records of Dublin* covers the whole period, medieval to nineteenth century. It includes the detailed 1585 written survey of Dublin's circuit, also published in the *CSPI* series.

The records for some other towns, such as the most prominent of counties Cork and Kilkenny, are readily available as edited collections in books or journals. They have survived best for the seventeenth and eighteenth centuries. They are valuable especially for evidence of the use and/or care of the town defences then and, by implication, in earlier periods. They also include quite detailed surveys of the walled circuits of Cork for 1733 and Galway for 1747, but the nature of the details provided is different from that of the earlier Dublin survey.

Town documents such as these serve, regrettably by their rarity, to illustrate the extent of loss elsewhere in Irish urban records. This problem can be made good in some measure by other sources such as the *Civil Survey* of 1654–6. This is particularly useful for the walls of Limerick, Kilmallock and a few other towns. On a lesser scale there is relevant material for many towns in the land deeds relating to the late seventeenth century Acts of Settlement, published by the early nineteenth century *Irish Record Commission*. For the earlier, immediately post-medieval, period there are documents relating to monastic houses in the *Extents of Irish Monastic Possessions*, 1540–1. Even a few survive for the medieval period from ecclesiastical estates in the Pale, for example the *Cartularies* of Llanthony and other major houses, particularly of those near Dublin. A more fruitful source of records, but equally uneven in its geographical spread, is secular estate-based material. Pre-eminent are the records of the Ormond (Butler) estates contained in the mainly medieval *Ormond Deeds,* 1172–1603 (ed. Curtis 1932–44). These cover large areas of counties Tipperary and Kilkenny, and isolated places beyond such as Arklow. Some documents relating to towns occur in the rather different, but still estate based, *Red Book of the earls of Kildare* (ed. MacNiocaill 1964) and in many smaller collections. These are most useful where the limits of urban lands are carefully described in relation to features such as the town wall, gates or ditches/fosses. In some cases they are accompanied by maps, as in Callan where land holdings, scattered throughout the town and dated by documents such as deeds to the late sixteenth century, are accompanied by an eighteenth century copy of a 1681 map (PROI MSS 2835 and 2841).

A further source of primary material are accounts of independent travellers and works of compilers of what might be termed early basic topographies. Camden's *Britannia,* published originally in 1587, and the anonymous *Description of Ireland* dated to *c.*1598 (ed. Hogan 1878) are two examples of the latter. This type of work reached a peak in Lewis's *Topographical Dictionary of Ireland* (1837), which contains many references to original documents including murage. Most have, however, to be used carefully because they are only as good as their base material, the sources of which are not often revealed. Even more so, travellers' accounts may be flawed by the quality of their sources and by the prejudicies of the authors, but these are usually apparent. The last major war of the seventeenth century, in which sieges of walled towns figured prominently, is well covered from both sides. Accounts of the events, such as those of the Williamite Story and some opposing Jacobite sympathisers, contain much that is useful. Story's work is illustrated by drawings, as is that of Dineley, whose journey through southern Ireland in 1681 foreshadowed many made in the eighteenth and early nineteenth centuries. The earliest of these are the most useful because of the subsequent disappearance of town walls. Some contain fine drawings by prominent artists like Petrie, who provided sketches for T. Cromwell's *Excursions through Ireland* (1820). Others are specialist works concentrating on antiquities, such as Wright's *Louthiana* (1748) and Grose's *Antiquities of Ireland* (1791–7, ed. Ledwich). This is an area where further delving might produce good results but it is a very large source indeed, with much that is also irrelevant.

Finally, work by historians, mostly since the turn of this century, both specific and general, is an important source. Of the general, Orpen's *Ireland under the Normans* (1911–20) remains basic for the early medieval period in spite of being updated and extended successively by Curtis (1938), Otway-Ruthven (1968), Lydon (1972; 1981), Frame (1982) and others. The Tudor and Stuart period has been re-assessed in the works of MacCurtain (1972), Canny (1976), Ellis (1985) and J. Simms (1969). The volumes of the *New History of Ireland* for the medieval and Tudor/Stuart periods (*NHI* II 1986; III 1984 resp.) now provide the best general historical source and the associated volume of maps (*NHI* IX 1984) is a useful addition. Much of the ground work on types of settlement or particular sites was also laid by Orpen and his contemporaries in local and national journals. It is being carried forward today by a number of geographers, historians and archaeologists whose works are used extensively in this study.

The point at which state and town records meet is in the charters. These were usually granted by the Crown to specific towns, but occasionally by major magnates too. One group of these, the murage charters, were often separate documents but the financial arrangements implicit in them were also sometimes included amongst the provisions of other, more general charters. Murage measures gave a town the right to spread the cost of defence beyond its normal resources in the form of a tax on its commercial life, involving thereby all those who traded at its market in certain named goods over a specified period. In the nature of taxation generally, the range of goods involved grew and the period lengthened, either in later grants or by means of successive extensions to existing ones, while exemptions also developed until the whole system became both cumbersome and relatively unproductive.

The murage charter was only one of a number of murage measures which will be discussed in detail in chapter 4. The fashionability of any particular type varied from time to time but most had a long life, some even being used in the early modern as well as the medieval period. In theory it ought to be possible to relate the granting of murage measures to stages in the development of a town wall system and its subsequent maintenance, repair following attack or extension. For the best endowed such as Dublin this is possible to some extent, especially when actual structures or sites are named in the documents. However, the usual formula employed is rather vague—'to inclose' the village/town/city both for 'its defence and that of the surrounding area'. Occasionally, as in the first known Drogheda charter of 1234, this is expanded slightly—to 'inclose their vill with walls' but the wording of many thirteenth century charters is too variable as well as vague to be regarded as significant. The fourteenth century charters often refer specifically to a stone wall which is rather more useful.

Murage, like other forms of evidence, is not used here in isolation but in conjunction with whatever data is available. It is, however, the most direct record for a study of town walls and, therefore, its inherent problems, as well as its potential, need to be appreciated. The presence of a single known murage grant in particular involves special problems of interpretation. There is rarely any way of knowing if it is a lone survival or the only one ever granted. If it is a case of the later then it may be taken as indicating an intention to wall which is of interest, and may be regarded as comparable to the many walling projects of the late sixteenth century, some of which also were not put into effect. Additionally, the medieval instances, illustrated well by grants for some of the smaller towns of county Limerick, such as those to Croom in 1310 and Garth in 1409, may indicate the use of murage funds for allied defensive works at the local castle, particularly if, as in these cases, there is no other evidence for a town wall. Where a series of murage grants are known, or even only one and a successor, as at Adare for 1310 and 1376, it seems reasonable to assume, in the absence of other evidence, that a town wall was built. It can then be dated tentatively to the intervening years unless the wording indicates that repair is involved.

Youghal displays well both the problems of the residual nature of Irish records and the difficulties of using murage evidence to date town walls. Its earliest known charter is dated 1275 and indicates that repair was involved, while the next known one is nearly a century older, 1358. A reference to a murage account for 1323 provides the only evidence for the intervening period. This cannot refer to the earlier (1275) grant because it was given only for seven years, unless it was considerably extended. This is not known but would not have been unusual. Thereafter, from 1374, varied murage measures are known to have been in operation at Youghal almost continuously, as at other major towns. It is particularly unfortunate, therefore, that the murage record for any town is likely to be most meagre in the earlier period just when it might be most useful for dating the initial building of the town wall. In the case of Youghal, the best that can be established from the early murage evidence is that the town wall was begun, and probably completed, before 1275. Similar lines of argument must often be applied, even in the cases of the most prominent medieval towns.

The gazetteer ends with a discussion of the walled town insofar as it has been possible to reconstruct it from the foregoing evidence. Wherever possible the various problems are considered and the relationship of the circuit to the present street pattern is reviewed. This relationship, which may change considerably with time, may also have a two-way aspect to it. The street pattern, for example, may have influenced the siting of gates or vice versa, and property boundaries may now indicate the former line of the wall because they were once related to it. Generally, an evolutionary approach is taken because a walled town was a continuum, not a static feature.

In concluding this review of the evidence, reference must be made again to Table 1.1 because its division into the two lists, A and B, is essentially an expression of the quality of the available evidence. It must be emphasised that this division should not be seen as immutable. It does mean, however, that for almost 60% of walled towns (list A) the evidence, although varying considerably, seems at the moment to be sufficient for them to be regarded as 'proven'. Conversely for the rest (list B) the evidence to hand is insufficient so that they must be classified as 'unproved' but not unlikely. Excluded from this is the appendix to list B where the evidence is very slight.

For list A sites the evidence consists of physical remains and/or a range of documentary material. Even so, the classification poses a few difficult cases, such as Athboy. There, the structural evidence is slight and equivocal but, in addition, there are a series of murage grants, one late-sixteenth century reference to the town as 'walled', and a number of property records in which two or three town gates are mentioned. A town which illustrates the dividing line between lists A and B is Tipperary, for which there are two successive murage charters, the first dated 1300 and granted for ten years and the second dated 1310 but for only three years. It is, therefore, assumed that a town wall was built, at least in part, although little is known about it from other sources. This assumption may not be justified but it makes for a clear division between those on list B with only one known murage grant. To that extent the separation may be entirely a matter of the relative preservation of records, but it is unavoidable in the circumstances.

List B sites are characterised generally by the paucity and/or equivocal nature of their evidence and, for those in the appendix to list B, the evidence is very slight indeed. The largest number depend on a single medieval murage record, such as the charter granted in 1286 for seven years to the fitzMaurice towns of Tralee, Mallow and Ard(fert). Presuming this to have been an initial grant—the wording is unspecific—it may be regarded as a means of providing the finance for a town-walling project, the result of which is unknown. Comparable projects continued beyond the medieval period of which Ferns and Burris are examples. Indeed, town walling seems to have survived as an element in town planning right to the end of the seventeenth century, as the example of Portarlington shows, although again with unclear results.

For a few sites, all in the appendix to list B, the evidence is based entirely on secondary sources of variable quality, or on enigmatic field, map or written evidence. Greater credence should probably be placed on the earlier accounts, if only that they may describe features then still visible, but later accounts, based perhaps on local tradition, should not be discounted either. Two county Cork towns provide illustrations of this. Rosscarbery (list B) was described in 1517 as 'a walled town with two gates and 200 houses (Hanmer, ed. Theiner 1864; *NHI* II 399), whereas Inishannon (list B app.) was stated in 1750 by the prominent historian Charles Smith, to have been 'formerly walled'. The one seems to have the quality of an eye-witness account and the latter of hearsay, but Smith can be proved reliable in such matters elsewhere, for example in the case of Buttevant.

Monaghan (list B) provides an example of map evidence (TCD MS 1209/32) for a walled town that is otherwise unsupported. Enniscorthy (list B app.) raises the problem of gate evidence, which of itself may not necessarily imply the presence of a town wall but may be related to later, unconnected toll collection. On the other hand more complex field evidence provided by walls and related structures is, also, not without problems as the example of Kells-in-Ossory (list B appendix) shows. It was described by Archdall in 1786 as an 'ancient walled town formerly of note'. This was repeated by later writers and so Kells was included in Fleming's *The Town Wall Fortifications in Ireland* (1914). The enclosure involved was actually the outer court of the priory, which stands half a kilometre from the medieval settlement site, and so the structure was part of a defended priory rather than a town.

As already indicated, many of the problems outlined above arise because of the residual nature of the documentary evidence and its uneven spread, both areally and through the centuries. The major centres are the best supplied, those in certain areas of the country are better off for some periods than for others, or have particularly useful records such as detailed early maps. These are problems for any historically-based study in Ireland. In some cases they may prove insuperable but in this particular work a degree of extrapolation backwards from the towns walled in the seventeenth century, for which there is a considerable body of contemporary evidence, may help to elucidate aspects of their medieval forbears.

CHAPTER 3

Comparative Study

This chapter is based entirely on evidence detailed for each site in the gazetteer, the purpose here being to consider walled towns as a group. Various aspects will be considered in turn—the sizes and shapes of the walled area and the circuit, the varied structural features of the wall and the topographic nature of the site. The discussion will be concerned largely with those in Table 1.1, list A, a total of fifty-six towns for most of which there is a considerable body of evidence. The section on structure, which will deal with the nature of the curtain wall and its associated elements—gates, towers or bastions, fosse and ramparts—will depend heavily on ten to twenty sites at which there are the best survivals of both fabric (ill. 4) and documentary evidence. These must serve to build up a picture of Irish walled towns generally. The towns of Dublin, Limerick

Table 3.1: Areas and Circuits of Town Walls

LIST A	AREAS IN HECTARES	CIRCUITS IN METRES
Adare ?	4	–
Ardee	25	1525(+625R)=2150
Athboy 2?	15+2=17	1400+425=1825(R)
Athenry	28<12(+16)	2000<1250,I 500
Athlone 2	6+4=11	625(+375R)=1000/875[1875]
Athy 2 ?	7+9=16	700+900=1600(R)
Bandon 2	6+10=16	625+875=1500(R)
Belfast ?	30	2000
Buttevant ?	5-15	600-800(+2-300R)
Callan ?	10-34	1000-1500
Carlingford ?	8-12	1000-1250=1350-1600 (+350S)
Carlow ?	13	1350
Carrickfergus	6+5=11	625>1000>1175
Carrick-on-Suir	12	875(+675R)=1550
Cashel	14	1550
Castledermot	15	1450
Clonmel	14	1050(+450R)=1500
Clonmines ?	8	–
Coleraine	14	1100(R)
Cork	14	1625
Dingle ?	4	875
Downpatrick ?	10	1200
Drogheda 2	32+11=43	1250(+775R)=2025/1125(+400R)=1525 [3545]
Dublin	6+6+8=20	875>1575>1750+I(575)
Dundalk 2	21+13=34	1800+1525=3400+I(125)
Dungarvan	6	950
Fethard	7	1125
Fore ?	14	1450
Galway	13	1325
Gowran	12-19	1350-2000
Inistioge ?	4-7	750-900(+125R)
Jamestown	3	750

and Waterford are used as case studies for particular features of the structure. From time to time comparison is made with examples from outside Ireland, particularly from England and Wales.

SIZE

Looking first of all at walled towns as complete entities the aspect of size may be considered under two headings—(a) the area enclosed by the wall or walls, and (b) the perimeter or length of the circuit. The details, as far as they can be established at this stage, are given in Table 3.1 and illustrated in different ways in Table 3.2 and Figures 3.a and 3.b. The values given for both area and perimeter are approximate, taken from the 25 inch OS maps and converted to metric. Occasionally, ground measurements are quoted in the gazetteer where these are available. In transferring the values to graphs and other diagrams, they have been rounded down rather than up (5.5 equals 5) and, where values are given in the gazetteer within a range, the lower value is used (10–12, using 10). Consequently, the values should be seen as conservative estimates and may well be underestimates. Areas have been calculated on the basis of a hectare grid. The

Table 3.1 *continued*

Kells	21	1650
Kildare ?	9	1000
Kilkenny 3	29+10+4=43	1550(+750R)=2300/750(+450R)=1200/ 625(+225R)=850 [2925](+750R)=[3675]
Kilmallock	13	1700
Kinsale +B	11+3=14	1300+625=1825+I(100)
Limerick 2	14+13=28	1650+1375=3025
Londonderry	12	1325
Loughrea ?	17	1075(L)
Maryborough ?	14	1375
Naas ?	13	1375
Navan	10	1125(+250R)=1375
Nenagh ?	10-15	1250-1500
New Ross	39	1575(+750R)=2325
Newry 2 ?	8+5=13	1100+800=1900
Philipstown ?	5-20	900-1600
Rindown ?	25	500(L)
Roscommon ?	20	1000(L)
Thomastown ?	7	700(+250R)=950
Thurles ?	8	750(+250R)=1000
Tipperary ?	15	1125(+275R)=1400
Trim 2	16+7=23	1175(+375R)=1550/600(+250R)=850[1775])(R)
Waterford	8+14=23	1200+1250=2150+I(300)
Wexford	12+13/17+8=25	875-1000+500-750>1250+I(250)
Youghal + B	17+1=19	1550+300=1750+I(100)

KEY

NB Values are simplified (ie 4. not 4.5), therefore totals can be greater than the apparent sum of their parts.

R   riverside wall
S   sea side wall
L   lough side wall
      – if bracketed (R) etc. not included in circuit values

+I   internal wall - value shown separately
+B   Basetown - value shown separately
+   separate walled areas
>   expanded walled areas *or*
<   contracted
[ ]   combined total for complex situations
/   to separate the different circuits.

perimeters include the space occupied by gates and towers/bastions, but not their projections beyond the line of the wall.

As already emphasised, neither the walled area nor the circuit wall is necessarily a simple feature, although there are many sites at which the town wall enclosed a single walled area, for example Cashel, Castledermot and Londonderry. At others, the original town wall was extended to give two adjacent walled areas and three perimeters—the original, the additional and the resulting combined. Waterford and Youghal are cases in point, Athenry represents the reverse because the original area was cut more or less in two in the sixteenth century, to give a reduced inner walled area on which attention could be concentrated and an outer one which could be left to act simply as a delaying mechanism. Yet, at Cork, the apparently simple, single walled area of the post-medieval maps may have originated from a doubling of the original, with the resulting intervening wall disappearing. This certainly happened on the north-west side of Carrickfergus in the seventeenth century. The same may be true of Wexford, Kilmallock, Kilkenny Hightown and Limerick Englishtown, all apparently simple single walled areas. At Dublin the picture is more complicated because there were probably two successive extensions to the original Hiberno-Norse walled area, the riverside wall of which survives still in part. Twin walled towns were made clearly distinct by the presence of the river between them but only a couple of them, Drogheda Louth and Meath and Kilkenny Hightown and Irishtown, were ever administratively distinct towns, until 1412 and 1574 respectively. The bridge-head suburb at Kilkenny Hightown, St. John's, was also walled in time but it was really as much a part of the main town there, as were the two walled areas at seventeenth century Bandon. All of these were separated by rivers but at Bandon there was an in-river defensive system, rather like a bridge, which may have existed elsewhere too. The two walled areas at Bandon were contemporary, but at Athlone the medieval walls seem to have been intended for the east side only. They were upgraded in the early seventeenth century but the western circuit was not made until the middle of that century, during the first of the major war periods. Possibly none of the three walled areas at Kilkenny (ill. 5) were strictly contemporary although the independent ones were both medieval. The tables and figures have been compiled to take into account the best established of these complexities so as not to deal with a simplistic, but unrealistic, optimum situation only.

AREA   Figure 3.a shows both (1) the complete walled area, whether simple or multiple in character, of each of the 56 sites and (2) the 75 individual walled areas which are known to have made up that total. The two patterns are, however, fundamentally the same with two-thirds of each falling within the range of 6–15 hectares.

Within this marked clustering the individual walled areas are equally spread between the lower and upper ranges (6–10 ha. and 11–15 ha.). Included are the single walled towns of Dungarvan (6 ha.), Fethard (7 ha.) and Navan (10 ha.), Carrick-on-Suir (12 ha.), Galway (13 ha.) and Coleraine (14 ha.), as well as the main towns at Newry (8 ha.) and Kinsale (11 ha.) and the Irish towns at Kilkenny (10 ha.) and Limerick (13 ha.). The combined walled areas feature only at the

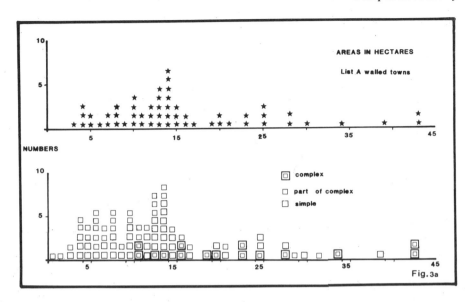

AREAS IN HECTARES

List A walled towns

NUMBERS

□ complex

□ part of complex

□ simple

Fig.3a

upper end although some, such as Carrickfergus and Athlone (11 ha. each), remained relatively small even after extension. Likewise, it does not seem as if Newry as a combined walled area of main and basetown (13 ha.) or, indeed, Kinsale similarly (14 ha.) was sufficiently large to leave this basic category. All these examples, scattered throughout the country and comprising medieval and post-medieval walled towns, show that a clear distributional element was not involved, either in terms of period or place. From the evidence below it will also be seen that this is a feature throughout the range of sizes, from the very small to the very large. It will be referred to again after these are discussed.

4 Athenry town wall with tower in south-west, outer side

33

Unsurprisingly, amongst the category 'very small' (1–5 ha.) there are no complex walled towns, either those with extended or double walled areas. Nonetheless, there are complete walled towns and not just small appendages, such as the basetowns at Youghal (1.5 ha.) and Kinsale (3 ha.). The best example of the 'complete' is Jamestown (3 ha.), whose walled area was created in the seventeenth century and is not in doubt, despite its minuteness. Less certain, but also possible, are the earlier walled towns of Adare (?4 ha.) and Inistioge (4–7 ha.). Originally too, Buttevant may have been of a similar size, as may some of the towns on list B, if they were walled. The map evidence for seventeenth century Monaghan, for example, points to an area of about 4 ha. Bridge-head suburbs were likewise small. Kilkenny St. John's (4 ha.) and Athlone West (4 ha.), both of which may be viewed in this way, were both very small, and so may have been Athboy East (2 ha.), if it was walled.

At the opposite end of the range (15–45 ha.), there is less obvious clustering but about 20% of the individual and 30% of the complete walled areas were that large. Of the latter not all were multiple in character as might be expected. Of course, there were combined towns, such as Limerick (14 + 13 = 28 ha.) and Trim (16 + 7 = 23 ha.), but amongst them, and sometimes larger, were some single walled towns too. Kells (21 ha.) and Loughrea (17 ha.) were amongst the more modest of these, but others, such as Athenry (28 ha.), Belfast (30 ha.), and New Ross (39 ha.), were formidably large. Even more striking, as Table 3.2 illustrates, is the frequency with which some town names appear twice, involving both an individual and the complete walled area. This is true for Dundalk (21ha. Lower/34 ha. complete), Drogheda (32ha. Louth/43ha. complete) and Kilkenny (29ha. Hightown/43 ha. complete). In other words, combined walled towns, double or treble, were not necessarily composed of small or medium parts. Some, such as Athlone, Trim and Wexford, were, just as, rather surprisingly, were the two most important medieval towns, Dublin and Waterford. Both of these are known to have been extended but their complete walled areas were not particularly large. Waterford, the great port of south-eastern Ireland from Hiberno-Norse times, at its fullest extent covered only 23 ha., less than Ardee (25 ha.) which was always a modest market town in rural Louth. but one that also may have been extended. The full size of Waterford's walled area is thrown into greater contrast when it is compared with that of its nearest and very active rival, New Ross (39 ha.), whose area was not apparently ever extended. Most striking of all is the full size achieved by much-extended Dublin (20 ha.), also Hiberno-Norse founded, and subsequently walled and developed later as the centre of the Anglo-Norman administration. Indeed, its two extensions, like its core, were each almost as modest as the one finally achieved by Carrickfergus in the seventeenth century. The resulting walled area still did not even match one part of its nearest neighbour, Drogheda—Louth side (32 ha.)—and was less than half of the combined Louth and Meath walled towns there (43 ha.).

Of course, the areal extent of built-up Dublin, or any other walled town, was not necessarily limited to that within the walls. The initial governing charters of Dublin, Cork or Limerick make that clear. The extension of the walled area was

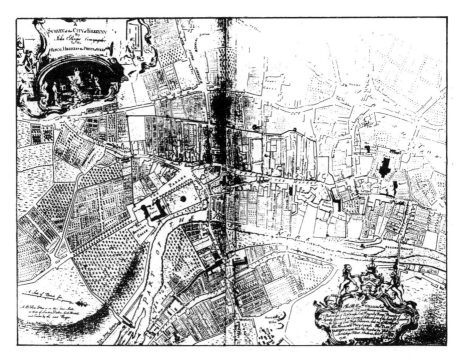

5 Kilkenny, 1758, from Rocque's survey of the city

but one of the possible defensive measures available to a growing town; Dublin in 1610 shows a common compromise measure, the use of suburban gates. The scale employed there was not matched anywhere else but both Kilmallock (13 ha.) and Ardee (25 ha.) had one gated suburb each in the seventeenth century, as possibly other towns had too. The maps for Kilmallock and Ardee serve to emphasise a further point—that even an average walled area need not have been wholly built-up but could include open spaces too, and still require an extension to the defended area.

The topic of distribution has already been touched on and will be considered fully in chapter 5 but it is clear from the examples already cited that no distinction can be made between medieval and later created walled towns on the basis of area size. The two walled towns of the Ulster Plantation, Londonderry (12 ha.) and Coleraine (14 ha.), were not conspicuously large, rather they were characteristic of the majority of their predecessors and little bigger than Carrick-fergus (11 ha.), for so long the key town of medieval Ulster. Nonetheless, the Stuart period towns show extremes too—Jamestown (3 ha.) was very small and Belfast (30 ha.) distinctly large. Its rather later walling was in response to a sudden and pressing sense of danger, produced by the 1641 uprising, just as the motivation for walling New Ross (39 ha.) in 1265 was related to fear, in that case induced by a local war. The resulting large walled areas may well reflect the strength of 'new' towns and a consequent optimism for future expansion. The same may be true of Athenry (28 ha.) and Ardee (25 ha.), and also of Kilkenny

Hightown (29 ha.) and Drogheda Louth(32 ha.) but, while the early and sustained economic vibrancy of the latter pair is not in doubt, nor their medieval status as major regional centres, that of the former is not well established. Ardee does not stand out so markedly in its regional context because some of its near neighbours were also large—Kells (21 ha.), Dundalk and Drogheda. Yet, not all the walled towns of the area ultimately known as the 'Pale' were so large, for example Navan (10 ha.) or Athboy (?15 ha.). As for Athenry, it was of course later reduced in size. Moreover, its contemporary and nearest major port, Galway (13 ha.) was average in size and never significantly extended. The sizes of walled areas were, therefore, highly variable. Most of the medieval examples were broadly contemporary, thirteenth to fourteenth century. The best distinction that can be drawn seems to be between the Hiberno-Norse established major towns and the rest— that is between Dublin, Waterford, Wexford, Limerick and possibly Cork, and the 'new' Anglo-Norman towns such as Drogheda, Dundalk, Kilkenny and New Ross. Furthermore, the early thirteenth century extensions of the generally small (*c*.6 ha.) Hiberno-Norse walled areas were also on a fairly modest basis. This happened twice at Dublin (6+8 ha.) and possibly twice at Waterford too (14 ha. addition in all). It seems likely that less freedom was available at these towns simply because their sites were already strongly developed over a wide area. In other words, the differences may often reflect the strength of constraint imposed by land ownership around each settlement, for example whether it was varied or in the hands of a single owner, either the town or the local lord. This could impose an additional cost on wall building if philanthropy, or just a willingness to cooperate, did not prevail. Such a situation is likely to have persisted at some towns until the sixteenth century dissolution of the monasteries released land near to many towns. The use of this land for subsequent reinforcements of medieval circuits is a striking feature of Irish towns, especially at Waterford. By then the effect at Dublin was only marginal because intensive urban development had spread so far beyond the walls. Clearly other factors may have been involved too—the prevailing financial climate; individual attitudes to the use of money which might range from parsimony to profligacy; the desire and capacity to impress; the need to plan for future expansion or to provide for an assured minimum food supply within the walls during emergencies. Any or all of these could produce different results within an area during the same period, and so they must underpin much of the variety detailed above.

In order to evaluate the size of Irish walled towns it is useful to consider those in neighbouring countries, however superficially. A visual comparison has been made with a small number, twelve, of English and European examples (Bradley, 1985 fig.17.4). This forms an interesting attempt, although the scale is tiny and apparently seriously underestimated—for Winchester a figure of 33 ha. can be measured while Turner (1970) gives a figure of 138 acres (55 ha.). Unfortunately, the gazetteer in Turner is very haphazard as regards details, so that the size of the walled area is given for only about 10% of the towns involved and a similarly small number are dealt with, also in an incidental manner, by Harvey (1911). He describes Totnes as 'probably the smallest' and Stafford and Rochester as 'amongst the smallest'. Beresford (1958, 181) gives figures of 4 ha. for Totnes and *c.*12 ha. for both of the others. In the same range Turner gives values which, when likewise converted, appear as Denbigh (4 ha.), Bath (9 ha.) and Cowbridge (13 ha.). Turner and Harvey quote slightly different values for Great Yarmouth (52/60 ha. resp.) but agree on Winchelsea (60 ha.), towns of the same order as Winchester but well above the Irish maximum. Winchelsea was regarded as 'too large' in 1414 (Turner 177) and it was proposed that its walled area should be reduced. There is a clear parallel here with Athenry more than a century later, but it is interesting that the Irish walled town was reckoned to be 'too large' at half the original size of Winchelsea. This impression of greater size on the larger island is strengthened when Dublin (20 ha.) is compared with London (130 ha.). It shows that London's area was clearly predominant, whereas Dublin's was not; this is even so when allowance is made for the greater size of apparently many English walled towns. Yet it is clear, even from so few examples, that the range of sizes was considerable in England too, even if it was of a different order to that in Ireland. The picture was also variable in that some prominent towns were comparatively small, for example Bristol. Although about twice the size of Dublin with which it had early close connections, Bristol was considerably smaller than Winchester or Chepstow, despite being, also like Dublin, much extended. Likewise, Southampton, another important port and one whose defences were the subject of much attention because of the frequent risk of attack by the French, appears to have been similar in size to Waterford. (These comparisons are drawn from Bradley 1985 fig. 17.4.) On the other hand, the majority of Welsh towns and those on the English border were small to medium sized, that is under 16 ha. (Soulsby 1983, 50; Butler 1985, 477–9 and maps; Wood 1962, fig. 2). The extremes there are represented by Chepstow (53 ha.) and Caernarvon (4 ha.). Conway, the other well-preserved Edwardian town of North Wales, was not quite so small, being probably at least 10 ha. (Delaney 1977, 39).

Speed's atlas (1610) provides inset plans for 67 towns, 51 English and 16 Welsh, the majority (66%) of which were walled, as were the additional 4 Irish towns. One interesting contrast, which can be made at this stage, is that very few of the English towns apparently had multiple walled areas and none of the Welsh. There were three English 'twin' walled towns then—Norwich, Bristol and York. Some towns may have had their walled area extended, losing part of the original wall and so the evidence of extension, by the late sixteenth to early seventeenth century, but of the towns in Speed only Berwick had two walled areas situated side by side. Platt (1976, 53) also notes that the extension of walled areas was rare in England, compared with the continent. The Irish walled towns, therefore while being probably often smaller than the English, seem to have been more intensively walled, at least at this period and possibly thus to have been closer to the European norm. Indeed, the contrast with Britain was to continue throughout the seventeenth century as new walled towns were created in Ireland or old ones modernised. In England only the elaborate new circuit at Berwick was built in the sixteenth century, in response to the continuing danger of attack from Scotland. Actually the walled area of Berwick was then reduced, just as Athenry's was.

Temporary fortifications enclosing larger areas were built at a number of English towns during the Civil War, for example at Bristol in 1643–5, but they seem to have been short-lived or relatively uninfluential (Jones 1946, 73).

As regards mainland Europe, Bradley (1985, fig.17.4) only gives three examples—Paris, Arles and Mainz—which were large or very large. Few authors dealing with towns comparatively are specific about the size of the walled areas, but it is likely that there was, throughout Europe as in Ireland, considerable variety and many apparent anomalies too. Mumford (1961, 208), for example, quotes values of 12 acres (4.8 ha.) for Basle, 50 acres (20 ha.) for Strasbourg and 550 acres (220 ha.) for Nimes. Beresford (1967, 254) regards area as merely a 'measure of ambition', given that it may be related more to the contemporary stage of development of the town. He suggests that new towns may have been prone to over-optimism and old towns to protecting what existed. He, and Delaney (1977, 39), rightly point out that the size of the walled area need not be a reflection of the density of settlement within and thus of the population defended by the town walls. Nonetheless, in the context of this study, a comparison of areas helps to break down the isolation necessarily involved, and provides a yardstick, however flawed, by which to judge the Irish scene. This does seem to suggest that the areas of Irish walled towns, single and combined, were not unduly ambitious. The case for ambition or pride being a factor in town walling will be discussed again because it is often raised, especially in relation to the transformation of an earthen into a stone enclosure. Moreover, given the lack of evidence for the structural reality of town walls at too many Irish sites, the actual walled area is more than usually significant. While the evidence it provides is not very strong, it does seem to point generally to a close relationship between the settled and the walled areas at most sites, because of the small to medium size of the majority of Irish walled towns, and of the known prominence of many of the larger.

PERIMETER   Although quoted here as approximate and conservatively under-estimated values the perimeters or circuits of the walled towns provide another basis for comparison, as well as some measure of the task undertaken at each site.

Clearly, a generally positive relationship may be expected between size of walled area and length of perimeter, and this exists—almost the same walled areas, simple or complex, appear at the top of both lists, that is those with areas above 25 ha. and perimeters above 2000m (Table 3.2). The combined areas at Drogheda, Dundalk and Limerick each had over 3000m of town walls. This is presuming that the two river fronts at Drogheda were completely walled at some stage, which seems likely.

The riverside, in fact, is generally the only complicating factor in a simple relationship between area and perimeter. Thus Kilkenny, the only town with three separate walled areas, had apparently a smaller total circuit (2925m) than those just mentioned. This is because about 1200m of riverfront along the main river Nore is excluded. In the mid-seventeenth century the riverfront at the Hightown was clearly open, with properties running down to it from the main street (Civil Survey 1654–6), but this need not always have been so. Probably only

Table 3.2: Walled Towns in Order of Size

AREA IN HECTARES		CIRCUIT SIZE (2000M+)
43	Kilkenny 3	I
43	Drogheda 2,	II
39	New Ross	V
34	Dundalk 2	III
32	(Drogheda Louth)	IX
30	Belfast	X
29	(Kilkenny Hightown)	VI
28	Limerick 2, Athenry	IV, X
25	Ardee, Wexford, Rindown	VII, –, –
23	Waterford 2, Trim 2	VII, –
21	Kells, (Dundalk Lower)	
20	Dublin, Roscommon ?	
19	Youghal 2	
17	Loughrea	
16	Athy 2, Bandon 2	
15	Castledermot, Athboy ?, Tipperary ?	
14	Cashel, Clonmel, Coleraine, Cork, Kinsale 2, (Limerick Englishtown), Maryborough ?, Fore ?	
13	Carlow, Galway, Kilmallock, (Limerick Irishtown), (Dundalk Upper), Naas ?, Newry 2 ?	
12	Carrick-on-Suir, Londonderry, Gowran ?	
11	Athlone 2, Carrickfergus, (Drogheda Meath)	
10	Navan, (Kilkenny Irishtown), Callan ?, Downpatrick ?, Nenagh ?	
9	Kildare ?	
8	Carlingford ?, Clonmines ?, Thurles ?	
7	Fethard, Thomastown ?	
6	Dungarvan, (Athlone East)	
5	Buttevant ?, Philipstown ?	
4	Adare ?, Dingle ?, Inistioge ? (Athlone West)	
3	Jamestown, (Kinsale Basetown)	
1	(Youghal Basetown)	

NB Only some of the double walled towns are listed both together and separately.

archaeological evidence will resolve this matter for most sites. There is some medieval documentary evidence for 'open' riversides initially. In 1324, for example, properties at Carrick-on-Suir were described as lying 'in length from the King's street . . . to the river called Le Soure on the South', while others lay 'in length from the King's street on the South to the stone wall [of the town] on the North'. A similar description is given for a Clonmel property *c*.1350. Yet it has also been stated that the 'town wall and towers along the quays there were levelled for river improvements, post-1756', and the late-seventeenth century maps show the riverfront partially walled. Likewise, the 1624 map of Waterford Harbour seems to suggest that Carrick-on-Suir was also by then walled along the river. To return to Kilkenny, no positive evidence for a riverside wall at the Hightown has been found and so it has been stated that 'no wall was built along the river' there (Bradley 1975, 211). However, there was a tower known as Evan's, in the grounds of the former friary by the river, which may have been the remains of the town wall or of a defended friary wall acting in the same way. A slightly earlier eye-witness account of the adjacent Irishtown of Kilkenny described it, at least, as 'washed by the river' on the east and 'defended by walls and turrets' on the west (Bishop Rothe, *c*.1625).

The evidence from these towns, and that of the stages by which a riverside wall was finally built at seventeenth century Athlone East, as well as at medieval Dublin, suggest that they may have been a common feature, if short-lived and reluctantly built. Indeed, Harvey (1911, 193) states that a complete circuit was the norm at single walled towns in Britain, even when the sea or a broad river formed part of the defence of the town, except at a few sites such as Tenby and double walled towns like York. None of the three English double walled towns illustrated by Speed—York, Bristol and Norwich—had a wall along the riverside then and Hull, a single walled town, had a wall along the major river but not along the minor. The sheer inconvenience of not having free access to the quay would be likely to cause it to be removed, however piecemeal, when the pressures of trade grew as a sense of danger waned. For Kilkenny more research in property documents for the medieval period contained in the Ormond collection might well prove Bradley's statement wrong, and show that, as at Clonmel, an early absence of a town wall by the river was followed by a later presence, of which Evan's tower was the sole survivor by the seventeenth century. Certainly, it would seem not unreasonable to have left the riverside wall to the last, because of the defence inherent in what was, in effect, a natural fosse and one often of considerable proportions. Therefore, riverside walls may have been considered unnecessary as well as undersirable by many towns until they were faced with a specific danger. This is what seems to have happened at Waterford in 1377, when it was attacked at the quay by foreign ships after which a riverside wall was built, and earlier in the century at Dublin, during the Bruce emergency (1315–18).

Despite the map and other evidence at Drogheda pointing to riverside walls, some less prominent double walled towns divided by a river may not have been completely walled as individuals, like their English counterparts. If they faced each other directly the separate walls could have formed in effect an unbroken circuit interrupted only by the river. The two points where the river 'cut' the circuit could have had a chain or other type of movable boom, or some more fixed structure, partially underwater, to prevent access to the walled area. The river itself was, as noted above, a form of defence in that it involved a change in transport, with boats being required by would-be assailants. These would be vulnerable to attack from the ends of each half circuit at the river, where there were often towers. In addition, they would be slow-moving, of limited carrying capacity and uncertain in terms of achieving a common landfall. At Bandon, to judge from the *c*.1620 and *c*.1630 maps, an actual continuation of the wall itself seems to have been intended. This would have required some type of opening for river transport, at least on the down-stream side, and was probably only feasible if the river was shallow or had islands. In medieval towns especially the size of the river too may have been a crucial factor, as well as the location of the town. Kilkenny and other towns situated far inland on the major River Nore, such as

Inistioge and Thomastown, may provide examples of walls being completed by the riverside much later than the rest of the circuit, if at all, for these reasons. However, towns on a minor river would seem more likely than not to have been fully walled, especially if the river was fordable, as it was at Ardee.

Sea walls fall into the same category as river walls and, again, the evidence is mixed. The town wall at Youghal, including that of the Basetown, was a complete circuit according to the map evidence, *c*.1587–1776, but it was not necessarily built as a piece. There is no evidence that there ever was a wall by the sea at Wexford and, possibly, at Carlingford too. There is, however, some vague map and street evidence pointing to a wall running southwards from the royal castle at Carlingford along by the sea, and a petition of 1537 may have been intended as the prelude to ending Wexford being 'open' on one, the sea, side. Dungarvan's circuit was complete, and generally this is the pattern, whether at sea or river ports—for example, Galway and ultimately Carrickfergus (ill. 6), or Cork and Limerick. At both of the latter the walls largely followed the outlines of the island sites, enhancing the natural defensive quality rather than relying on it. This, again, suggests that a complete circuit was the stronger likelihood generally.

Of course, such completion may have been more apparent than real, given that the economic pressures on the sea or riverside walls were the strongest and often resulted in the cutting of private 'doors', if not the actual removal of sections of the wall. Cork provides a good example of the problems, its town wall being entirely a riverside wall. In 1286 and 1291 licences were given to citizens to 'break the walls', on the latter occasion specifically so that a ship might be launched, but provided that the damage was made good. The eighteenth century records list many instances of more permanent breaches or private gates and passages, but still apparently bearing the responsibility for restoration, if so required. A problem, also illustrated by the Cork records of the seventeenth century, was the vulnerability of riverside walls to physical undermining by the

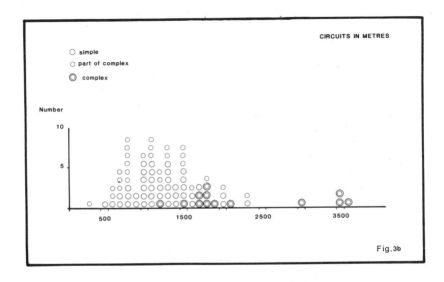

Fig.3b

ever-present flowing waters. This too, elsewhere, may have encouraged the early demise of riverside or sea walls.

Using, therefore, the potential as opposed to the known perimeter would add Ardee, Trim and Wexford to the 2000–3000m group, but would make the combined circuits at Kilkenny by far the largest at over 4000m. Carrick-on-Suir's perimeter would almost double in size (875 to 1550m) but the increase at Carlingford and some other sites would be less significant and would not alter their classification. The number of really large circuits (over 2000m) would change slightly, increasing by about 5%.

The great majority (over 75%) of all walled areas had perimeters within the range 500–2000m. They are more or less equally distributed between three sub-divisions of that range—500–1000, 1000–1500, 1500–2000m—as figure 3.b illustrates. Below them there were only the Basetown (300m) at Youghal and the east side of Athboy (?450m), if it was walled at all. Amongst the smallest perimeters (500–1000m) were possibly those of the two parts of both medieval Wexford and Hiberno-Norse Dublin, and of its later extension, Tudor Dingle and both parts of Athlone—the medieval/Stuart East and the seventeenth century West. Likewise, no distinction can be made in the middle range (1000–1500m) between medieval and early modern. Coleraine and Fethard were close in size of circuit, although the Coleraine wall was never completed along the river as intended. The two separate circuits of the twin walled areas at medieval Trim, facing each other across the Boyne, were not very dissimilar, the northern medium sized and the southern small, as were the two walled areas alongside each other at sixteenth century Newry to judge by the map evidence at least. Londonderry's seventeenth century circuit was also modest and similar to that of the medieval Irishtown at Limerick (1375m). Likewise, the circuits of the original Hiberno-Norse and the additional Anglo-Norman towns at Waterford were each of modest lengths.

This raises the question of joint or internal walls which in Waterford's case (300m) are included only in the figure for the original circuit. Just a few are known and they varied in length from Dundalk's 125m and Kinsale's 100m to Dublin's 575m. The adjacent walls at Newry were however totally separate although closely parallel structures, as were the comparable walls of Kilkenny Hightown and Irishtown along the Bregagh river.

Amongst the last sub-group (1500–2000), the large as opposed to the very large circuits (over 2000m), there were some large individual walled areas such as the maintown of Youghal, both parts of Dundalk and Kilkenny Hightown (if its riverside is not counted). Also included in this group for a special reason was Drogheda Meath (11 ha., 1525m). Here the complexity of its shape was the main factor leading to a large perimeter. The same was true for Cashel (14 ha., 1550m), but by the same token, a simple smooth outline such as that of Kells had a reverse relationship. Its area was slightly more than Dublin's full extent but its circuit slightly less (21: 20 ha. and 1650:1750m). Also within this range of large perimeters were Ardee, Kilmallock and Limerick Englishtown, but the only post-medieval representative was Bandon's complete circuit.

The very large circuits (over 2000m) have been referred to at the beginning of the section and are high-lighted on Table 3.2. They were relatively few in number but included the circuit of Drogheda on the Louth side alone, those of Athenry (max.), Belfast and New Ross, and the combined circuit of Waterford. If riversides are counted a few, such as Kilkenny Hightown and Ardee, would join this group. The largest of all (over 3000m) were only combined circuits—those at Limerick, Dundalk, Drogheda and, possibly, Kilkenny.

As for English examples, there appears not surprisingly to be a tendency towards greater length than was the case in Ireland but the sample of 20 (including 3 Welsh), derived from the Turner and Harvey gazetteers, is too small for certainty. Of these 50% had circuits over 2000m, most of which were between 2000 and 3000m and 25% each had circuits of 1000–2000m and 500–1500m. The largest included London, Colchester, Canterbury, Chester and Newcastle-upon-Tyne, all about 3240m, with York (4455m) and Coventry (4860m) being larger than even Kilkenny at its potential maximum. Norwich, also large (3645m), was a twin walled area but did not have a riverside wall in 1610 (Speed map). What may have been the middle range of English circuits included those at Shrewsbury (1620m), Hereford (1646m) and Southampton (1822m). The Welsh towns predominated amongst the smallest range—Chepstow, an incomplete circuit, consisting of 1123m, Conway 1280m and Caernarvon 732m. Totnes was again distinguished by its small size with a circuit of 594m.

Speed 1610, in the text accompanying each map, quotes figures for the perimeters of 14 of the 44 towns illustrated as walled. A couple are quoted in English miles and the rest in 'paces'. Some of the figures can be cross-checked with Harvey or Turner but, while some seem to agree—those for Shrewsbury and Hereford in particular—others do not—Southampton and Colchester are considerably underestimated. Consequently, it is probably better not to use Speed's figures, although, as they cover over a quarter of the walled towns illustrated, they would have allowed a larger sample than those provided by either Turner or Harvey.

SHAPE

The shape of Irish walled towns, while varied in detail, was generally basically square or rectangular (fig.3.c). Those at major rivers tended to lose some angularity for a more semi-circular shape. This was true of New Ross, where the outline had a broad curve, but only partly true of Drogheda Louth. The opposing Drogheda Meath, while possibly initially rectangular, was ultimately highly irregular. Perhaps the most varied shapes were those of towns not sited close to major rivers, such as five-sided Athenry, diamond-shaped Castledermot, almost circular Kells and the irregularly shaped Tipperary towns of Fethard and Cashel. As with Drogheda, the twin walled areas of Limerick were quite different, the Englishtown triangular and the Irishtown square, but both irregularly so. Dundalk's two walled areas were more similar, in that both were irregular

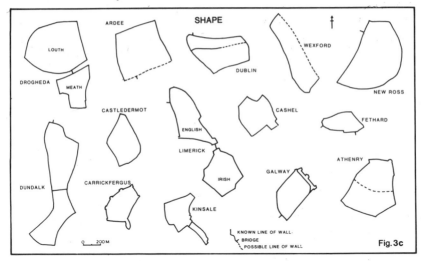

Fig. 3c

rectangles, but they were related rather indirectly due to a change of alignment of the underlying ridge, unlike those at nearby Newry or at Wexford. The slight change in shape, from square to rectangle, was often a feature of double walled towns. The small Basetown at Youghal and Kilkenny St. John's were both almost square while their respective, large main towns were rectangular. The Irishtown at the latter was markedly more irregular than the other two and so there was considerable diversity of shape at Kilkenny.

Truly regular shapes were rare and, not surprisingly, appear to be related to the later walled towns of the post-medieval period. Jamestown was the most regular, but also one of the smallest and latest, but others, such as Maryborough and Port-arlington, were intended to be regular to judge from the map evidence. However, the actual shape of Bandon was a considerable modification of the early, regular plans, and even Londonderry (ill. 7) achieved only a distorted regularity. This was largely due to alterations made to the line in order to take advantage of the features of the ridge site. In terms of shape detail, the protruding angular bastions, characteristic of this and other later circuits, tend to distinguish them clearly from their medieval predecessors. Yet, they were just the lineal, if rather exaggerated, successors of medieval towers and so their distinctiveness was really a matter of style rather than shape. Of course, some medieval circuits, such as Athlone East and Limerick Irishtown, were modernised in such a way but their basic shape was not really changed.

Many medieval walled areas were extended, as already indicated, but again such a process had different results at different sites. The possible extensions at Cork and Wexford maintained the original shape by the simple process of continuing the existing lines. The later extensions at Dublin and Carrickfergus also reinforced the existing, less regular, shapes by the same means. At Waterford, in contrast, the later walled area was ultimately vaguely rectanglar, placed partly along the shortest side of the original triangular area. The result was a totally irregular shape for the combined walled areas.

The term 'circuit' implies a circular shape, yet this was clearly not the norm for Irish walled towns. It is probably derived more from the fact that a wall surrounded a town and could be walked around—on top of, inside or outside. The earliest map of Drogheda, admittedly only a rough sketch, gives such an idealised picture—a town composed of two semi-circles separated by the river—but the documentary evidence shows that this is unlikely to have been true, even in 1574 (Thomas 1975, 181). Concentric town walls, which add to this circular aspect and were characteristic of some major European walled towns such as Paris, are conspicuously absent from the Irish scene. The seventeenth century lines at Limerick Irishtown did have this effect but they did not enclose a substantial additional area. In fact, they may have caused the destruction of buildings or even streets that had arisen close to the medieval wall. The same may have been true at other towns during the end of the seventeenth century although it is not known if any of the new lines were fully concentric. Small survivals still exist at Ardee and Kilmallock, but at Galway the new developments, which were more elaborate like those of Limerick Irishtown, were restricted to the east wall only (1651 map). The only other instance of an 'outer' wall that might have been concentric is the one described, all too briefly, for Buttevant (Smith 1750 I 313). Unfortunately the dating of the inner and outer circuits and their relative extents are not known from this or other sources.

Turner (1970, 55) describes the outline of English and Welsh town walls very briefly as 'almost always either rectangular or roughly circular'. The few English examples in Bradley's comparative map (1985 fig. 17.4) suggest a picture closer to the Irish. They show evidence of much small-scale variation, ranging from subtle alteration of a geometric figure, such as the rectangle at Dorchester-on-Thames, to considerable distortion of the same ideal at Southampton, due there largely to the influence of the outline of the coast in the SW corner. Exeter had a regular geometric shape—semi-circular like New Ross—but Bristol was much extended and highly irregular. Harvey (1911, 200–220), in similar vein, indicates the general shapes of the English and Welsh towns as 'square, rectangular or circular', but the most useful work for comparison is Speed's (1610) atlas. In it the shapes of 44 walled English and Welsh towns are clearly illustrated in their post-medieval state, and shown in a style similar to that employed for the 4 Irish examples—Dublin, Cork, Limerick and Galway. Similarities can be drawn between Fethard and Stamford, two small towns with irregular shapes, and Kells and Chichester, both generally circular and quite large. In the same simplistic way the regularity of Ardee's square shape was similar to that of Winchester, and of Cork's river-modified rectangle to Southampton's. Likewise, New Ross's broad semi-circle was like London's or even Hull's, viewed from the minor river. At the level of detail the elaborate, 'modern' style of Berwick's sixteenth century circuit, which was unique in England (Beresford and St. Joseph 1979, 193–5, figs. 79a–b), can be seen as a forerunner of seventeenth century Londonderry and other later Irish walled towns.

However, these similarities are largely superficial, derived to some extent from comparing similar sites, especially those without a marked variation in slope and/or with a dominant water element, such as a major river or the sea. Site alone cannot account for the individuality of shape at Irish, or indeed British, walled towns. The dominant feature is in fact the sheer variety of shape, especially in terms of detail. It is hardly an exaggeration to say that no two walled towns were alike in this respect. Yet clearly, there was the possibility of common developers, both between the mainland and its colony, and within Ireland itself. Not only was the town used as a tool of colonisation in the thirteenth century in particular, but the major landowners had extensive estates on both sides of the Irish Sea. Furthermore, these often included more than one Irish town—Galway and Loughrea were de Burgh towns, Drogheda Meath and Trim were de Lacy creations. There were many others, including the three fitzMaurice towns linked by one murage grant in 1286—Tralee, Mallow and Ardfert (list B). The initial development of a town and its original walling were not necessarily coincident in time, especially in the Middle Ages, but the capacity undoubtedly existed for the repeated use of a small number of expert builders and designers, perhaps even some who worked extensively for Edward I in Wales and France. Therefore, despite appearances to the contrary, a degree of planning, and even some uniformity, may have been characteristic of medieval walled towns initially. Indeed, it is not impossible that applications for murage grants were supported by outline plans at least. The careful administration of murage accounting, which is clear from the documents, suggests so and inspection on the ground may well have required plans for reference.

There is one map in the Hardiman collection (TCD MS 1209/76) which seems to be a prototype for a seventeenth century walled town and there may have been medieval equivalents. Yet, the post-medieval walled towns that were built exhibit as a group almost as much variety as their predecessors, while retaining distinguishing, common characteristics of style and a greater degree of regularity of shape. Alternative designs are known for Bandon (TCD MSS 1209/39, 41–2), both highly regular, but the reality on the ground was clearly a modification. This is most striking at the church in the southern walled area and is comparable with a major irregularity in the medieval circuit at Cashel. It suggests that pecularities of land ownership may be significant for individuality of shape. Again, there is evidence in support of this from the seventeenth century for the delay in commencing building at Londonderry, compared with Coleraine, was said to have been due to 'the greater difficulty' experienced there in acquiring land rights (Milligan 1949–50 I 17).

The time factor may have been important, too, for allowing variety to develop both in overall shape and details. There are two ways in which it may have had an influence. Firstly, progress on building a medieval town wall may have been slow. Bradley (1975, 93) has suggested about one hundred years for Kilkenny Hightown, using some internal evidence supported by comparable time-scales which have been indicated for some English towns by Turner (1970, 50). This matter will be discussed in the next chapter but, if true, at issue is probably completion to the planned 'strength and style', rather than the long existence of a circuit with actual gaps in it, which would have been next to useless. Such a time-scale does highlight the considerable capacity for small-scale alterations to the original scheme which could give rise to much of the variableness under discussion here. Factors which might encourage such modifications *en passant* would be land-holding considerations, particularly with regard to the church or the major landlord, and questions of ease of access, some of which might also be associated with such owners.

Secondly, because the medieval walls, in particular, stood for so many centuries they experienced much repair activity. Normal weathering contributed to this, also possibly poor materials or workmanship, but in Ireland attacks by enemies were a particular, additional and recurrent problem of the later Middle Ages. The resulting repair work might well lead to minor modifications or even major ones, if the line had proved to be especially vulnerable because of some locally based factor, which could then be at least partially remedied. Major extensions were another consequence of a long time-scale. In fact they provide one of the few contrasts between the medieval and early modern walled towns, in that the latter were not extended. New lines of fortifications were proposed for Londonderry after the siege (1705 map) but they were not built. They were intended very much as outer and extremely elaborate lines of defence which would link the walled town with a series of new forts. Extensions also could alter the shape to give much irregularity, particularly at the macro-level as, for example, at Waterford and Kinsale (ill. 8), but this did not invariably follow. The examples of Cork and Wexford, where a simple shape was maintained despite being enlarged, have already been quoted. Combined walled towns such as those at Kilkenny and Drogheda were really a special case because they were in fact separate circuits that just happened to be adjacent. The very different shapes of the walled areas at these sites was partly the result of extensions and partly of major differences in the underlying topography. The latter was also the main cause of the major contrasts in the shapes of Limerick's walled English and Irish towns.

Such highly individual responses suggest that the overriding consideration may have often been to have a settled area enclosed rather than to produce a line of maximum defence. No doubt care was taken to achieve both, wherever possible, but to the community an undefended and heavily settled suburb might have seemed a greater danger than a weak defensive line. Extensions, which show up most clearly as oddities in the shape of a walled town may, therefore, have a different, but still defensive, significance. The shape of the walled area may thus mark stages in the growth of the town, coupled with periods of fear. If the extension was on a generous scale it may indicate a sense of optimism that growth was possible in the future, or a sense of forboding that the extra space would be needed for an influx of refugees from the surrounding area. As the colony shrank, such optimism was often found to be misplaced, but this was not generally reflected in the shape. At least, there is no evidence of town walls being reduced for this reason, although some may have faded away, particularly at sites on list B. Indeed, the older lines were often retained, as for example at Waterford and Dublin, and were found to be useful as inner defences. Elsewhere, inner lines were later built. These are known to have existed at Dundalk and Limerick

Englishtown and they may have been quite common. But they, and the new inner wall at sixteenth century Athenry, have little relevance here because they did not alter the shape of the walled town in the way that extensions did.

Perhaps the most important result of a consideration of shape is that it indicates that the capacity for change was considerable, that in fact a town wall was not as rigid a structure as might be supposed. The changes might be based on defence considerations but they might just as well be derived from matters of convenience. A walled town was still a functioning town in which ease of access and land-use considerations were of day-to-day importance, while those of defence were for the future or at worst the short-term present. For the medieval period, there are no maps of the original walled areas so that it is not possible to measure the extent of alteration from the original shape, or the deviation from a geometric norm. Nonetheless, there is sufficient documentary evidence to confirm that the highly individual shapes were not necessarily the original. Archaeological work in the future may indicate more satisfactorily the detailed evolution of the shape of some walled towns.

STRUCTURE

The term 'town wall' is used to refer to the whole circuit, irrespective of the structural nature of the curtain wall—earth, wood, stone or a combination. It comprises, in addition, the possible external fosse and internal rampart, gates and towers or bastions, and associated small outer lines of fortification or forts. Towers and gates are dealt with separately here after the curtain wall where all the other features and their relationship with castles or large forts are discussed. Again, it must be noted that the detailed information recorded in Table 3.3 is only available for less than half of the towns on list A and even then, with a few notable exceptions, it is based on small amounts of physical remains, surviving or recently uncovered (Table 3.4). In addition, while some of the documentary evidence for medieval towns is contemporary, the most useful, the maps or surveys, is, as already emphasised, post-medieval. The Tudor/Stuart walled towns fare better, having maps generally contemporary with their defences and detailed accounts of the work in progress or on completion.

CURTAIN WALL   The simplest form of circuit, an earthen bank, produced by digging a boundary ditch, and probably topped by some sort of wooden fencing was, as already indicated in chapter I, not necessarily the prerogative of towns, although it may have often been their initial defensive line. There is evidence from Waterford of such a structure. It was created in the twelfth century on top of some dwellings and re-levelled later in the century so that its outer edge, reinforced by gravel, could provide the foundation of the first stone wall. There is similar evidence for Drogheda Meath where an earthen rampart and ditch seems to have predated the thirteenth century stone wall on the east side. Therefore, this may have been quite a common procedure, with only the earliest and/or most vulnerable towns going through the intermediate structural stages seen in the three successive and parallel Hiberno-Norse waterfront walls at Dublin.

The intensive excavations carried out at the Wood Quay site in Dublin, 1969–79, have been most productive for the elucidation of early town wall development (O'Riordain/Wallace, 1971–85). The first wall (Ia) was very similar to, if older than, the Waterford example but its late tenth century successor (Ib) was a more complex feature. It consisted of a bank of mixed earth and gravel with a core provided by a post and wattle fence, the whole bonded together by estuarine mud and protected from the river by an outer breakwater of post and wattle. This was re-used by the third wall (Ic), dated to *c*.1000 and built riverside of its predecessor. As might be expected it was more formidable and sophisticated again, the earthen bank including gravel and stones reinforced by layers of brushwood, covered by estuarine mud and crowned by a post and wattle palisade, later replaced by a wooden stave wall. It is possible that such a development, at least as regards the bank, only happened at Dublin along the waterfront of the Liffey, and that the rest of the earthen circuit there was simpler, basically of Ia construction, on top of which was a palisade or stave 'wall'. In other words, it may have been very similar to the earliest structures at Waterford and Drogheda.

Such ditch-and-bank circuits never quite died out as complete or partial town defences in Ireland, or indeed in England and Wales. Harvey (1911) notes seven examples including Cambridge, Portsmouth and the highly planned Flint. There are doubts as to whether the late thirteenth century new town of Winchelsea (Turner 1970, 176–9) ever achieved the stone wall intended to complete its earthen defences. In Russia all town walls were wooden except those at Moscow, Smolensk and Novgorod (Gutkind 1946, 355). Indeed as many as 25% of the sites on list A may not have had walls of stone. Amongst these are places like Callan where a 'section of the town wall' of unspecified form has been described as 'removed recently', but where documentary evidence from the fifteenth century onwards refers only to a 'common ditch'. The seventeenth century map of Callan fails to clarify the matter, the line shown could be either a ditch and bank or a stone wall. The nearby town of Gowran had a composite wall to judge from its early eighteenth century map—'town wall' on one side and 'rampart' or 'trench' on the other—but its fifteenth century murage grant specified a 'stone wall', for which tolls were allowed for forty years. Of course, a complete stone wall may have been built, part of which had disappeared by the eighteenth century, or else a compromise was made when the toll revenue failed to come up to expectations. A further Co. Kilkenny example is Inistioge for which there is no map evidence but a number of post-medieval documentary references to the 'wall'. These imply stone but might refer to the wall of the priory rather than the town.

The ditch-and-bank type of structure actually had something of a revival in the 17th century. The reason for this re-emergence of essentially earthen defences was largely the introduction of cannon which required a firm, but broad and therefore expensive, base on which to operate. Not all medieval stone walls had sufficiently broad wall-walks to accommodate cannon. Earthen structures also had the advantage of entrapping cannon balls, rather than causing them to

Table 3.3: Structural Features of Town Wall

	1	2	3	4	5
LIST A	FABRIC	DETAILS	MEASUREMENT IN METRES *	GATES	TOWERS
Adare	S				
Ardee	S+F+(E)			4+1P+1Ex	
Athboy	S			3?	1
Athenry	S+F+E+	Int Ramp	3.5-4.5h in 6-7h out 0.6w.	4+2I?+3P	6-8
Athlone E	S+F+(E)/	E Int Ramp.	3-4h,1w.	2-3/1-3	6/5B
W	E+F	W Hedge on Ramp.	F 2d.		
Athy	?			1	
Bandon N/S	S+F	Batt, slate WW-ext St.	10-15h, 2.5w.	1+3P/ 2+1P	3/3B
Belfast	F+E	Ramp, stones, trees.		3	9-10B
Buttevant	S			2?	
Callan	S?+F			5	
Carlingford	S			3-4	3?
Carlow	S			3-4	
Carrickfergus	S<-E/S<- E/W+F	Batt, lst/sst.	3-5h, 2w. F1d,5w. fd 1.5-2.4w, 1-5d.	2+2Q	6B
Carrick-on-Suir	S	WW		4	3
Cashel	S+(E)	'good'		5	2
Castledermot	S+F?			3-4	
Clonmel	S+F?+(E)	Batt, Arch.		4+1Q+1P	7-10
Clonmines	S+F			1	1
Coleraine	F+E	Sods/hedge -Ramp, Pal dams -Fosse.	E3.5h,3w. F2d, 12 w.	2+1P	9B
Cork	S+F	Batt, lst, BB,WW- ext St.	6.4h,1w. special fd.	2+1Q+5P	14
Dingle	S			2-3?	3-4?
Downpatrick	S+F			1+?	
Drogheda L/M	S+F+(E)	Batt,Arch. WW.	5.4h,1.5w.	4+3P+I /3+2P	12/6
Dublin	S<-E/W+F	Batt,Ramp, BB, Butt, stairs in T.	3.5-5h, 1.5w.	7+3I+?Q+8 Ex	14
Dundalk L/U	S/E+F	Composite		3+1P+I/3	5+
Dungarvan	S			2+2P?	4
Fethard	S+F(R)	lst	1.5-2.4h now.	4+1P	5
Fore	S?+F+E			2	
Galway	S+F+(E/S)	Batt, ramp, WW, ext stairs in T.		3+2Q+BR	12
Gowran	S/E+F	Composite		2+1Ex?	
Inistioge	?S			2-4?	

1	2	3	4	5	
LIST A	FABRIC	DETAILS	MEASUREMENT IN METRES *	GATES	TOWERS
Jamestown	S+?			3	6B
Kells	S			5	1+
Kildare	S?+F			3	
Kilkenny H/I/J	S+F+(E)	Batt, BB, lst.	3.5h now.	6+1P+I/3/ 1+P+1Ex	5/?1
Kilmallock	S+F+(E)	Batt,WW,	6.h, 1-2h now.	4+1P+1Ex	4
Kinsale	S+F+(E)			4+2Q+I	15
Limerick E/I	S+F+(E)	Batt, lst, WW, Ramp.	5h,1.6-2w. shallow fd.	3+I+4Q +BR+4P/4+2P	17/10
Londonderry	S+F	Batt, BB, sst, Ramp-stone faced.	6-7.5h. 4-9w ramp.	7	2T+10B
Loughrea	S+F			3+1P	1
Maryborough	S?+F				
Naas	S?+F?	?Int Ramp.		6?	
Navan	S			3	1+
Nenagh	S?				
New Ross	S+F+(E)	Ramp, marble. F 6w.		5+3-4Q	7
Newry	S?/E+F	Batt.		4+I	2
Philipstown	S?+F			2?	
Rindown	S/F		4.5h,1.2w.	1	3
Roscommon	E?+F			2	3B
Thomastown	S			3-4	2-14?
Thurles	S?			2-3	
Tipperary	S?			3-4?	
Trim	S+F			4+1P+1Q	2
Waterford	S+F +(E/S)	Batt, Ramp, WW, BB, shale/lst.	5-6h,1.8w.	5-6+3I+6Q	19
Wexford	S+F	Int Ramp.	1.2-1.4w excav.	5+1P+3I+2Q	5
Youghal	S+F +(E)	Batt, Butt, WW.	2.4-5h, 0.6w.	2+I+2Q+1P	13

NOTES

(1) E: earthen, in seventeenth century at least, face sometimes strengthened by sods and stonework
(E): later addition, radical change from previous form.
W: wooden   S : stone
F : fosse or ditch, (R) river as fosse   ? : unknown; or unproven if used with 'S' or 'F'

(2) Arch : arches in wall   Batt : battlemented top   BB : battered base
Butt : buttress(es)   Ramp : rampart   WW : wall-walk
fd : foundation   Pal : palisade   T : tower
St : stairs   lst : limestone   sst : sandstone
int/ext : internal/external
Composite : wall in some sections of stone and others earth and/or fosse

(3) * measurements are for stone wall unless indicated otherwise
E : earthen structure   F : fosse   fd : foundations
h - w - d : high - wide - deep   excav : excavation details

(4) Values are given for MAIN GATES first, where it is possible to distinguish them, and then for quay Q, internal I, postern P, gate on bridge BR, and external Ex.

(5) Values are given for the maximum known towers (or bastions B if mentioned) excluding gate towers.

NB: The numbers of gates and towers have been established by evidence available so far but not all were necessarily present at any one period. Most of the evidence is post-medieval.

6 Carrickfergus, *c*.1612

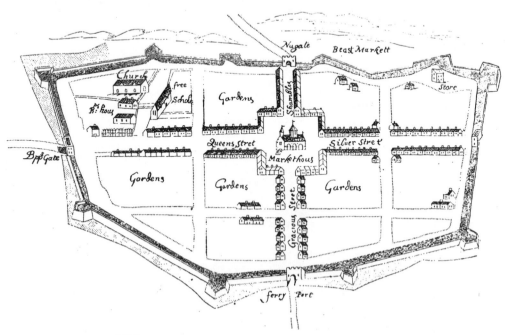

7 Londonderry, 1622/25
from Raven's plan

ricochet with unpredictable results as stone could. Internal ramparts could be used, rebuilt or introduced, for example at Wexford and Limerick Irishtown. Small external 'rampiers' and flankers could be added to medieval circuits, like those at Drogheda Meath, Ardee, Kilmallock and Galway. Stone walls and fosses were intended for both the earlier plantation towns of Maryborough and Philipstown, but it can only be proved that the associated forts were actually built of stone. At the same time Carrickfergus's medieval wall (ill. 6), which was still not unlike the earliest at Dublin and Waterford, was upgraded and extended twice, becoming, first of all, a larger earthen rampart with a wider ditch, and then a totally stone structure. But the town walls of Belfast, Athlone West and Coleraine were never more than earthen bank-and-fosse structures, although internally strengthened with stones. Lines of quick-set hedge were now favoured as additional bank top or slope defence and they, too, may have been common earlier. Trees even appeared at Belfast, but probably only later and for aesthetic rather than defensive reasons.

The Coleraine 'sod' wall may be compared with the contemporary and nearby Londonderry stone wall to judge the extent of such a sophisticated but earthen structure (ill. 7). Its general width of 3m was not much less than the minimum of 4m for Londonderry, although in places this is now as much as 9m wide. The height of the Coleraine rampart (3.5m) was only half that of the Londonderry (6–7.5m). These measurements are taken from the 1611 survey which, perhaps optimistically, described it as a 'good rampier of earth and sods'. Two years later, while describing it as 'handsome', a report also noted that it 'should have been built of stone' and should have been of smaller circumference. By 1616 'the needless charge' of keeping earth walls repaired was voiced. The next report, 1618–19, noted again the erosion problems. It also complained, firstly, that the bulwarks were inadequately small for the cannon likely to be required; and, secondly, that the gates which served as watch houses were very vulnerable, because they were made of timber instead of stone. By 1629 only this last complaint was actually accepted and acted upon. The argument put forward was that the wall had been built according to the specifications of the government's own surveyor of forts and so these criticisms were unjustified.

The Londonderry stone town wall was composed of a rampart with a core of earth, bounded on the inside by a retaining stone wall and on the outside by the town wall (ill. 9). This, the outwardly visible stone wall, rose above the rampart to give cover to men and machinery behind it, as its medieval equivalent, the battlemented parapet, had done earlier. It can be seen, therefore, as an improvement on the Coleraine wall in that it was stronger and less vulnerable to weathering. Yet, as the maps show, the fabric difference did not involve a stylistic change. In fact it was, as the murage grants also suggest for the medieval towns, the result of a conscious evaluation of the defensive needs of the town and the area as a whole. In this case the aim was to have one at least highly defendable centre in north Ulster. This role Londonderry provided in 1689 for Coleraine too, which was then abandoned because of the inadequacy of its wall in view of the nature of the expected challenge.

53

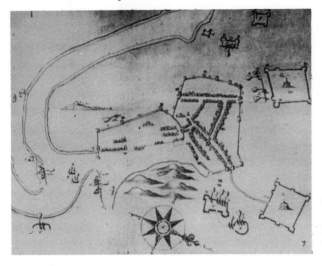

8 Kinsale, 1601 from a contemporary plan by Baptista Boazio

The vast majority of walled towns on list A (at least 70%) did have, what may be called, the 'traditional' or 'expected' stone town wall or walls. Many of these dated from the thirteenth and early fourteenth centuries. Furthermore, at five or six of the sites on list B stone town walls were planned at least. The features of these walls will be considered now as they appeared to later cartographers and writers, and as their surviving fragments above and below ground indicate today. Limerick will be used as a case study because of the quality of evidence available for it—architectural and archaeological, cartographic and written surveys, including pictorial views—and the extent of surviving fabric. The last is largely due to the neglect of the two walled towns when the new one was built in the eighteenth century. In addition, Limerick's town walls were in active use until the very end of the seventeenth century and so span the full period under consideration, including possibly the Hiberno-Norse (for the Englishtown area), although this has yet to be proved.

The sense of enclosure is particularly strong in the earliest, perspective maps of *c.*1587. One is the work of Francis Jobson (ill. 10) and the other is from the *Pacata Hibernia* series. They are fairly similar in style and could be different versions of the same map. In both the view is taken from the west, the Shannon side, and so it shows the outer side of the west wall and the inner side of the east. A sense of enclosure is also provided by the much later, 1685, Phillips sketch of the west side of Irishtown, and by Story's view of the 1690 siege which shows the whole of the east side, with the lines of bombardment. This was concentrated on the bridge linking the two towns, on the SE corner and on two projecting points, one each on the Irishtown and Englishtown walls. It was able to over-ride the medieval stone town walls and the flanking, probably mostly earthen, seventeenth century defensive line which ran along the outer edge of the fosse. A similar missile attack had, the year before, caused most of the damage to Londonderry. This view also gives an impression of a highly concentrated settlement within the

9 Londonderry
town wall rampart
above New Gate

walls, as do the perspective maps even more vividly, but the early seventeenth century plan-style maps show that there were gardens too, associated with some houses, and open spaces around churches and within the castle. All agree, although it is more obvious on the plans, that there was open space towards the wall along much of the eastern side of Englishtown and on both the east and west sides of Irishtown.

The medieval stone curtain wall at Limerick (ill. 10) was sufficiently wide to accommodate a wall-walk above which, on the outer side, rose the battlemented parapet. This allowed for offensive action from the town while providing protection for the defenders. Three styles of parapet are shown on the *c*.1587 maps in which the lengths of the solid sections varied and the number of loop-holes that pieced them. The largest appear to have been roofed and they, at least, may have been corbelled onto the outside of the wall. They could have provided better shelter for guards and a more effective means of defending the face of the wall. Only the Jobson map appears to show one on the Irishtown wall and it may, in fact, have been a different feature, perhaps a ground-level projection such as a small quay. At the same point the *Pacata Hibernia* map indicates a gateway—the East Water Gate. The maps show no visible means of access to the wall-walk, presumably it was reached via the gates and/or towers. No doorways are shown on the inner sides of the latter but Leask (1941, 103) found evidence of stairway access in a tower on the east side of Irishtown. The towers, and even more the gates, are shown as rising above the wall battlements, the more formidable being twice its height. There appears to be a distinction between the inner and outer sides of the wall, the inner being composed of larger and the outer of smaller blocks of stone, set in regular horizontal courses, except for the Englishtown wall along the Shannon from the bridge to the harbour. Whether this is an artistic device or a real distinction it is impossible to say, but it is the opposite of what Lynch (1984) found in one excavation.

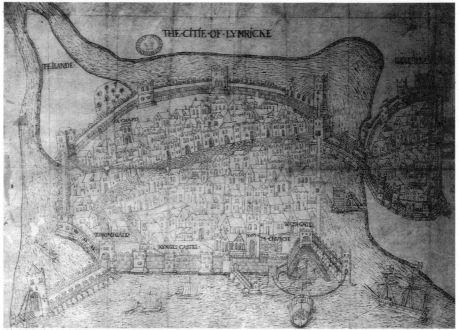

10 Limerick, *c*.1587

The west wall of the castle was very much part of the town wall and in no way projected to interrupt the line, but the battlementing and wall-walk seem to have been missing at the Franciscan friary in the south-east corner of Englishtown. Other maps also show the friary buildings outside but not as precisely adjacent to the town wall as do both the 1587. The friary's stone buildings could have acted as a forward defence and the wall-walk might have continued around its boundary wall; this is not shown because it would have been largely invisible from the angle of view. The defended harbour was formed by two additional walls extending at an acute angle from the quay below the town wall at the Water Gate. There were three to four simple arched openings in the Englishtown wall giving access to the fosse and to mills in the Shannon, including one from the castle. The final feature of note is the wall projecting around the southern gate of the Irishtown as an outer defence with three simple openings in it. It was lower and less elaborate than the medieval barbican at Drogheda Louth and so it probably represented an intermediate stage of forward gate defence, a late or post-medieval device and the lineal antecedent of the more elaborate fore-gate bastions of the seventeenth century. Then, too, the wall itself was enclosed by increasingly elaborate lines of defence made of earth, or earth and stone, and separated by fosses. These came to surround the Irishtown in particular because of its perceived role as a forward defence of the Englishtown, which had the stronger island site, but there were more isolated lines there too in the east. The late seventeenth century maps of Phillips and Goubet show Irishtown looking like a many-petalled flower, for which the medieval stone wall delimits the settled centre.

The fabric of the parts of the wall which still survived fifty years ago was studied by the antiquarian architect Leask, and a small additional section was revealed recently by the archaeologist Lynch (1984, illustrated in pl.VIIa). The sections concerned were parts of the east wall of Englishtown and of the east and west walls of Irishtown, the excavations being on either side of the West Water Gate there. The structure was found to be remarkably consistent, comprising of a wall, about 2m wide, with a core of mortared limestone rubble, faced inside and out with cut limestone blocks set in clear courses. In the area north of the gate there was no batter to the base of the wall, although there was to the south, but the upper part was off-set giving a small ledge. Lynch regarded the foundations as 'shallow', a maximum of 0.5m. They consisted of either mortared masonry or unmortared blocks loosely set with small stones, resting directly on boulder clay,

Table 3.4: Surviving Structures

TOWN	TOWN WALL			TOWERS	GATES
	almost complete circuit	short stretches of circuit	fragments		
Athenry	*			6	1
Athlone East		*		1+2B	
Carlingford		*			1R
Carrickfergus		*		3B	1A+excav
Clonmel		*		4+1B	1R
Clonmines		*		1?	1
Drogheda L+M		* +excav			1+1F
Dublin		* +excav		1 T/B	1A
Fethard	*			2	1
Fore			?		2
Galway			*	1T/B	
Jamestown		*			(1A)
Kells			?	1	
Kilkenny H+I		*		3 T/B	1A
Kilmallock		*			1
Limerick E+I		*		5(3+2)	1+excav
Londonderry	*			7 B	7A
Loughrea			*		1?
Navan				1	
New Ross			*	2	
Rindown		*	3	1	
Trim			*	1?	1
Waterford		* +excav		6	2 excav
Wexford		* +excav		3	1
Youghal		*		3	1R+1A

?: possible
excav: excavation
B: Bastion (under Towers)
T/B: Tower altered partly or wholly to Bastion

A: Archway restored
R: Gate house restored
F: Foregate or barbican

Fragments of the town wall are also visible, but generally in degraded form, at ARDEE, BANDON, CARRICK-ON-SUIR, CASTLEDERMOT, CASHEL, DINGLE, KINSALE and THOMASTOWN; excavations have been carried out at CORK. A possible base of a tower exists at ATHBOY and a possible gate house at THURLES.

which rises away from the gate site. The wall, which still survives there to *c*.5m in height, may reach close to its full height in the most southern stretch—Leask (1941, 107) noted there 'two small wrought stone corbels of a small machicolation'.

Turning now to the stone walls of other Irish towns attention will be given first of all to the physical structure and the dimensions, and then to the other features, many of which are similar to those of the Limerick walls. Tables 3.3 and 3.4 summarise the structural features, both known and surviving.

The preferred building stone seems to have been limestone, which is hardly surprising given the geology of lowland Ireland. An exception was Bandon whose walls were made of 'thick, black slate', available from two local quarries. The limestone boulders on the surviving sections at Carrickfergus tend to be rounded and set in a mortar, with smaller stones partially filling the gaps, but not clearly 'coursed' as the Limerick wall was. The outer side has a marginally more consistent and smoother face than the inner, and the top, the battlemented but by now rather degraded part, is set as a clear course above the rest. Carefully cut sandstones were used to face corners of the bastions. The surviving stretches of the town wall at Athenry and Fethard look similar, being composed of large and consistent blocks of limestone. The sections of town wall surviving at Waterford and Kilkenny seem to have a preponderance of angular or 'squared' blocks of dressed stone, especially towards the base, the least disturbed part. A concentration of larger blocks towards the base has been noted too at Youghal (Buckley 1900, 157). At Waterford shale is interspersed with the predominant limestone. However, the structure of few Irish curtain walls has been studied in detail, Fleming (1914) in particular was more interested in the gates and towers. Even the Londonderry wall has been described only briefly—as 'split-stone rubble, laid in lime mortar' (Rowan 1979). The Cork excavations revealed 'two well-built faces, mostly of limestone, with a rubble core held together by a lime and sand mortar' (Hurley and Power 1981). This is basically consistent with the Limerick evidence and most of the above. The degree of 'coursing', or setting of consistent blocks in horizontal layers, was obviously variable, being very evident at Dublin near the castle, but less evident in some of the other surviving stretches. Its significance cannot be assessed at this stage. It suggests careful initial building, but equally it may have resulted from later repair or even rebuilding. Perhaps more interesting is the evidence from recent studies of both the Cork and Wexford walls (1985 and 1976 resp.). These indicated that repair or rebuilding was made to look consistent from the outside, but was in fact inferior internally, being thinner than the original. In the case of Wexford, the new section was only half the original thickness and its masonry was less good. As time went on such a ruse probably became quite common and was not an unreasonable economy, so long as it remained generally unknown.

There is some evidence for the dimensions of these town walls, especially their width. Out of a dozen examples half had walls of 1–1.5m wide, including Dublin, Drogheda, Wexford, Waterford and Cork, with the walls of Youghal and Athenry just under 1m wide. Medieval Limerick, and seventeenth century Carrickfergus and Bandon were unusual at 2–3m wide, and Londonderry the

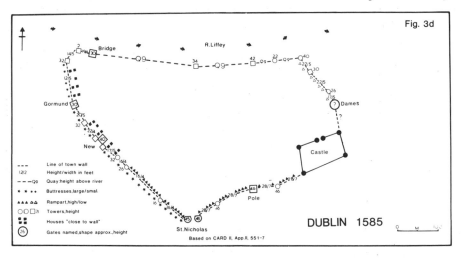

Fig. 3d

DUBLIN 1585

Based on CARD II, App.II, 551-7

Line of town wall
Height/width in feet
Quay:height above river
Buttresses,large/small.
Rampart,high/low
Towers,height
Houses "close to wall"
Gates named,shape approx.,height

ultimate at over 4m. Except in the case of the latter, such widths would allow for a narrow wall-walk, unless it was partially or largely a wooden addition extending inwards. This seems to have been the case at Youghal, where its post-holes survive in the inner face of the wall. A series of arches set against the wall on the inside may have been the solution at Drogheda Louth, as the 1749 map shows very clearly. A few of these survive at the St. Lawrence Gate and they may have been a feature at other towns. The 1673 map for Waterford suggests so for the south part and there is some surviving evidence for the west wall too, as there is possibly for the churchyard area of Clonmel. Arching served to strengthen the wall while reducing costs and allowing for easier cutting of loopholes. At other places, such as Wexford and Dublin, an earthen rampart provided high-level space within the wall as well as strengthening the structure. This particular solution, seen now in degraded form at Athenry, came into favour again with the use of cannon and was restored or built anew at Dublin and Limerick Irishtown, ulti-mately being incorporated in the very wide wall of Londonderry (best illustrated in the 1618–19 map). Stone arching may also have been used elsewhere then to strengthen the old medieval walls which had not been built with cannon-fire in mind.

The height of the curtain wall is less well known but seems to have been generally 5–6m. It was so at Dublin, Drogheda, Waterford, Cork, Limerick and Kilmallock. The Londonderry walls are only slightly higher today at 6–7.5m. For Bandon in 1622 heights quoted at 10–15m may contain a certain element of exaggeration, or may include the depth of the fosse outside.

These measurements are approximate and can only give some slight indication of the scale of work involved. They need not have been consistent over the whole circuit, indeed the fragments surviving may not be the most characteristic. Consideration of the evidence in the 1585 written survey of the Dublin wall may serve to indicate the range of variation within a simple circuit (fig. 3.d). It is assumed that a foot meant the same then as now and this measurement has been converted to metric here. The Dublin wall was then generally 1.2–1.5m wide, the common width above, except on the south side where it reached 2m. The height varied between 4.8m and 6m, also as commonly above. The exception once more was on the south where it was again formidable, at 8m. In the NW corner too there was a marked difference, the wall was only 3–4m high, possibly due to degradation by floods which was not made good because it was not considered a vulnerable area.

Very few measurements are readily available for comparison. Turner (1970, 48 and gazetteer) quotes work on the Berwick wall in 1360 as involving a structure approximately 5m thick at the base, thinning to 2.5m at the top and reaching to 10m high. This was, therefore, considerably more formidable than the majority of the Irish seem to have been. But, a surviving section of the Winchester town wall at the bishop's palace is described as standing to a height of 6.10m, apparently complete and showing evidence of patching with three different mortars— Roman, thirteenth century and late fourteenth century—and she considers the Norwich wall, standing in sections to 3.5–4.5m, to be close to its original height. Its width is not given but the wall-walk was 1.2m wide and supported by arches, as possibly at Drogheda and a feature also seen at Southampton (Turner pls.17 and 25; Platt 1979, fig.24). A greater variety of stone would seem to have been employed in England and Wales, including flint rubble, which again is not surprising given the more varied geology. The plates in Turner's book, such as those for Newcastle, Southampton and Caernarvon tend to emphasise a regular, coursed structure of squared stones, although the regularity is less marked at Conway and apparently lacking altogether on the inside of the Norwich wall (pls. 11,25,29,34,37,17).

Returning to the Irish town walls for which there is evidence, the following comments may be made as an extension to the picture given by the case-study of Limerick (Table 3.3). At thirteen towns the stone wall is known to have ended with a battlemented top, generally rising above a wall-walk. The crenellations are usually shown as simple, except on the 1602 map of Cork which shows a variety similar to that at Limerick—the longer sections pierced by two or three loop-holes or slits of some form. Again, it is impossible to decide whether this was the reality or a case of artistic licence. The western Basetown wall at Youghal is like-wise shown to differ from the rest on the c.1587 map, but otherwise the battle-menting there is consistent and simple. Later on, in plan as opposed to perspective maps, especially those of the Down survey, a line indicating castellation was sometimes used to mark the wall, suggesting that this was indeed how most town walls ended vertically. The 1602 Cork map also suggests the presence of loop-holes or embrasures lower down in the curtain wall and similar evidence has been found in remains of the wall at Waterford, Kilmallock and Kilkenny. Such features might be later rather than original, and only possible where the wall was arched or was otherwise thinner than usual.

Access to the wall-walk seems, generally, to have been via the towers but the 1602 Cork map and the later ones for Bandon (ill. 11) show external stairways too, the latter entirely so on either side of both gates and towers. The height of the

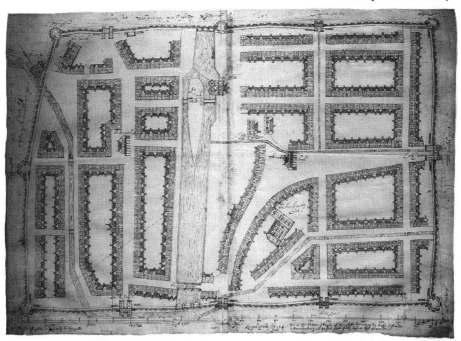

11 Bandon, *c*.1630

wall-walk varied in the south-east area of Galway and flights of steps on the walk solved that problem, according to the 1651 map. This map also shows clearly, as did earlier ones, the external wall around the main east gate with two side openings, and the wall-walk there supported by arches. As at Limerick Irishtown, but not apparently at Youghal's North Gate, this feature was further protected later by an outer line of fortifications which here ran the length of the east wall, with four-sided bastions at the two corners and across the outer gate defence. Further small projections which occurred here and at other towns will be discussed with bastions. Only the Bandon maps of 1620–30 indicate an extension of the curtain wall across the river, although similar devices may have operated in medieval times at sites such as Trim. The Bandon wall is shown as an unbroken line supported by pillars in the river with, on the later map, the wall-walk also continuing uninterrupted. Finally, strengthening of the curtain wall and the provision of access to it was also provided by internal ramparts at fourteen sites and probably many more.

Each section of the Dublin wall is described in detail in the 1585 survey. A quotation taken at random will serve to bring together the various features already described, and lead on to a discussion of others at the base of the wall and outside. The area chosen was in the SW beyond the main southern gate, St Nicholas, and involved a considerable length of wall. It was 238 foot [*c*.70m], had a thickness of 4.5 foot [1.3m] and rose to 16 foot high [4.8m] 'besides the garettes' [battlements]. The rampier within was 15 foot thick [4.5m], and 'near as high as the wall in [sic] the inside, besides the buttress which is at the bottom of the ditch to the foundation of the wall 19 foot good [5.7m], by estimation'. Here

61

12 Small tower astride town wall in west, inner side, Wexford
13 Waterford mural tower, called 'French', in south-west outer side
14 'Butter Gate', Drogheda, *c.*1925
15 New Ross mural tower in south-east, outer side

12

13

14

15

there seems to be an indication that the ditch or fosse, although protecting the wall by making access difficult, could lead to problems especially for the wall's foundations. Other evidence of external buttresses supporting the wall is to be found at the surviving internal wall at Dublin, although they may be more recent and are not associated with a fosse, and similarly at Kilkenny Hightown on the north side. Buttresses survive on the west wall at Youghal and seem to go down into the fosse, now infilling. Mural towers, such as those along this wall, served the same role by helping to strengthen it. Another apparently common feature was a 'battered' base to the wall, possibly extending up from the foundations and strengthening the wall by its inward and upward slope. This has been found at

Cork in excavation, as at Limerick, and also at Dublin, Waterford and Kilkenny. The island site at Cork, close to sea-level, produced its own engineering problems with regard to the foundation of the wall. In one area at least these were resolved by using a base of brushwood and moss for the stone wall to sit on above the river mud (Hurley and Power 1981).

At Cork, as for parts of Limerick, the river provided a natural fosse but elsewhere one had to be dug, at least for part of the circuit although, doubtless, the natural lie of the land was utilised wherever possible to minimise the work involved. There is evidence for a fosse at well over half the towns on list A. Probably most had one, but the evidence has been lost because the feature was inclined to fill up, both naturally and by the actions of citizens who were inclined to use it as a rubbish-dump. It is in fact the digging of the fosse in 1265, preparatory to building the town wall, which is retailed in the famous poem about New Ross. Some of this account may be apocryphal but there is still evidence of a fosse on the east and north sides there. On such a steeply sloping site it would have been necessary, if the fosse were to hold water, for there to be a system of sluices, like those later built at Coleraine. It seems probable that all fosses were intended to hold water, or at least to be capable of doing so, but they were often allowed to dry up and grass over. Then they could also be used for other purposes, such as grazing, as well as the less savoury one referred to above.

Finally, as at Limerick, castle walls might form part of the town wall. Dublin was a close parallel but the more usual case was that of a castle attached to the town wall but somewhat separate from it. This was the situation at Carlingford, Carrickfergus and Dungarvan—all royal castles like those of Dublin and Limerick—but also at seignorial towns such as Kilkenny, Athenry, Trim, Wexford and Drogheda Meath. The later medieval tower-houses too may have been associated sometimes with the wall, especially by the water front, for example at Youghal and possibly Carlingford. At the later walled towns of Maryborough and Philipstown forts replaced the medieval castle and were also sited either along one wall or towards a corner. Similar structures, known as citadels, appeared beside or close to medieval town walls in the seventeenth century, often at gates. At Galway one was built within the circuit at both the East and Bridge gates and at Clonmel similarly but close to the harbour. In contrast, at Waterford the large St. Patrick's citadel was built without the main west gate but it was also set against the medieval curtain wall.

Two features of the town wall, which might be regarded as mini-castles, will now be considered in turn—towers and gates. It is these which chiefly interested Fleming in his work on town-wall fortifications in Ireland (1914). Most of the structures he illustrated were of the medieval period—Waterford and Wexford are particularly well covered, but the seventeenth century circuits of Londonderry and of Carrickfergus are featured too.

TOWERS Towers, and their successors bastions which are discussed later, occurred at the corners of town wall circuits, where the curtain wall changed direction, and along straight sections as flankers. In either position their primary

16 Kells mural tower with projection on inner side of uppermost level

purpose was to defend the adjacent curtain wall by providing 'forward' positions from which the outward face of the wall could be covered defensively. Stone towers could also strengthen the curtain wall physically and wooden full or half-towers could provide shelter for guards on normal, rather than emergency, duty. Open-backed, or half-moon shaped, towers in particular made the sectionalising of the wall easier and so the containment of attackers who got on to it. This was because the wooden connections for the wall-walk within them could be readily removed leaving a stretch of wall isolated from the town. Complete square or round towers could also provide covered and concealed stairway access to the wall-walk. All shapes of towers that rose well above the wall level could defend the adjacent wall-walk, and act as look-out and signalling posts for the system as a whole.

Towers survive today (Table 3.4; ills. 12-20) at thirteen towns and there is evidence that they once existed at a similar number, together accounting for 50% of list A. At a further ten towns their place was taken by post-medieval bastions. It seems, therefore, reasonable to assume that all town walls had towers and/or bastions, although the numbers at each probably varied considerably. Only one survives at Kells and is not otherwise recorded, while as many as nineteen are indicated by some of the Waterford map evidence. A total of forty towers survive in varying stages of completeness, the collection of six at Waterford being the best. Six also still stand at Athenry but the five at Limerick are poor fragments by comparison. Otherwise some individual towers remain in substantial form, for example at Youghal, New Ross, Clonmel, Kells and Kilkenny and, altered to a bastion, at Dublin. These represent a survival rate of about 30% on the basis of the maximum number of towers for which there is evidence at each site. This may be as realistic a basis as that of using a notional number such as four or eight towers per circuit. Post-medieval Dublin is known to have had 14 towers, Drogheda Louth 12 and Meath 6, and Fethard 5. Therefore, taken together the surviving towers would represent a mere 7% of the known total for these four towns. The frequency and distribution of towers along a circuit will be considered again with that of gates at the end of this section because most gates were, in a sense, specialised towers. Together they both reinforced and sectionalised the system and, indeed, changed roles sometimes, either when gates were let into mural towers or were closed so that their structures acted in turn as towers.

The six Waterford towers (all illustrated by Fléming 1914, 12–19) will be used as a case study, with additional features noted from elsewhere and compared with the details given for the fourteen Dublin towers described in the 1585 survey. The Waterford survivals include four corner and two flanking or 'on the wall' towers. The distinction involved slight differences in shape with circular changing to semi-circular or square to rectangular due to the different locations. At corners, the line of the wall changed through acute or obtuse angles. This change was to some extent hidden in the body of the corner tower. It, therefore, both strength-ened a particularly vulnerable point and provided defensive cover along two different lines of wall. The Waterford corner towers comprise three circular and one square. The latter, known as 'Beach', is the least well preserved and is now relatively inaccessible. Of the circular towers, the 'French' is particularly high, rising from a slightly pedimented base to *c.*20m, and even so may not be quite complete. The best known, 'Reginald's', is almost like a martello tower of more recent times in being lower, broad and slightly tapering, but its site is the oldest, being of Hiberno-Norse origin. It has been altered but not radically changed from its early medieval state, and it alone is still in use. It is *c.*12m in diameter and *c.*16m high with, in addition, a conical roof inside a corbelled, battlemented top. Such roofs feature on many of the map-views of round towers, often being topped by flags or weather vanes, while rectangular towers seemed to have had simpler roofs. A similar battlemented top can be seen on the last of the surviving Waterford towers, the 'Watch', allowing for a wall-walk inside it. It is three-storied, as was fairly usual, with a series of embrasures for each floor. There is a door at the base although this was more often at first-floor level, as at the 'Beach', so that it could be approached by a ladder which might be secreted when necessary. Embrasures or loop-holes for use with bows, sometimes now altered to narrow windows, are common on all the towers but the Watch tower also has wider loops for cannon on its first floor. It has been dated to the late fifteenth century but it is not known if it was new then or a rebuilding of an earlier structure.

The flanking towers, ideally evenly spaced along the wall between the corner towers, had a similar cover role and sometimes also masked smaller changes in the alignment of the curtain wall. To achieve cover they, too, usually projected beyond the wall line, having the wall at their back. They could also be open-backed with the wall continuing, as it were, around their projecting sides. Some open-backed towers are shown on the 1602 Cork map. Both types seem to have

17 Mural tower, Athenry

18 Mural tower, Waterford

19 Mural tower, Waterford

20 Mural tower, Youghal

existed at Athenry, but only the former at Waterford. As many of the other towers survive only in a ruined state it is difficult to tell which was more usual, or even to be certain of the original shape sometimes. Early drawings, which provide a source of knowledge of some which are by now even more dilapidated, tend to show only a view of the outer side, the more imposing but often the less revealing one. Also, it is very possible that ostensibly open-backed towers may have lost their back walls through decay or actual removal of the stone-work. A further type is illustrated by one of the flanking towers at Wexford. It is essentially a half tower, rising above the wall but sitting astride it, supported on the outside by corbelling and on the inside by a pillar and a flight of steps. There is some map evidence from Galway and elsewhere that half towers may have been quite common. They were, in fact, repeated on the seventeenth century Londonderry wall in the form of two guard houses.

One of the Waterford half-moon flanking towers is semi-circular, while the other is rectangular but complex. It is known as the 'Double' and stands in a curiously contradictory position as a projection on an indented part of the south wall. It rises to two different, but apparently complete levels, hence its name. It may be, in part, a tower-house, perhaps built against a mural tower at a point where the line of the wall was later changed. On the other hand, a large rectangular or square mural tower, once left isolated by the removal of the curtain wall, may well be mistaken now for a late-medieval tower-house. Such structures are seen on Speed's 1610 map of Dublin along the River Liffey but they, at least, are known from documentary evidence to have been mural towers. The origins of similarly-placed 'towers' at Inistioge and Thomastown are not known but may well be comparable. Dating by a study of the structures may help to resolve the problem and possibly also indicate whether there was a riverside wall at either of those sites.

As already indicated, towers often served as access points for the wall-walk but most of them rose above the level of the curtain wall by a half to one third of their height. They tended to be tall and thin like the French Tower and the best at Athenry, or broad and shorter like Reginald's Tower or Talbot's at Kilkenny. The Kells (Meath) tower has a rare detail, a corbelled projection at the top floor level which may possibly have been a garderobe or an additional defensive device. The greater height, of course, gave better views into the surrounding area, better points of projection for weapons and for signalling within the system, while the greater depth provided stability for the curtain wall and space internally for use as a muster point or guard house.

The 1585 survey of the Dublin wall gives the most detailed picture yet available of towers. Being clearly measured it can be taken at face value, as opposed to the details on some of the early maps for other towns, although to do them justice some of them may be equally correct. Fourteen towers are noted with measurements given for thirteen, the exception being described as a 'house'. It may have been on the site of a former tower but clearly was no longer regarded as part of the defences. In fact it was situated in what was by then the least strong, but also the least exposed, part of the wall, the NW corner. Twelve towers rose above the curtain wall and only one, towards the SW, was level with it, obviously no longer functioning as it was described as 'earth filled'. Two of the towers along the quay, one square and one rectangular, were much larger than the rest and may have been by then much extended. The lower, Prickett's, was similar in height to the majority of towers on the circuit but it had an additional turret on its eastern side and one window. The other, Fyan's, was amongst the highest at 12.6m, although not as high as two semi-circular towers on the south side which rose to almost 14m. It had four stories, each with windows, but lacked the loop-holes and battlements of the others.

Two examples, taken again at random, illustrate the varied dimensions and design of Irish mural towers—'tower in Mr. Fagan's possession [on west wall near to New Gate] is a round tower without, and square within, and neither vault or loft, but a way going up unto the top, being 10 foot [3m] square upon the top, with a garette and five loops in the way going up, and the tower 32 foot high [9.6m] and 2 foot thick [0.6m], besides the thickness of the stairs'. The adjacent wall northwards was 17 foot high and southwards 16 foot, so that the tower was half as high again. On the other side of New Gate, the nearest tower was a third higher than the adjacent wall (20–22 feet) but the same actual height as Fagan's— 'in Mr. Fitzsymon's possession is a square tower, four story high, with three lofts and no vault, two loops in the lower story, three loops in the second story, four loops in the third story, and four loops in the fourth story, the tower 32 foot high [9.6m], 16 foot square [4.8m] and 3 foot thick [almost 1m]'.

These two were actually typical of the majority of Dublin's towers, both in area and height, and in that their external shapes were different (fig.3.d). Five of the Dublin towers were square or rectangular, like Fitzsimons, and seven semi-circular, like Fagan's. Only one was truly round. Clearly, they were similar to those surviving at Waterford and elsewhere, and the many, both round and square, shown on the post-medieval map-views, such as those for Limerick and Galway.

Mixed designs of towers was also a feature of some English walled towns, in particular of York and Southampton. Turner (1970, 58) also shows that there were many minor differences, even where there were basic similarities of shape and period, as for example at the west wall of Newcastle-upon-Tyne. This seems to indicate the absence of a single design plan. However, she does suggest a sequence of style from an early broad but shallow, semi-circular or half-round, type to a later deeper D-shaped but also basically semi-circular form. The change appears to have come about 1260 and to have lasted until the late fourteenth century, when rectangular towers became more common. If this was generally proven, it would suggest much new building or rebuilding of towers at Dublin, Wexford and elsewhere occurred in the fifteenth century. This may well have been the case as it was a period of limited resurgence in Ireland generally, charac-terised by much new building of houses and churches. Moreover, by then mural towers and other parts of a circuit, might well have been in a poor state structurally due to age alone. It would also point to the antiquity of some of the surviving towers at Waterford, but one of the round type, as noted above, has been dated to the late fifteenth century. This is a subject which, clearly, needs the attention of medieval archaeologists or architects as a matter of urgency, before surviving Irish mural towers deteriorate further or disappear altogether.

BASTIONS   A bastion is defined as a 'pentagonal projection from a fortification' (*OED*). In fact its fifth side was often provided by the town wall itself although at gates, such as St. John's Limerick Irishtown, a bastion could be set ahead of

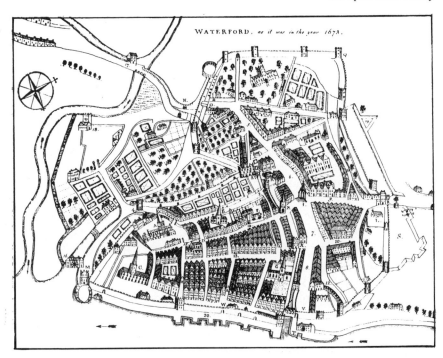

21 Waterford, 1673

the rest of the system and connected only by a narrow walled passage. Normally it was characterised by two, often short, parallel sides emerging from the back wall, followed by two generally longer sides which met at an angle. Depending on the size of this and the other angles, between the 'short' and 'long' sides and the wall, the whole structure might be broad or sharp featured. The latter tended to be characteristic of corner bastions and the former of flanking. It was, therefore, comparable with the subtler shape changes seen in tower design but such a regular geometric shape did not, in fact, mark it off from towers, for they too were basically geometric in outline. However, this was a more obvious feature of bastions because they were less high and more extensive areally. The reason for both changes lay in the introduction of cannon which, while being more powerful, adaptable and intimidating, also needed more room for manoeuvring.

Small cannon could, and were, introduced into existing towers, the example of the Watch Tower in Waterford was noted earlier. Many towers may have been strengthened, and consequently altered to a greater or lesser extent, to accommodate cannon, including the so-called 'bastions', really stone towers, at Kilkenny and Clonmel. A more interesting development was the addition of bastions to the existing town wall circuit, leading to its re-emphasis. Such an addition involved a whole new circuit at Limerick Irishtown but was often a more piecemeal process, as for example at Galway where the east wall only was involved. The beginning of this process can be seen at Waterford in the *c.*1590 and 1673 maps (ill. 21) where vaguely circular or D-shaped structures can be seen in front of

Reginald's Tower and between the Watch Tower and the southern gate, St. John's. By the mid-eighteenth century the former, which did not even rise as high as the town wall beyond, had disappeared but the latter, made of stone and known as the Watergate Bastion, had by then a more regular straight-sided appearance and possibly an additional function as a dock (1745 map; Kerrigan 1985,14). Waterford also acquired two more elaborate, fort-like structures generally known as citadels. These can be seen as sixteenth and seventeenth century castle-building exercises in that they provided bases for garrisons as well as strong 'points of last resort'. One was located beyond the curtain wall but the other in the west, which was mentioned above, used as its back the town wall which there contained two medieval towers, one square and one round (1685/90 maps).

Simpler, generally largely earthen, structures called block-houses were probably often built at vulnerable points, especially on rivers, for example at New Ross. Elsewhere, at major strategic sites such as Cork and Kinsale, forts separate from the town wall were the solution. At Clonmel, to judge from the 1691 map, two internal corner towers acquired additional, angular bastions, and a flanking bastion was also built. At the same time three corner towers, including those at the river, were left apparently untouched but bastion-type structures were built in front of the three gates. The sum total of these changes, at least on paper, was given a sense of unity by the redevelopment of the fosse. However, the only survival, of what looks like a fairly elaborate system, is the internal corner tower referred to earlier. It alone did not have a bastion planned for its exterior but it was possibly lowered and strengthened. This suggests that the map may have been a design for the future rather than a picture of reality. It is, nonetheless, interesting as a possible 'modernisation' scheme for a medieval circuit.

The medieval wall of Athlone East does show signs of having been 'bastionised' or, perhaps, even totally re-built in the seventeenth century. The medieval castle in Athlone West was also modernised by then. The various maps for Carrick-fergus, in particular the 1580 and 1612, show clearly the transition from medieval corner tower, generally round, to angular bastion. Yet, at Bandon the process was apparently stalled, if not actually reversed. The 1613 map shows modern bastions but the 1620–30 maps more medieval circular structures, both at the corners and on the sides. They may well have been lower than their forerunners and the plan-style maps do make clear that they were intended for cannon emplacements. The reason for the change in shape is not known. The earlier, 1581, map for Roscommon did include similar, circular bastions but the Ulster towns all had angular bastions as did the later seventeenth century creations, Jamestown and Portarlington (list B).

The common number of bastions was six, four at the corners and two on the long sides which, with gates on the short sides and possibly also centrally on the long, gave an even cover for the wall. They appear now more regularly spaced than medieval towers, but this may be the effect of the shorter passage of time and of the often more regular circuit. Jamestown had this number. It was, to judge from the later map evidence, perhaps the purest, bastioned circuit to be built, but only the down-graded remnants of its north-west corner area now survive. The less regular circuit of Londonderry is due to a close adaptation to local topography. The flanking or side bastions there are generally shallower than the corner, although fundamentally of the same shape. There is another variation in the form of broad, but shallow, rectangular 'platforms' or abbreviated bastions. These exist on the west side, perhaps as an economy feature made possible by the steeply sloping terrain there. Elsewhere, simpler triangular structures, known as ravelins, took the place of flanking bastions, for example on the south wall at Drogheda Meath and at Ardee (1657 maps). Similar triangular side bastions were a feature also of Belfast's defences and those planned for Portarlington, although there were also large and elaborate corner bastions of the Londonderry type. The purpose of all these, as of their medieval predecessors, was to enhance the defensive quality of the circuit. They were, however, often extensive structures, sometimes wholly or partially of earth and so they lacked the adaptability for other uses which towers had. Consequently they were removed at most towns except in areas where there was little pressure on land use as, for example, at Ardee and Kilmallock where their remnants still survive.

GATES   Just under thirty gates survive, generally now as isolated structures except at Londonderry (Table 3.4). As most circuits had a minimum of four gates, these represent about 12% of the minimum total for list A towns. This is a rather better notional survival rate than that for towers, and is more realistically based because the data are better for gates. In addition, the foundations of three gates have been revealed briefly in recent excavations—at Carrickfergus, Waterford and Limerick—and six more are known in part from nineteenth and early twentieth century illustrations. Some of these are reproduced in Fleming (1914) which has drawings of twenty gates in all. The most comprehensive source, however, is the collection of map-views, although the accuracy of their mini-pictures must be carefully evaluated. In some cases the gates do indeed appear to be shown symbolically, for example in Speed's 1610 map of Limerick. Yet, the pictures given on the two *c.*1587 maps for the West Water Gate at the Irishtown there are verified by the results of recent archaeological work and by the Phillips elevation drawing of 1685. Consequently, the different styles of some of the other gates shown on the early maps may be taken at face value too. Unfortunately, later maps generally show gates either symbolically or in plan. As a result, little is known of the vertical style of the gates which survived at Kilkenny into the eighteenth century and probably at many other towns. In addition, the only detailed architectural evidence involving measurements and giving a complete, rather than a one or two sided picture, is the 1585 survey of the Dublin wall. Figure 3.e contains plans of five Dublin gates, based on this survey, set alongside diagrams of some other Irish town gates.

The term gate, like town wall, is used throughout this work generally as a convenient shorthand for what may have been a simple or a complex feature. In reality what was involved was a break in the walled circuit, a gateway or passage, whose prime purpose was to allow access between the enclosed, defended area and its surroundings. Therefore, whereas a tower was essentially

71

a strengthening of the curtain wall, a gate, by its nature, was at least initially a weakening of the whole system. Consequently, it needed, firstly, a device to stop the gap or passage and, secondly, a means of defending such an inherently weak point. The former might be achieved by the use of one or more structural devices— a side-way moving gate or gates; an upward moving drawbridge, especially if a fosse existed; a downward moving portcullis. The last required a structure above the passage, usually referred to as a gate house, tower or even castle. Actually it might be only skin-deep, merely a sham feature involving just an outer but imposingly-styled wall. At its simplest, therefore, a gate was an opening in a town wall, generally arched to allow for the continuation of the wall-walk above. In such a case the curtain wall itself provided the surround of the gateway and the means of hanging or securing the actual wooden gate or gates. These might also be reinforced with sheets or bars of iron. The simplest of official town gates, as opposed to private posterns or doors in the curtain wall, were often those leading on to the quay as the map evidence for Galway, Youghal and Waterford in particular indicates. Presumably, this was, again, a case of seeing the river as an additional defensive device, with the wall-walk and battlements above the gate and the nearby mural towers being regarded as sufficient to defend the opening. Such a simple opening with a ship unloading at the adjacent quay is illustrated in a late-fifteenth century Flemish painting (Platt 1979, fig.73). Nonetheless, more elaborate, quay gates are also known to have existed in Ireland, for example the main water gates at Limerick Englishtown and Cork, both apparently comparable with the main land gates at these towns.

The considerable variety of form illustrated by these and other Irish town gates was derived mainly from the development of both the side walls and the area above the gateway or passage. This could be merely facial decoration but even then, there was a range of possibilities. These are displayed well by the simple, so-called 'canal-style', new nineteenth century gateways of Londonderry and the more formidable, late eighteenth century rebuilding of the Bishop's Gate there. This saw the replacement of the original gatehouse by a high ceremonial archway, with pedestrian passages cut through the broad side walls (Camblin 1951,pl.42). The North Gate of Carrickfergus has been similarly, if more modestly, restored but it may never have been more than a simple opening to judge by the 1612 map. As such it is comparable with the battlemented Water Gate surviving at Youghal (ill. 31) and those shown on the 1651 Galway map. Further development of the side walls tended to separate them from the curtain wall, forwards and/or backwards. At its simplest this made for stronger structures, deeper than the curtain wall even if not rising much above its level. An example, that survived until recently, was the North Gate at Jamestown (ill. 29) which was similar to the probably earlier Three Bullets Gate at New Ross (ill. 28), known only from drawings (Fleming 39). In a more complex form, development of a simple gateway allowed both the building of a substantial gatehouse above and the erection of two sets of gates at the inner and outer ends of the deep passage way. Further, there was then space available in the side walls within the gateway for sentry or toll-collector's alcoves and for stairs to give access to the gatehouse above. Even if there was no gate

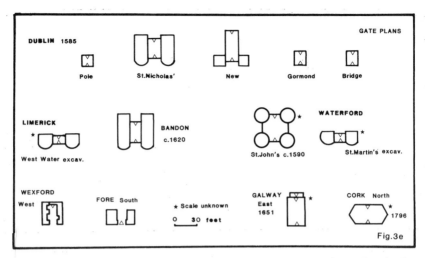

Fig.3e

house the space above could be used to house the portcullis and to maintain the wall-walk as a continuous system. In addition, given its possibly greater size than a normal mural tower, the gate house could more readily serve as a muster point for a garrison or a guard house, as one did in seventeenth century Coleraine.

The West Gate at Wexford is illustrated in elevation and plan by Fleming and used on figure 3.e as typical of such single-towered gates, although it is one of those cases where it is difficult to distinguish mural tower from gate—it may well have fulfilled both roles at different times. A less equivocal example but one also illustrating the capacity for change, given the long time span, was the North Gate at Athlone East (ill. 32)—known again only from eighteenth and nineteenth century drawings. It was of a similar style, being a square or rectangular structure with a narrow, rounded gateway arch and three floors above, topped by a corbelled battlement. This gate stood slightly in front of the town wall and rose well above it and the adjacent two or three story buildings. It may have survived from the Middle Ages and been rebuilt in the sixteenth century but, apart from details such as sets of windows instead of loop-hole openings, it was typical of many single-towered gates shown on map-views of Cork, Limerick, Galway and Waterford. It was also similar to some of the Dublin gates and, probably, to many known only by name at other Irish walled towns.

One probably modest version survives, the Tholsel Gate at Carlingford, but its ruins have been evened off and simply roofed in slate. Its rounded gate arch narrows the street to a single width and it has an external stairway on its wider, eastern side. This feature may be recent, or originally it may have led only to the curtain wall, because it occurs too at the West Gate, Southampton (Turner 1970, pl.27), a gate apparently of broadly similar style and scale. A further stage in the degradation of a single-towered gate was the complete removal of the gatehouse, as happened with the rebuilding of the four main and original early seventeenth century gates at Londonderry. When first built, they were apparently very close to their medieval forbears. The 1611–25 maps show them as battlemented gate houses with drawbridges, rising slightly above the level of the wall. The removal of the gate houses in later centuries allowed the production of a very consistent, extended series of gates at Londonderry. The original are only distinguishable from the new ones of the nineteenth century by virtue of being the main gates, and so more elaborate. Basically, they are all now gate archways or simple, but variously decorated, openings. They indicate that gates could become simpler as well as more complex with time, especially when their defensive role ceased to be of paramount importance. This has the effect at Londonderry of emphasising the curtain wall and the sense of demarcation provided by it now, because the gates now tend to merge with the wall.

A similar fate may have resulted in the present form of St. Audeon's Gate, Dublin, which is broadly similar in structure to the Londonderry gates. The two gates at Fore, the North Gate at Fethard and the Butter Gate at Drogheda Meath are now poor ruins but their former shapes can be established to some extent (Fleming 28–9; 32). They are all of a similar scale and have rounded but narrow gate arches, like those described for Carlingford and Athlone. The southern gate at Fore (ill. 30) and the Fethard gate, in particular, show signs of substantial depth within the surviving side walls, which, while presenting a flat face to the outside, include a stairway at the former. Both the Fore gates have a minimum passage-way of 2.6m wide (Leask values), which is comparable to that of the West Gate, Wexford, and even of the larger gates described below. The Butter Gate at Drogheda Meath is a mere arch now, like the northern at Fore, but a photograph dated *c*.1925 shows a much more substantial and interesting ruin (ill. 14). Built on the steeply sloping west side of the town, its battered base can be seen on the outside. The relative positions of the rounded gate arches suggest that there may have been steps within the gateway. The front wall was slightly cut off at its outer limits to give a three-sided face, but the structure was basically rectangular. Long arrow slits point to a medieval date. Only the inner gate arch on the higher part of the slope now survives and it is questionable whether this was really a gate or an adapted mural tower. Like the equally problematical West Gate, Wexford, it is located off the present street system and not far from a known main gate, St. John's. Furthermore, the Butter Gate is sited on a steep slope, a location more typical of a tower. Even so, as a tower with a postern doorway or as a gate it may well have been used as a toll point for butter because this might have involved only pedestrian traffic.

Other single-towered gates survive more intact or even redesigned. The North Gate at Athenry reaches to two stories above a slightly pointed gate arch which, again, reduces the street to half its width. The West Gate at Clonmel (ill. 22) has been remodelled and now has a nineteenth century gothic-castle design to it. Its gate arch is slightly pointed too but it is broad enough to allow for footpaths as well as single-file road traffic. Its original form is not known but by its setting, closing off the broad main street and rising above the three and four-story build-ings attached to its sides and obscuring the town wall, it perhaps most successfully conveys the sense of enclosure that must have been common to walled towns at their peak. A similarly tall, apparently single-towered gate sitting astride the main

22 West Gate, Clonmel, rebuilt 1831   **23** The Clock Gate, Youghal, pre-1777 (from Fleming 1914)

street is the Clock Gate at Youghal (ill. 23). Its rebuilding as late as 1777 is even more curious because it was located then, and for long, on an inner part of the town wall, although it had once been the main southern gate. Its earlier form will be discussed below but the rebuilding has resulted in a very tall single tower of four stories, topped by a cupola and clock above a broad rounded gate arch. Like the Clonmel gate, it both achieves a sense of enclosure and provides an imposing entrance even though it actually interrupts the long narrow main street. Its rebuilding at a time when the other main gates of Youghal were being removed is especially curious and, perhaps, points to a certain capriciousness affecting the survival of town gates. It now serves as a museum but its former role as a prison can hardly have been so important as to require its rebuilding *in situ*. The usefulness of gates as toll collection points may have been significant here and elsewhere for the preservation of town gates.

The fullest development of a single-towered gate can be seen in the elongated, but differently arranged, rectangular gates at Galway and Cork. The East Gate, Galway, while being earlier a square or rectangular structure, like the other main gates there and the above, had by 1651 been developed backwards, into the town along the main street. The two main Cork gates, earlier round or square structures, were redesigned even further in the eighteenth century and largely lost their defensive role. Their re-structuring was sideways which made them large, formidable entrances. The South Gate was four stories high, excluding a deep but apparently unbattlemented pediment, and five bays wide above a strongly decorated gateway entrance. The North Gate was of a similar width and height but had a lozenge rather than rectangular shape, having triangular 'extensions' on each side, one by then partially hidden by adjacent buildings. Again, the gate entrance was accented architecturally and there was a pitched roof but no battlements (1796 Grogan paintings, in Pettit 1977, 160).

24 The North Gate, Kilmallock, outer side, from an 1822 print

Finally, in the context of single-towered gates, there is the possibility not only of gates being derived from towers (or 'vice versa' as already noted above) but another type of transition, which needs to be discussed too. This was due to the close structural similarity, both in scale and style, between some single-towered gates or mural towers and late-medieval tower-houses, particularly towers or gates that were rectangular or square in plan. (Leask 1944, 75; Murtagh 1983–4,355). Tower-houses were defended private houses and this provided a functional link too because individual town wall structures, such as gate houses or towers, could also be adapted for this purpose. The gate at Loughrea may be a case in point. It appears to be a square gate house with a rounded gate arch and battlemented top, not dissimilar to West Gate, Wexford. Yet, it could have been a tower-house into which a gateway was inserted because it is situated to one side of a secondary street. Although rather isolated from other buildings, it certainly looks now more like the individual tower-houses still standing along the main streets of Galway, Carlingford and Ardee, than a town gate. Of course, the exact line of the Loughrea street may have altered with time and, as it led from the castle, it might have been important once. Another example, but in reverse, is the King's/Queen's castle in Kilmallock, presumed now to be a tower-house but sitting astride the main street as if it were a gate (Bradley 1985, 482). Actually, it is in a suitable position for a northern gate if the town was once smaller as it may well have been. Following an extension of the town wall, it might have been rented as a dwelling.

The ultimate development of the side walls in particular resulted in what might be called 'twin-towered' gates. In fact they presented a face composed of three elements—the two side towers and the intervening wall. This joined them and might be either skin deep or the front wall of the gate house. At the gateway level the towers provided more room for sentries and toll collectors, and for stairways

76

25 Barbican of St. Laurence's Gate, Drogheda, 1834

to even more space for defence and other use above. Such a lateral complexity could be matched by complexity in depth, allowing for a 'double' gate as a maximum development. The front section of this might sit ahead of the curtain wall, sometimes beyond the fosse, in which case it was generally known as a barbican. The finest surviving medieval Irish gate, the St. Lawrence Gate at Drogheda (ill. 25), appears to be such a foregate feature, but it is not known how it connected with the wall itself. It now stands *c*.10m outside the wall line. The side towers are basically circular and complete but there is no gate house between them. There is a 'sham' wall which provides room for the portcullis and allows for the battlemented wall-walk to continue across the top of the whole structure. St. John's Gate at Waterford (*c*.1590 map) apparently had a similar outer barbican which was repeated at the wall level to provide a 'double gate' in effect. This may have been so once at Drogheda too, in which case it must have been a truly massive structure. Alternatively there, the gate passage itself may have been linked with the wall, with or without use of the space above the arch for a gate house. Double gates not only impressed by sheer size and complexity, they provided a trap internally, as did all barbican-type features, where assailants could be contained temporarily and, hopefully, eliminated before they reached the street system and could disperse throughout the town. The later rectangular extensions of the town wall, noted earlier for Youghal's North Gate, Limerick Irishtown's St. John's Gate and Galway's East Gate, had much the same effect. Such foregate walls were, in effect, low barbicans but generally with only simple entrances made more sure defensively by being set indirectly to one side so that they could not be easily forced. They provided more space internally for defenders at ground level or just above which was necessary for using cannon. An alternative was to have an inner gate, a barbican in reverse. This seems to have been the purpose of the structure that stood across across the street a short

26 Blossoms Gate, outer side, Kilmallock

distance inside the West Water Gate at Limerick Irishtown (1590 map).

The foundations of the West Water Gate at Limerick was revealed in excavation (Lynch 1984). It provides a good example of a twin-towered gate especially as its elevation is known from drawings. It was composed of two D-shaped towers set against the town wall. Consequently they stood out from it like a pair of mural towers. The excavations at St. Martin's Gate in Waterford indicated a broadly similar structure (Moore 1983). There, the side towers were not identical, possibly because one of them had a corner position on the original triangular shaped town wall. It may, in fact, have acted also partly as a mural tower, or even actually originated as such. The surviving plans for a 'gate at Bandonbridge' (c.1620–22) show how a pair of fundamentally circular-shaped gate towers could be developed backwards to give, in effect, a basically square gate house. This allowed for a narrow gateway, with outer and inner gates, and access to the towers in the flat back-ends, as existed also in the two medieval examples. Indeed, although it is not known if this plan was put into effect, the gates shown in elevation on the 1620–30 maps of Bandon are remarkably like the 1685 drawing of the West Water Gate at Limerick Irishtown. So, as already illustrated by the original Londonderry gates, there was continuity in design from the medieval to the early seventeenth century.

Other points of interest arise from the gate excavations at Limerick and Waterford. Evidence from both indicates that, while the gate was part of the original plan, it was let into the town wall at a later stage, the curtain wall being left thinner for that purpose. The foundations of the twin-towers at Waterford were deeper (by 1.4m) than that of the wall, presumably to carry the additional weight. One gate tower there rested on a raft of timbers above the underlying boulder clay, while at Limerick the more fully excavated tower had projecting footings. The stone-work of the outer faces was superior to that of the inner, implying the work of stone craftsmen and a desire to make an impressive structure.

The cores of the tower walls were similar to those of the curtain walls, being generally composed of mortared rubble. The gateways were of similar widths to those of single-towered gates noted above (2.4–2.6m) and there was evidence for a portcullis at Waterford. This gate later went out of use, was closed up and much rebuilt. Consequently, its medieval elevation is not known, but it is unlikely to have looked originally very different from the Limerick gate and others illustrated on map views, or, indeed, from the St. Lawrence Gate barbican at Drogheda Louth.

The surviving, but partially ruined, Blossom's Gate at Kilmallock (ill. 26), was also originally twin-towered. Only one of the D-shaped side towers stands but the central wall above the rounded gate arch appears to be intact and to have had a corbelled pediment. Battlements as such are not visible on either the tower or the central wall, possibly they have been evened off. The other main gate at Kilmallock, the North (ill. 24), is shown clearly on the 1602 map as a similarly twin-towered structure, although by the nineteenth century only its gate arch and central wall were intact (Fleming 43–4). Its side tower then reminded viewers of a minaret, being square in section but broad at the base and narrow at the top, where there was a roofed 'look-out' area. The two Kilmallock gates seem to have been of similar size, two storied above the gate arch, which was rather pointed in shape at the North Gate. The surviving one is on a similar scale to the North Gate at Athenry which was described earlier because it may never have had side towers. Both narrow the street but because it is less ruined, Blossoms Gate (ill. 26) at Kilmallock is the more impressive, both in terms of height and solidity. Of course, it is seen against two-story buildings whereas the St. Lawrence's Gate, Drogheda, remains impressive even when compared with the three or four story buildings near it. Another twin-towered gate, known from nineteenth century drawings, is the Fair Gate at New Ross (ill. 27). It would probably have been very similar to the Kilmallock gates, having D-shaped side-towers. It apparently had a gate house with a barbican-type structure which extended backwards beyond the level of the backs of the side towers (Fleming 38).

Evidence from maps, particularly the perspective rather than the plan type, indicates the existence once of a number of other twin-towered gates, including the Clock Gate at Youghal (*c*.1587 map) whose medieval form was, therefore, quite different from its present. The two southern gates at Waterford, St. John's, whose barbican has already been described, and the Colbeck were probably similar, round or D-shaped twin towers (*c*.1590). The latter is shown as having conical roofs on its towers, very like the adjacent mural towers. Neither Cork nor Galway appear to have had such twin-towered gates but Dublin did, and a seventeenth century painting of Kinsale suggests that such gates may have existed at other towns too. In the latter case the side-towers seem to have been square rather than round. It is impossible to calculate how many twin-towered gates there were but, given the possibility of transformation from twin-towered to apparently single-towered by the survival of the central gate house only, it is probably higher than the map and other evidence presently suggests. What is clear is that by the end of the Middle Ages a considerable variety of gate forms existed.

Very few of the gates already described have been measured at all and so the

27 The Fair Gate, New Ross, *c*.1850 (from Fleming 1914)

details given in the 1585 Dublin survey are quoted now to give more reality to the diagrams, drawings, photographs and discussion above. The eastern gate, Dame's, is the only main one omitted from the survey. This is unfortunate because it was probably impressive, being then the most direct point of entry for the king's representative en route from England to the castle. However, like Limerick and Youghal, the other Dublin gates were varied. There were three simple, single-towered structures which were similar in scale—Pole on the south, Gormund on the west and Bridge on the north; and two that were more complex, both twin-towered but different—St. Nicholas' on the south and New on the west (fig.3.d).

The Pole Gate was described as 'a square tower with two stories, the lower story upon a vault with three loops, and the upper story a timber loft, and the wall 6 foot thick [1.8m] and 14 foot [4m] square within, and the tower 46 foot high [13.8m], besides the garettes, from the foundation of the wall, with a portcullis for the same'. In size it was not dissimilar to the nearby D-shaped tower and, like it and the next southern gate, it rose above the curtain wall by a third of its height. The other single-towered gates were not so high but neither was the west wall beside Gormund Gate, while the town wall from Bridge Gate along the quay had

28 The Three Bullets Gate, New Ross, from a 1914 sketch

gone by then altogether. These gates were rather larger in area than Pole Gate, being *c*.25 sqm as opposed to *c*.15 sqm.

The main southern gate, St. Nicholas', the survey says 'hath two round towers without, and square within, and the said gate placed betwixt both the towers, every tower three heights, whereof two lofts and four loops in every tower, the wall 5 foot thick [1.5m], 39 foot [11.5m] in length one way and 18 foot broad [5.4m] the other way, and the tower 45 foot high [13.5m], with a portcullis for the same gate'. These seem to be broadly similar to the dimensions of the Bandon gate drawings which allowed for a depth of 44 feet for the side towers and widths varying from 12–15 feet (internal measurements).

New Gate, the main western gate, had square-shaped twin-towers of '12 foot [3.6m] square within the wall', three stories high and 'topped by two small turrets'. It represented, therefore, the other major possibility in that, firstly, the towers were apparently of a square shape; and, secondly, the depth was provided by the central gate house. This latter allowed, as already noted, for an outer and inner gate with the intervening passage acting as a mini-barbican in that 'the gate house stands betwixt both the said towers . . . 40 foot one way [ie backwards, 12m] and 15 foot [4.5m] an other way'.

The form of the newer, seventeenth century, east gate at Dublin, Essex, is not known but when it and the, now at least, simple arched gateway of St. Audeon's on the inner wall are included all the main types of gates are seen to have existed at Dublin. A further possibility, double bridge gates, may also be represented there and certainly did exist at Limerick, Cork and Galway. These generally took the single-towered form and so were not a new type. They were really an extension of the barbican or foregate device in a more open form and surrounded by water. There was usually a gate tower at both ends of the bridge and, at least at Galway, one in the middle too.

A further type of gate, specialised more by its location than its structure, existed at Dublin and some other towns, possibly at more than are yet known. This was the suburban or external gate. At Ardee and Kilmallock in the seventeenth century they were apparently very similar to the other main gates at those towns. Speed's map of Dublin, 1610, suggests that this was so there too, although all the Dublin gates tend to look the same on this map, which, clearly, they were not: No less than eight are marked but only one named. It is conceivable that they were just the closest to the centre of a series of outer gates, which were erected at stages along main streets as the city expanded further and further beyond the curtain wall. They may be viewed as a minimum defensive or toll device made feasible at Dublin at least by the intensity of the urban development. Elsewhere, they may have been associated with earthen defences although none are shown on the Ardee and Kilmallock maps. Each stood at the entrance to the only extra-mural development of those towns.

Clearly, gates were more complex than towers, both in their function and structure, although they shared some features. Consequently, it is not surprising that there was some switching between them; instances have already been noted from Waterford, Wexford and Drogheda. The use of the term 'blind' in a gate name, for example at Ardee, may sometimes indicate a change of use when the gate was closed, or blinded, and became in effect a tower instead. It could, of course, be opened again when priorities changed, and so there may have been some considerable fluctuation in function over the centuries between gates and towers. This introduces the problem of the minor gate or postern. It might be official or unofficial, a modest gate house or a gate in the side of a tower, but it could also be simply a passage cut into the curtain wall and closed by a gate or door. Yet, such minor gates could have a significance for street development in the long term, even if they were originally essentially private openings, such as those leading to the many churches adjacent to town walls. They make for difficulties in counting the number of gates that each town had because they may appear more significant on maps than they really were, and because they probably fluctuated in number. Some may have been quite short lived while others may have been upgraded in time to augment the system of main gates.

The cutting of minor gates, probably often only for pedestrian and small cart traffic, emphasises the restrictive aspect of a walled circuit. However, there were also instances of internal gates. Some of these were on a redundant section of the town wall. At Dublin, St. Audeon's is the sole survivor of possibly four such gates and there were three at Waterford. Elsewhere, additional internal gates seem to have been created to be used similarly for the defensive purpose of sectionalising parts of the town, and/or to act as toll points. Examples of these may be the three internal gates of Wexford, apparently located at ward boundaries along the main street; New Gate in Limerick Englishtown, also on the main street; and those at Galway, apparently situated even in the nineteenth century at entrances to side street blocks. In contrast to the gates on former sections of the circuit, some of these may have been relatively recent, possibly erected to overcome the problem of toll evasion caused by infiltration through a decaying town wall, or one riddled with private and unguarded posterns. Both these problems were cited in eighteenth century records for a number of towns including Galway.

Turning briefly for comparison purposes to English and Welsh town gates, a number are illustrated by photographs and some by diagrams in Turner (1970, fig.2). A change in style is suggested from the square/rectangular plans of single-towered gates, exemplified by the twelfth century gates in York, to D-shaped twin-towered gates common at the Edwardian Welsh towns. The latter might be associated with barbicans or not, and lasted from the late thirteenth to the late fourteenth century. Thereafter, there seems to have been a return to the original rectangular style with single or twin towers. Also in the later Middle Ages, gates which did not protrude from or interrupt the wall so much apparently became more common, one at least of these was a water or quay gate reminiscent of the Londonderry gates in their present form (Turner 7–Hartlepool's Sandwell Gate). Unfortunately, the re-occurrence of the more rectangular style makes for difficulties in any attempt to date gates on the basis of style. Clearly, again, there is no substitute for detailed structural or archaeological analyses of individual sites in Ireland. Turner (67) draws attention to the sophisticated nature of gates, as opposed to other town wall structures, and points out also the complications that frequent

29 North Gate, Jamestown, with town wall on either side, pre-1973

30 Gate in south-east wall, Fore

31 Water gate on sea wall of main town, Youghal

rebuilding cause for attempts at dating. She cites evidence of gates being built in stone prior to the town walls, for example at Norwich and Newcastle in the thirteenth century, and at Sandwich even in the fifteenth century. This may also have happened often in Ireland but there is little evidence as yet, except possibly for Callan, and for the slightly different case of the outer, suburban gates of Ardee and Kilmallock which were probably built of stone. Turner (71) also suggests that by the late Middle Ages gates were designed or altered with factors such as toll collection and 'making a good impression' gaining ground on the original consideration of defence. In Britain, as in Ireland, gates figured prominently on town shields, possibly because they were picturesque (Speed 1610). Doubtless this use also reflected the prestige value of a really formidable gate such as York's early medieval Walme Gate (Turner 1970, pl.12) or later medieval Micklegate Bar (Platt 1979, fig.101). Some of the best in Ireland, including the New and St. Nicholas' gates at Dublin, were probably comparable with the major English or Welsh medieval town gates.

In considering the frequency of gates in Irish circuits, numerous gates must be viewed as a development from a basic group of two to four major gates. Cork, given its island site, was not necessarily typical but illustrates the minimum situation. It had two major land gates, both also bridge gates, and probably contemporary with the construction of the town wall. There was a major water or harbour gate too which gave access from the internal harbour to the main river. The tributary which fed the harbour entered the circuit through an opening or arch, a feature that was theoretically, if not effectively, a gate. Small diversions of the River Corrib entered the Galway circuit by similar means, probably for local industrial purposes such as milling or fishing. At Cork the late sixteenth-early seventeenth century maps indicate up to five posterns but do not appear to agree on each, while the 1733 survey notes ten 'large passages' through the wall and five 'slips or gates'.

Probably a theoretical four main gates is not unrealistic given basically rectangular or square circuits. Seventeenth century Londonderry had four main gates originally and so probably had medieval Fethard. Three would seem to have been a common minimum, as exemplified by medieval Drogheda Meath and seventeenth century Jamestown. More than four was not unusual, particularly where there was the need for one at the river bridge and at the quay, or a long circuit was involved. Clonmel, Kells and Wexford provide medieval examples but, for the later period, even the combined circuits at Athlone and Bandon may not have had as many as four main gates, let alone more. There may have been an approximate correlation between the medieval status of the town and the number of both main and postern gates. Dublin, Drogheda (Louth), Kilkenny (Hightown), Limerick (Englishtown especially) and Waterford all had over four main and many minor gates of varying types by 1600. Nonetheless, at any town the actual number of 'active' gates may have varied over the centuries, rising during periods of vibrant economic activity and falling during periods of war. Those shown on a map can, therefore, only be taken as true for that date unless their use is documented in other sources.

A sea or riverside site compounded the problems of identification by greatly increasing the possibilities. Waterford, for example, may have had as many as five water or quay gates on the River Suir alone at some point and Limerick Englishtown's total varied from two to five. Furthermore, no such gates may have existed at Waterford before the quayside was walled post-1377, or some may have always terminated streets leading down to the quay, even when it was not walled. Post-medieval Limerick had one major watergate giving access to the harbour in the Shannon, and there was an opening nearby leading to a mill in the Shannon which had a gate set back in the street behind it known as the Bow Gate. Beyond this again there was the more obviously private postern in the castle wall which formed part of the town wall there. On the other side of the harbour towards the bridge to Irishtown there were two gates later where towers, possibly with postern doors or small gates in them, are shown on the early maps. On the east side of Englishtown there may have been at some stage as many as four minor gates, only one or two of which may have provided general access, the others acting as posterns for the two friaries located there.

The building or rebuilding of gates in the seventeenth century, and more especially in the eighteenth century, is generally known from documents. The use of the term 'new' is of course strictly relative. It may refer to a late-medieval additional gate, as on Waterford's west wall, but in Dublin's case it seems to indicate the early medieval rebuilding of the main west gate. Little has been done to date the surviving structures except for the barbican at Drogheda. Bradley (1978, 118) gives it a mid-thirteenth century date, largely on stylistic grounds, but compares it with two English gates known to date from a century later—West Gate, Canterbury (1380) and Land Gate, Rye (*c*.1350)—(Turner 1970, 152; 160–1). As a fore-gate it may well have been an additional structure and so not a true guide to the date of the actual opening as such. The excavations carried out so far have produced a thirteenth century date for the Waterford gate and a fourteenth century for the one at Limerick Irishtown. These dates are useful in that they serve to confirm what is already known regarding the dating of their respective circuits and to identify the gates as original, but the study of gates, or gate sites, at less well documented towns might be even more fruitful for dating a circuit.

More precise dates have been established for many of the Dublin gates from documentary evidence. Unfortunately, none survive and it is not even certain that their structures, detailed in the 1585 survey, were the original in most cases. Consequently, it is not possible to employ this detailed and potentially useful information to date, by cross reference, gates at other towns which were stylistically similar. Dating gates is not only of intrinsic interest, it is necessary for studying the ratio of gates to circuit at particular periods and has implications for the development of street systems.

It is clear however that, by the late twelfth or early thirteenth century, there was one gate for each straight stretch of landward wall at Dublin. Two additions were made as the wall was upgraded on the south and extended on the west soon afterwards. These numbers give approximate ratios of 1:500 and 1:375 metres respectively along the landward circuit. Along the riverside the frequency was

32 North Gate, Athlone, outer side, from a *c*.1820 engraving

much higher, a ratio of 1:190 due to the presence of at least three quay gates which can be dated to the period 1195–1240. Such precise dating is not possible at any other site yet. Even at Waterford none of the gates, unlike the towers, can be related to the Hiberno-Norse circuit as the original three at Dublin can, and so it is not possible to make a basic distinction. Post-medieval gates can be dated there and elsewhere with more accuracy but less usefully. At Londonderry the original ratio was 1:335, reduced to 1:190 when three new gates were added in the eighteenth and nineteenth centuries. Broadly similar values to that for seventeenth century Londonderry can be obtained for medieval Kells and Cashel. Both had five gates by the 17th century which at the former, a simple circular circuit, produces a ratio of 1:335 and at the latter, a more complex irregular circuit, a ratio of 1:310. These values are also broadly comparable with the later for Dublin and, indeed, with the earlier if it is assumed that originally Kells and Cashel had only three gates—1:555 and 1:510 resp. There is no evidence that such an assumption is correct but it is not implausible. Medieval Galway had four gates giving a ratio of 1:330 which is reduced to 1:265 by the addition of another quay gate. Four gates at Fethard give a relatively low ratio (1:280), but at Kilmallock a high one due to the differences in circuit length (1:420). A system of four gates was often related to a cross-shaped street pattern. Where a walled town had an elongated shape, with a single dominant street crossed by a number of side streets, there was a tendency for a large number of gates in the long wall. Kilkenny Hightown and Wexford are examples, with three and four gates respectively on their long west walls, giving intervals overall nearer to 1:200m.

Taken alone, that is without consideration of tower intervals too, such relationships are largely indices of convenience or ease of access. They display a considerable uniformity but, as always with averages, they may disguise disparities, even major ones. This is less so in the case of a few, original, gates but is quite marked when additional gates are taken into consideration. Londonderry is a good example because two of its later gates were created in the north-west corner between the north and west gates, because of the extra-mural growth of the town there. At medieval Dublin gates on the east and south walls were spaced equally at *c*.150m either from each other, the castle, the south-east corner or the river, but there was a long stretch of more than 300m of the west wall by the Fair Green where there was no gate at all (fig.3.f).

From a defensive viewpoint gates and towers need to be considered together because their roles were similar up to a point. The twenty-four towns illustrated in Table 3.5 are those with reasonably full evidence for circuit length and numbers of towers/bastions and gates. Less than a quarter had high ratios, that is over 1:150. These values imply a low frequency of towers and gates on the circuits and the towns involved were generally those with spacious walled areas, for example Athenry, New Ross and Belfast. Low ratios of under 1:100 were twice as common and included the post-medieval circuits at Dublin, Galway and Limerick, and the later circuits of Athlone East and Londonderry. Amongst the rest the frequency of towers/bastions and gates was broadly similar at Drogheda, Kilkenny, Carrickfergus and Coleraine. Clearly, there was no marked disparity between the medieval and later walled towns in this as in so many other respects.

Similar data are not readily available for British towns. Turner (1970, 58) quotes numbers which give ratios for towers only ranging from 1:62 for Southampton, 1:85 Hereford, 1:120 Great Yarmouth to 1:130 Newcastle. At Southampton there were twenty-nine towers and seven gates which, if combined, reduces the ratio to 1:53 and for Hereford, with four gates in addition to seventeen towers, the comparable ratio is 1:75. Hereford was similar to Waterford

Table 3.5: Ratios—Tower/Gate: Circuit (in metres)

Athenry			1:165
Athlone	1:80 E	1:125 W	
Bandon		1:125 N	1:175 S
Belfast			1:200
Carrickfergus		1:110 (Stuart circuit)	
Carrick-on-Suir		1:120 (excl river)	
Clonmel		1:100	
Coleraine		1:100	
Cork	1:96		
Drogheda		1:110 N, 1:130 S	
Dublin	1:83		
Dungarvan			1:160
Fethard		1:100	
Galway	1:74		
Jamestown	1:83		
Kilkenny		· 1:135 H	
Kinsale	1:90		
Limerick	1:66 E, 1:98 I		
Londonderry	1:85 (4 gates)		
New Ross			1:193
Rindown		1:125 (1 side)	
Waterford	1:92		
Wexford	1:90		
Youghal	1:97		

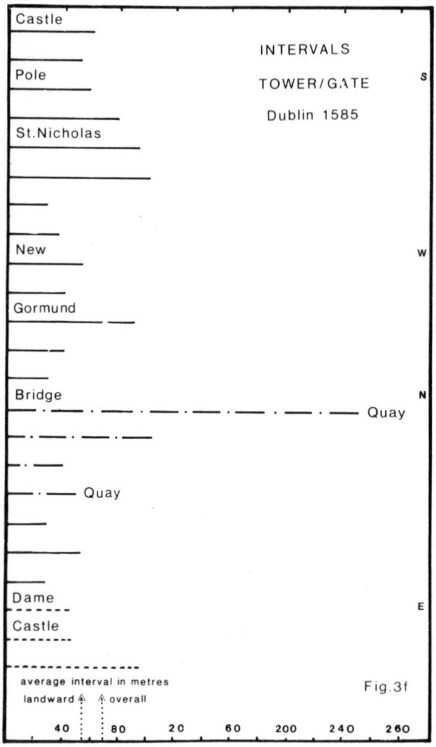

INTERVALS

TOWER/GATE

Dublin 1585

Castle

Pole

St.Nicholas

New

Gormund

Bridge — · — · — · — · — · — · — · — · — Quay

— · — · — · —

— · — · —

— · — · — Quay

Dame

Castle

average interval in metres
landward ↑ ↑ overall

Fig.3f

40 : : 80   20   60   200   240   260

(1:92) in the number of towers and main gates but its circuit was considerably shorter, 1584m as opposed to 2150m. Southampton had a longer circuit, 1782m, but one still only comparable with that of Youghal rather than Waterford. Nonetheless, it had apparently a much larger number of towers than Waterford and so a much lower ratio. It is not possible to draw sound conclusions on the basis of such a small sample but it does provide a different view to that of the circuit evidence. If these towns are typical then English circuits were, in contrast to Irish, more heavily reinforced by towers at least, while the Irish seem to have had longer circuits due to their marked tendency for extensions. Irish towns may, therefore, have been much walled but not necessarily very strongly so, unless the evidence for many more Irish towers has been lost completely.

Dublin had, in Irish terms, a strongly reinforced circuit. Figure 3.f illustrates the details of it as given in the 1585 survey. The values plotted are for the actual distance between towers and gates (converted to metric). Consequently, the average is lower than the ratio acquired by dividing the total number of gates and towers into the full length of the circuit. The pattern impresses most, perhaps, by its variability. A tendency to longer intervals is noticeable in the south but the most striking features are the very long section of quayside east of the bridge without a tower and the concentrations of gates in pairs to the south and west. There is no evidence from the medieval records for Dublin to indicate that there were any other towers or quay gates along the Liffey waterfront which might have been removed by 1585. It is not impossible but equally not very likely given the good quality of the Dublin records. The riverside wall, of course, had been removed by then leaving the towers and the Bridge gate to defend the waterfront as isolated structures, perhaps linked by rows of warehouses. This illustrates a phase which may have developed at many Irish walled towns due to the pressure of economic factors, or may have always been the situation if their circuits were never completed. Even then gates may have had an important role and a long-lasting one because of their use for toll collection and the general control of traffic.

The names of many Irish town gates are listed in Table 3.6. Some are self-explanatory and often refer to economic activity related to the area of the gate, for example Fish and Ferry, or to a prominent structure nearby such as the Castle

Table 3.6: Gate Names

NORTH	17	Great	1
EAST	7	Little	1
SOUTH	6	Ald	1
WEST	15	NEW	7
WATER	19	King	2
BRIDGE	7	Bishop	2
QUAY (KEY)*	7	Earl	1
Ferry	2	Maiden	1
Waterbailiff	1	Butcher	1
Custom	1	Sunday	1
Marine	1	ABBEY/ PRIORY	5
Strand	2	Friars	3
Mill	1	Nuns	1
Fish	1	Clare	1
Market	2	White	1
Fair	2	Black	1
Green	1	Trinity	2
Cow	2	Our Lady (Dame, Mary)	4
Sheep	1	Maudlin/Magdalen	2
Goose	1	St Catherine	2
Swan	1	Bride	1
Blagh/Blossom	2	JOHN	9
Bow	1	Peter	1
Iron/Clock	1	James	2
Spital	3	Patrick	3
CASTLE	6	Nicholas	2
Butter/Buttress	1	Martin	2
Pigeon Castle	1	Lawrence	1
Magazine	1	Paul/Pole	1
Cannon/Canon ?	1	Audeon	1
Porte/Drawingbridge	1	Werburg	1
BLIND	6	Personal names	32
Wick(et)/Postern/Sallyport	4	Famous events	3
Head	1	'Next' town (excl. Dublin)	12
Upper	1	Dublin	10
Lower	2	Local area (incl. manor, street and features other than any listed above)	29

* Includes Londonderry gates known as Shipquay and Ferryquay.

or Abbey. Some gates had more than one name, a few seem to have even been extravagant in this regard, although all the names were not necessarily in use at the same time. A typical case is the Bridge Gate at Dundalk which was also known as the North and the Water. All of these names were derived from the location of the gate. This was the most common basis for a name and usually took the form of North, East etc. In some cases one name may be a corruption of another, for example Butter or Buttress at Drogheda Meath. This gate was also known by the name of the area beyond it—Bebeck. The nearby main west gate there was named after the adjacent priory—St. John's and many other gates had saint's names for similar reasons. These sometimes took the form of 'Black', 'White' etc. depending on the religious order involved. Personal or family names of individuals also occurred and those, perhaps, generally commemorated the financiar, builder or embellisher of the gate or the mayor in office at the time. Cappock's Gate at Ardee may be a case in point. Such a name could possibly be used to date the gate but this would need good documentation. A name may also indicate the gate's status, for example Great, Blind, Postern.

The New Ross gates illustrate the extreme of multiple names with a total of fourteen names for five gates. The most named, the Maiden/Market/Fair/Earl's/ Bishop's Gate, does have its story told by its names, and so such excess is not without interest. It seems that it may have been associated originally with the ladies of the epic poem, hence Maiden; it led to both the Market place within and the Fair Green without, although 'fair' may be used in the aesthetic sense because it was regarded as the finest of the gates by modern writers; it also led to the Earl's manor of Old Ross; and it was probably rebuilt in the fifteenth century by the Bishop of Ferns who was then resident in New Ross.

The term 'gate' is ubiquitous; the alternative 'bar', common in York and eastern England, has been found only so far in Ireland in medieval references for Clonmel and Kilkenny Hightown (Walkyn's Bar). One of the suburban gates at Dublin was known as Crocker's Bar and it may have been used more frequently than these few examples suggest.

SITE

Site factors of significance for town walls may be considered under two main headings—physical and human. The former involves such topographic features as the slope of the ground and the nature of the associated water bodies, the sea, lakes or rivers. The latter includes a range of facilities resulting from human activity within the area of the town—harbour, through-routes, market place, parish church, religious house, castle and/or fort. Both of these groups were capable of alteration with time, but the influence of any one could be extraordinarily long-lived. The sea and river frontages of towns, for example, were particularly prone to change as the result of naturally occurring degradation or accretion. Yet, even where in addition artificial reclamation has been substantial, as at Dublin, the effect has been to maintain the existing line by parallel development. Of course, some sites have been altered radically when streams have been diverted or have disappeared through culverting. Likewise, the parish church, may have gone through many different architectural stages but its basic location rarely changed. Even when the building has been deserted, the site is often left untouched, if sometimes substantially reduced in area and so its influence survives. Other structures have tended to disappear altogether, particularly small castles or tower-houses which may once have been related to the circuit.

Not all of the 'human' elements in the local urban landscape were necessarily significant at each site. The parish church, for example, was often close to the market place at the centre of the town, and the castle or 'abbey' might be some distance away. Then none of these would have been directly related to the town wall although they might have influenced indirectly the siting of gates serving routes leading to them. Yet, in many instances one or more were adjacent to the town wall, either externally or internally, and the town gates might provide direct access even to the market place from the harbour area. The most important site factors are illustrated in Table 3.7. They will be considered here in turn, although they are often intimately interconnected.

SLOPES   The nature of the underlying land surface is obviously of importance both for ease of movement within a town and for the line of its town wall. The possibilities vary from the basically flat site to the one with steep slopes lying in a number of directions. Loughrea and Londonderry may be taken as examples of the extremes. There is a 5m OD variation within and just beyond the Connacht town but the Ulster one has a ridge site with a maximum variation of 30m OD, involving substantial slopes on three sides. But, within the walled area of Londonderry, the site is much flatter because the walls were built along the outer edge of the ridge, in other words utilising the local topography to its maximum defensive potential.

A fairly simplistic 3-fold division has been used to classify sites—weak or basically flat, moderate, and strong or steeply sloping. An indication is given of whether there is a dominant slope, usually towards a river or the sea, or a ridge/ knoll type of site in which there are a number of slope directions. Downpatrick is the sole example of the reverse situation, a hollow site where the direction of the many slopes is downwards towards the centre of the town, although Kinsale has some similarities, its site being amphitheatre shaped. Gradients have not been cal-culated for each site because of the numbers involved and the amount of internal variation possible at each site. The division is based on overall figures of up to 5m OD variation for 'flat' sites and more than 10m OD for 'steep' sites. Limerick represents the intermediate or 'moderate' category. There is a variation of 7m OD is general at both the Englishtown and the Irishtown, despite their contrasting site configurations—a ridge at the former and a single slope at the latter. The ridge type of site was obviously eminently defensible and was used not only at Limerick and Londonderry but at Dublin and Waterford, defended like Limerick from Hiberno-Norse times, and at Drogheda Meath, Navan, Galway, Kilmallock and Dundalk. In some cases, like the last, the ridge itself was only a slight feature

Table 3.7: Site Factors

	RIVER/SEA/LOUGH			TOPOGRAPHY	CASTLE (FORT)	RELIGIOUS HOUSE
Adare	R			+>	I ?a	E3
Ardee			r	–	E	Ia+E
Athboy			r	–	E	Ia
Athenry			r	–	IaC	Ea
Athlone E	R			+>		Ia Ea
W	R			+>	IaRoyal	Ia
Athy	R			–	E	I2?
Bandon	R			+>	I	
Belfast	R			–	I	
Buttevant			r	–	Ia?	I+E
Callan			r	+>	E	?+E
Carlingford		S		*>/–	IaC Royal	Ea
Carlow	R			+	Ea	?
Carrickfergus		S		–	Royal Ea	E2
Carrick–on–Suir	R			–	Ia <– E	I + E
Cashel		–				E1+2a
Castledermot			. r		I ?	E2a
Clonmel	R			–	Ia+fort C	Ia+?
Clonmines			r	–	I ?	I ?
Coleraine	R			+>	I fort +E	(I)
Cork	R			–	Ia+forts E	E5
Dingle		S	r	*>	I?	?
Downpatrick			(nr)	*	E	E3
Drogheda L	R			*>		I 4a+E
M	R			*>/–	IaC	I 2a+Ea
Dublin	R			<+>/–	IaC Royal	?Ia+E8
Dundalk			r	–	E	E2
Dungarvan	R/S			–	IaC Royal	E
Fethard			r	+>		Ea
Fore					E	Ea
Galway	R/S				I+forts I+E	E3a
Gowran			r	–	Ea	Ea
Inistioge	R			+>	I?	I?
Jamestown	R			–	I?	

but significant, given the surrounding marsh land. At single slope sites it was desirable that the ground should level off ultimately so that the town wall could be placed in such a way that it would not be 'over looked' from the area beyond. This was possible at Drogheda Louth, Youghal and Carrick-on-Suir but less easily achieved at New Ross and Limerick Irishtown. Depending on the circumstances, a very high and/or very broad wall with a large fosse could overcome this problem in medieval times, but it became a serious defect once bombardment from a distance became possible. For this reason in the seventeenth century of a line of forts was built on the rising ground which continued beyond the town wall of Limerick Irishtown and, lest these should be taken, elaborate outer defensive lines were developed at the medieval wall itself. At almost totally flat sites such as Athenry's a lack of height could be a problem too. There a rampart was built

	RIVER/SEA/LOUGH	TOPOGRAPHY	CASTLE (FORT)	RELIGIOUS HOUSE
Kells	(nR)	+	I	E 2a
Kildare			IaC?fort	E 1+2a
Kilkenny	R	2*>/–	IaC	I 2a+E2a
Kilmallock	r	–	E	Ea
Kinsale	R	+>	I? forts	E Ia+EA
Limerick E	R	<+>	IaRoyal+E forts	I 2a+Ea
I	R	+>	Iafort+E forts	Ea
Londonderry	R	<*>	E fort	
Loughrea	L	–	I	Ea
Maryborough	r	–	?Ia fort	
Naas	–	+	Ia?	?I 2+Ea
Navan	R	+>	E	Ea
Nenagh	(nr)	–	E?	I?+Ea
New Ross	R	*>	E	I 2a+Ea
Newry	r	<+>	I	(I)
Philipstown	r	–	?Ia fort	
Rindown	L	–	?Ia Royal	Ea
Roscommon	(L)	–	Ea Royal	E
Thomastown	R	+>	E	E?
Thurles	R	–	?I	E
Tipperary	r	+>	E?	E
Trim N	R	+>		Ia+Ea
S	R	–	IaC	Ia
Waterford	R	<+>	I?+forts E1+1a	I 2+1a+E
Wexford	R/S	–	IaC	E2a
Youghal	R/S	*>	I?(BaseT)	I+E2a

NOTES

1   R = major river; r = minor river; – = no river; S = sea; L = lough; n = near, ie c.1km

2   (a)   Nature of slope: weak   = – (less than 5m OD);
                                                moderate   = +(5–10m OD); * = strong (more than 10m OD).
      (b)   Dominant direction of slope: single   =>; multiple = <>.

3 & 4   I = inside; E = outside; a = adjacent to; C = corner of town wall.
           Religious house – only one involved, I and/or E, unless indicated.

in association with the wall and an extensive outer fosse created but this seems to have been a rare occurence in Ireland.

Basically, most sites have gentle topographies, although some small-scale, strong gradients may still be involved. This is often the case at a major river where closeby the site may be quite flat but away from it the slope may steepen considerably, as it does at Drogheda and Inistioge. Steeply sloping sites as such are not very common, accounting for only about 15% of those on list A. More than half are basically 'flat' sites and at 30% the slopes may be described as generally moderate. This pattern is also true of the post-medieval period with all three types represented by the newer walled towns.

Composite sites often resulted from extension of the walled area. Dublin and Waterford both provide examples here. The extension beyond the initial ridge sites took place in Dublin's case in the area reclaimed from the River Liffey, and in Waterford's on the only landward side of the Hiberno-Norse town. There, the line of the west wall had originally been at the end of the ridge but the new wall had to follow a less naturally defensible line, on rising ground to the west, except in the north-west where it utilised a scarp line towards the river. It is, therefore, perhaps not without significance that the most formidable of the seventeenth century additions to Waterford's medieval circuit was the large St. Patrick's citadel, built on the outside against the middle of the west wall and beside the main gate there.

It would be wrong to assume that apparent idiosyncracies in the shapes of walled towns were necessarily related to changes in slope. Occasionally however they were, for example at Drogheda Meath. There, to the east and partly to the west, the wall closely followed the natural escarpment but the site of the castle towards the edge of the escarpment in the west was an additional factor.

RIVERS, LAKES, SEA   The presence or absence of substantial bodies of water, whether sea, lake or river, is clearly closely connected with the nature of the slope. The sea and a major river are broadly comparable, except for the daily rise and fall in the level of the former, although rivers experience this too in their tidal stretches. Town walls by the sea or a river could help to hold off abnormal rises of tide but were also subject to the effects of such continual movement of water on their structure, especially their foundations. Indeed, the highest flood levels are still often recorded on surviving mural towers at Rhine and Danube towns. At rivers, of course, there was the additional possibility of having both banks settled, giving a pair of double or twin-walled towns, as for example at Drogheda and Trim, both on the River Boyne. At many more sites there was a dominant walled town with a suburb beyond the bridge, or at the opposite ferry-point. This might still have had some form of defence, such as a tower at the nearest end of the bridge, as was the case at Carrick-on-Suir in the seventeenth century. In time the bridge-head suburb too might be walled, an example being the suburb of St. John's opposite to Kilkenny Hightown.

A number of the towns have river meander sites. Drogheda is a case in point with the Louth town occupying the regularly graded 'slip-off' slope, and the Meath town the complimentary escarpment side. Few such sites are as strongly developed topographically as these and no Irish walled towns occupy dramatic meander loop sites, as do Durham and Shrewsbury. The only possible exception is Rindown which, as a peninsula in a lake, has a similar shape, if not a comparable range of altitude. There, the town wall survives at the 'neck' of the peninsula only and may never have been completed because the surrounding lake provided some defence.

The vast majority of walled towns had river or sea sites. For the medieval towns this meant access to water transport of some sort and potential for fishing and milling developments. Only 14% are not associated directly with a river, however minor. Even some of these are not far from one; for example, Downpatrick is now only a kilometre from the River Quoile and so was once able to have an out-port facility there. Others, like Kells and Naas, are in a major river valley if not actually at the river. A further 12% have sea or estuary sites, including some of the prominent early Anglo-Norman or Hiberno-Norse towns— Wexford, Carlingford, Carrickfergus and Youghal amongst others. Less prominent and relatively small in number are the 4% with lake-side sites—Loughrea and others in Connacht. In contrast, sites at small rivers account for 25% of the total. Some of these were navigable tributaries of major river systems, for example Athboy's river is a tributary of the Boyne. Ardee is on a relatively minor river by constrast with the Boyne, but one also draining directly into the Irish Sea and so useful in earlier times for small-scale river transport. Athenry is in a comparable position in the west.

The most striking figure is the 45% of walled towns which are at major rivers, as defined in the Atlas of Ireland map 22—a catchment area of over 500 sq km. These range from Hiberno-Norse towns such as Dublin on the River Liffey, Limerick on the Shannon and Waterford on the Suir, through the Anglo-Norman walled towns of which New Ross and Kilkenny on the Barrow/ Nore and Trim and Drogheda on the Boyne are the most prominent, to the seventeenth century plantation period towns such as Jamestown on the Shannon, Londonderry on the Foyle and Coleraine on the Lower Bann. It is clear, even from this brief resumé, that some rivers were dominant and this becomes even more striking when they are looked at as systems with their tributaries included. Thus, above Waterford there were directly on the Suir the walled towns of Carrick, Clonmel and possibly Thurles, with Fethard and Tipperary on tributaries and Cashel only 5km from the main river. These alone account for 12% of the list A total. If the Barrow/Nore river system, which also drains into Waterford Harbour, is included the concentration is increased further, in fact doubled, and much of the south-eastern quadrant of Ireland is involved. Similar, if less spectacular, concentrations were found in the Boyne/Blackwater system and amongst the series of south bank tributaries of the Shannon estuary. List B towns show a more even spread having about 30% at major rivers, 25% at minor rivers, 20% at the sea, and 25% unconnected directly with water but a few near lakes.

Many sites have composite water features. Small streams to the north and south at Youghal allow for water-filled fosses on a steeply sloping estuary site. Similarly at Coleraine the minor Mill Brook valley on the north side was enhanced to form the ramparts there, with the brook acting as the fosse. In a slightly different way the expansion of Kilkenny Hightown was taken to the 'natural' boundary of the tributary stream and the town wall between it and the older Irishtown was built beside it. At Londonderry the main river surrounds the walled town on two sides and on a third an area of bog provided a further natural defence. The elongated north/south line of Kilmallock may owe much to the adjoining small stream and to the presence of a shallow lake on the opposite side. Riverine island sites, such as Cork or Limerick Englishtown, had in effect 'walls of water' before circuits of earth or stone were built. Again, the influence of the natural line was strong and the line of the town wall largely derived from it.

A price had to be paid for such wholly or partially natural defence in erosion of the circuit's fabric, in difficulty of expansion of the walled area and in access to the areas beyond, which had to be limited to occasional bridges or the inconvenience of ferries. Thus, the nature of the site might reinforce the confining aspect of the town wall itself, adding to the potential for concentration within the walled area. Details of a river's configuration, such as areas of maximum depth, beaches or islands, could also affect the disposition of mural towers, gates related to quays and bridges, and defended harbours. Through these an influence could be felt in the street pattern both in its major and minor elements. The bridge gate and the major street at Ardee are both related to an island in the small River Dee, and the separate bridge and quay gates at Clonmel are likewise associated with different sections of the larger River Suir.

HARBOUR   Port facilities made waterside areas the most active in the town, apart from the market place. For this reason, especially at navigable rivers, which includes all the major, there was a strong force operating against having waterside walls. It has already been discussed in the section on size with regard to whether circuits were generally or always complete. However, specialised defensive structures such as gates were useful as control points for harbour as well as other administrative purposes, and so they may have existed both before and after waterfront walls. This was essentially a compromise situation allowing at the same time a degree of defence and/or of control as well as easier access to warehousing on land beside the river or sea. At Trim there was both a Water and a Bridge gate even though the riverside was probably not walled. Only one simple walled town, Athenry, had a river flowing through it but it was small and probably useful only in medieval times for small trans-shipment craft. The river there still enters by the castle and leaves through a gap in the opposing southern town wall, rather as a tributary of the Lee did at Cork. In the latter case the larger river was utilised to form an inner harbour, from which access to the main river was via a major watergate for ships. There are records of such a feature existing too at Clonmel and Waterford by John's River, the tributary stream. Both of these seem to have been much smaller harbours, probably providing only docking for one or two small boats, perhaps for specific items like fish or for the boats of toll collectors. There may have been inner harbours at other walled towns.

The alternative situation seems to have been a harbour area developed externally by quays built at the base of the town wall, either alongside it or at right angles to it. The former was the position at Dublin by 1585 where the quay was 'nine foot high from the channel to the pavement'. At contemporary Galway short jetties projected from the riverside wall and at Youghal they formed a small, almost enclosed, square harbour. There, and at Limerick Englishtown, the outer ends of the quays had their own defensive structures in the shape of towers. The harbour entrances between these were capable of being closed by means of booms, and at Limerick there was also covered access along the quays. Entrance to the walled town was effected then by means of a major quay gate from the harbour or by minor water gates elsewhere along the river or sea walls (*Pacata Hibernia* maps *c*.1587). It must be expected that in such an active area the details of the quay and other facilities, including the town wall, varied considerably over the many centuries involved, both to accommodate changes in water transport and economic activity, and as a result of flood damage or reclamation projects. In fact the defended harbour at Limerick Englishtown disappeared altogether in such a development in modern times, while the quay area of Dublin was being moved further and further north from as early as the Hiberno-Norse period, largely so as to make the shallow River Liffey a more effective port facility. However, outports such as Dalkey (list B) were needed in time.

CASTLE/FORT   There were castles at or near most walled towns, including those on list B as well as list A, but only about 25% of them were connected directly to the town walls. They varied both in date of initial construction and in status. Some of the earliest pre-dated the town wall, not only in the form of motte and bailey structures of the early Anglo-Normans, but in that of the even earlier Irish *dún* or *caisleán*. The de Lacy castle at Drogheda Meath is an example of the former and the O'Connor stronghold at Athlone of the latter; both were built in the twelfth century to defend river crossings and incipient urban settlements.

Strong stone castles were a feature of the next century, the strongest being the royal castles most of which are associated with the reign of King John. One was built across the River Shannon from Athlone and at six other walled towns— Dublin, Dungarvan, Limerick, Rindown, Carlingford and Carrickfergus. At each of these, except Athlone and possibly Rindown, the royal castle was attached to the town wall, indeed it was an integral part of the circuit. A corner position, as at Carlingford and Dublin, was the more usual but at Limerick Englishtown the castle's west wall formed part of one of the long sides of the circuit without interrupting it in anyway. It was close to the Shannon bridge, although that had its own defensive gate towers too. Dublin's castle, set above the harbour of the tributary River Poddle, was in one of the least exposed positions, while those at the other ports were at outer, waterfront corners. The actual connections between the town and castle walls at Dublin have been excavated recently and were found to be by means of arched walls across the castle moat (*Med Arch* 1987). The nature of the site at Carrickfergus did make for the slightest of connections, the seventeenth century town walls along the two sea fronts came up to the neck of the rocky promontory on which the castle is situated, but for long it may have been the only formal defence there.

Not every royal town had a major castle. Cork seems to have had a modest one, King's, beside the inner harbour close to the wall. A tower near the Water Gate entrance to the harbour was known as the Queen's Castle in later centuries; it may have served customs collection rather than a purely defensive garrison role. Waterford appears to have been a more extreme exception, a royal town and a port of prime importance but without a prominent royal castle, although no fewer than three kings visited it briefly in the Middle Ages. There is a reference to the King's castle in 1215 (*CDI* I 576), but its site is uncertain. Apparently, it did not survive to play a major part in the defence of the town.

A much larger number of castles were seignorial seats and the best of them, too, were formidable. Some, like those at Athenry, Kilkenny, Wexford and Trim, were attached to their respective town walls, again usually at corners in the circuit, and often near, or at, the waterfront. The castle at Carlow, sited on an island, had perforce to be slightly set apart from the walled town. Generally there was much variety within this group. A simple example was the small stone castle at Drogheda Meath, placed on top of de Lacy's original motte and close to a corner of the town wall above the bridge. More elaborate castles, such as those at Adare and Croom, are still today impressive ruins, but their connections with their respective town walls are not known because the latter have not survived.

Croom is a list B town because, unlike nearby Adare, with which it is linked in its only known murage grant of 1310, there is no evidence at all that the stone town wall provided for was ever built. This raises the possibility that the castle sufficed to protect the small urban community and even that murage money was deflected to its defence. Contemporary evidence from Leighlin, another list B town, suggests that this was a strong possibility. There, permission was granted to transfer the murage funds in order to finance the strengthening of an existing tower (?castle), because the amounts produced by the murage charter were proving so small (*CPI* 43). Murage was granted then, too, to the settlement at Newcastle Mackinegan, on the opposite side of the Wicklow massif, but this royal castle was frequently itself the object of official financing and so would have been un- likely to have required such deflection. This, and other examples like Carlingford and Dungarvan, suggest another possibility—that a walled town may be seen as an extension of a castle, in effect an inhabited outer bailey. In fact, the analogy with a castle was made later by the Waterford authorities in an application for aid. They described the town as 'only seven acres within the walls, like a little castle' (*CPR* 1374–7, 146). This may have been a considerable underestimate of even the Hiberno-Norse walled area (8.5 ha.) but also it may have been a ruse to strengthen their case.

As already noted, by then Waterford probably lacked a substantial (royal) castle and so did many other walled towns. Indeed, many never seem to have had one. Included amongst these are most of the prominent episcopal towns, such as Fethard and Cashel, although they did have bishops' houses, and a number of other towns located principally in early-settled parts of eastern Ireland. These were associated with major manors but located away from their centres, either slightly (*c*.1km distant) as, for example, in the cases of Clonmel, Thomastown, Ardee, Navan and Athboy, or further away and clearly the result of deliberate planning, as in the cases of Dundalk and New Ross. At Carrick-on-Suir the original castle was on the opposite bank to the town, but it was rebuilt much later as a 'manor house' in a corner of the walled area. The manorial presence at Dundalk may have manifested itself in the form of an agent's office which, in the later Middle Ages, possibly took the form of a defensive tower-house. A town gate house or mural tower could have served such a purpose too. Few instances have been found except possibly the east gates at Loughrea and Thurles. Major magnates such as the Desmond fitzGeralds, whose interests were widespread and included a number of walled towns, certainly had bases in them, for example in

Youghal and Kinsale. Others were the de Burgh residences in the centres of Galway and Loughrea. Some of these castles were, at least later, of the tower-house type, but they have tended to disappear or their exact location to be uncertain, so that the nature of their relationship to the town wall is now unclear. Tower-houses too might belong to bishops or to rich merchants, like those that survive at Galway and Ardee, but these examples are situated on the main street and so have no relationship with the town wall. It could be argued that the need for such strong dwellings within such towns suggests that their walled circuits were not as effective as they should have been. This may have been true but these tower-houses may also have been simply the standard type of house being constructed then by those who could afford, and perhaps required for business reasons, a fire-proof building. There is also some evidence to suggest that they may have helped to defend open sea or riversides, for example at Carlingford and Inistioge, or even walled waterfronts such as Youghal's.

In contrast, looking at the towns of England and Wales as illustrated by Speed (1610), the close association of town wall and castle is very marked. Only about 25% of the English and 20% of the Welsh walled towns shown had no castle by then, as opposed to the mere 25% of Irish which are known to have had a castle connected to their walls. A number of the British towns had their castles projecting beyond the walls, for example London, Bristol, Berwick and Brecon. At others such as Southhampton and Exeter the castle was set along the walls or more often, as also in Ireland, in a corner of the circuit, for example those at Carmarthen, Oxford and Chester. The castle at Newcastle-upon-Tyne overlooked the bridge, as did the one at Drogheda Meath, but at Norwich it was in the centre of the town. Possibly the closer connection of castle and walled town in Britain had more to do with the earlier urban development there and the administrative system based on shires and shire towns, than with the rate of decay of Irish town castles. The many small Irish castles set at a distance from their respective walled towns adds to the contrast.

In the sixteenth and seventeenth centuries interest on the part of the government revived and a spate of strategically inspired fort building affected the major walled towns. At new towns such as Maryborough and Philipstown the fort repeated the royal castle pattern, being placed along one wall or in a corner. In the case of Roscommon the old medieval royal castle provided the focus for a new walled town, as it may have done originally in the thirteenth century. The royal castle at Limerick Englishtown was partially modernised by one tower being altered to a bastion. At established towns fort-like structures were often attached to part of the town wall and large forts were also built near major towns, as indicated earlier. At Galway not only were two inner citadels built, again close by the main east and west gates, but also three large ones outside and away from the town wall. As with the royal castles, these were garrison centres and somewhat independent of the town; indeed, they now also came to have the role of monitoring the loyalty of the citizens or encouraging it by their very presence, as well as defending the town from external attack. At a restricted site such as Cork's, or an intensively settled extra-mural area such as that around Dublin, the forts were built well away from the walls and generally in relation to the river approaches.

In some places, such as within Clonmel and at Leighlinbridge, as in the area beyond Galway, monastic land provided convenient space for fort developments. Yet, the new towns of the Ulster Plantation, Londonderry and Coleraine, kept to the more civil pattern of a walled town with a modest garrison house, and thus continued the rather weak link between walled towns generally and castles or forts in Ireland. Forts apparently unconnected with towns were also built. In the case of Charlemont there is a map which suggests that a walled town was intended beside it, just as it was at the more modest fort of Monaghan (list B and appendix). But, no fort was built at Jamestown or Bandon, although one was originally planned at the latter to judge from the 1613 as opposed to the 1620 maps. In only a few other walled towns castles were modernised, particularly by changing towers to bastion-type structures. This happened at Kildare but the elaborate plans for redeveloping the Carrickfergus royal castle at the end of the seventeenth century were never realised. The solution at Athlone, a town of major strategic importance with a royal castle also still standing, was similar—to reinforce, modernise and extend the walled area. There, certainly, the new but small walled town created around the old castle does look like an extensive outer bailey, and so some of its medieval antecedents may well have been intended.

RELIGIOUS HOUSES AND PARISH CHURCHES   Religious houses of many different orders were a prominent feature of medieval life. Their extensive tracts of land had an influence on towns which often extended long beyond the post-medieval dissolution of the orders. Few medieval walled towns lacked an abbey, friary or priory, Carlow and Dingle appear to be the exceptions. Possibly the records are missing but this is unlikely because religious records are better than many in Ireland. Leaving out the post-medieval walled towns on list A, a few of which, such as Newry, were developed at former monastic centres, about 35% had one religious house and 30% had two. A further 20% are known to have had three and most of the rest had four, five or even more. Not all of these hundred or so houses were situated within walled towns, but all were close by and many were adjacent to the town wall. The use of their lands in later years as the sites for forts or for town development has just been referred to but, in medieval times, the extensive grounds and strong, stone buildings of most must have been of use too when a town came under attack. Indeed, sometimes their buildings were strongly fortified, not only at a rather isolated settlement such as Fore in Co. Westmeath but at towns like Dundalk and Inistioge. One has even been mistaken for a walled town, so extensive and well-fortified was Kells-in-Ossory's priory (list B app.).

Religious houses can be seen, therefore, as providing a means of reinforcing the walled town, however unintentionally. From the map evidence it looks as if the wall-walk of the Englishtown at Limerick may have continued round the boundary of the Franciscan friary, which was adjacent but extra-mural. Of course if an adjacent, external property was taken it might prove a grave danger to the town. It is possible that the town wall of Ardee was extended eastwards for this reason. The Carmelite friary at its south-eastern corner may originally have been extra-mural. At Drogheda Louth the friary church in the south-east corner was actually built against the town wall and so permission had to be requested for its east window to be cut into the wall.

At a few towns monastic churches seem to have acted as the parish church. This would have made ready access from the walled area important, if the church was outside as it may have been initially at Drogheda Meath, and it could also have had an influence on the siting of gates. It is noticeable how the town wall at Cashel loses its smooth line apparently in order to enclose the parish church and its graveyard. On the whole, externally situated 'houses' are often found to have been located close to main gates, like the two at Kells (Meath) near the east and west gates. Those whose property adjoined a town wall, either internally and/or externally as, for example, at Limerick Englishtown, generally had private postern gates in the town wall, for which they were presumably responsible. The surviving Sheep Gate archway at Trim may have been one such.

Access to parish churches within towns was usually achieved directly from the main street or market place or indirectly via a short intervening street from it. In towns that were not very large or 'deep' this meant that the churchyard, if not the church itself, occupied a corner of the walled circuit or part of one side as, for example, at Fethard, Castledermot, Carrickfergus and Wexford. At Youghal the church tower seems to have acted as an additonal defensive structure. At about half of the list A towns parish churches occupied such positions and so, this church land too could provide both open space next to the town wall, useful for access to the walls and for assembling forces, and strong stone buildings which, if tall, could also provide views over the wall.

Another point of contact was provided by parish boundaries. Today, the line of Waterford's circuit coincides throughout with parish boundaries and may have always done so. Some of these parishes have additional extra-mural areas, but at Wexford the four small intra-mural parishes run successively from the line of the long western town wall to the sea, and are entirely contained within the once-walled area. Yet, at Limerick the modern parishes cut across the site of the town wall. At Dublin there is considerable coincidence, partly parish and partly ward based, and at Londonderry the walled town comprises a complete ward. Further study could be carried out here, in particular by using the medieval parish boundaries where they are known. Current parish boundaries are only shown on OS maps for those towns designated as 'urban districts'. It is possible to envisage a close relationship between a single parish, or a group of parishes, and a walled town because of the convenience of using such a visible boundary as the town wall. However, this could only happen if the parish boundary post-dated the construction of the town wall, which seems generally unlikely to have occured. If town walls succeeded earlier enclosure lines or ancient boundaries then a relationship would have been more likely.

Some coincidence can also be seen between a townland boundary and the line of the wall, especially at Athenry where the walled town and the townland are the same, and at Thomastown where this may have been so too. To a lesser extent this is also true at Dundalk, Ardee, Trim and Kinsale. In reverse, either parish or townland boundaries may help now to indicate the line of a town wall that is otherwise unknown, if their antiquity can be proved and a strong connection established generally.

ROUTES, FAIRS AND MARKETS Most walled towns were on the major route-ways of medieval Ireland, or were major ports from which these routes fanned out. Many were connected by a series of routes based on the rivers of eastern Ireland for which the ports of Drogheda, Dublin, Wexford, New Ross, Waterford, Cork, Limerick and Galway acted as their crucial links with the world outside. A few other walled towns were related to the earlier Celtic route system based on inland political and religious centres. Kildare was a case in point while at Cashel, Naas and Downpatrick the two route systems met. Through-routes often may have influenced the general position of main gates but they are unlikely to have had a precise impact, because the detail of the routes could usually be deflected relatively easily. Indeed, it is possible that areas or points of local interest such as the towns, fields and fair grounds, as well as nearby churches or castles, were as significant, if not more so, in influencing the siting of gates and the roads to them. The position of a bridge connected to a through-route may have had, perhaps, a potentially stronger impact but many bridges disappeared in the course of time and were not necessarily rebuilt exactly *in situ*. This was the fate of the bridges at Athlone, Thomastown, Inistioge and Adare. Others were not rebuilt at all for centuries, for example those at New Ross and Coleraine. Fords often had an early influence and islands in rivers too were capable of a local, if indirect, impact through their association with fords, bridges, harbours and milling activity or weirs. Ferry points were probably more influenced by gates than vice versa.

Market places, either streets or open spaces, were usually located towards the centre of the town and so can have had little direct effect on the town wall. Fair greens, however, were different, generally being located outside the town and sometimes alongside the wall. The fair green at Dublin is a good example. It lay below the long stretch of the western wall which had no gates and may, indeed, be the reason for the long distance between the main south and west gates. The fair green at Kells had a similar location. Given the great antiquity of many fairs, they may have had a marked influence, causing routes to be deflected and hence indirectly affecting the location of gates.

Walled towns in Ireland, as elsewhere, were distinguished essentially by the experience of enclosure that they shared. The form this had on the ground at each site, its degree of completeness and its duration were all capable of much variation. This was in part due to period, which might be common to many towns, and in part to the setting of each, which was always likely to be highly unique at least in detail. The variety so derived, as well as the common traits, underlies the factual approach of this chapter and of the gazetteer.

CHAPTER 4

Creation and Use

CREATION

The creation of town walls is considered under five main headings—(a) the preparations made on the ground; (b) the financial arrangements provided by different types of murage measures; (c) the actual building in progress; (d) the costs involved; and (e) the time taken. Most of the evidence for the last three comes from the post-medieval period but there is one direct account for the medieval period of the beginning of a town wall project. This is the poem which tells the story of the digging of the fosse at New Ross in 1265 (Shields 1975–6, 24–33). Regrettably there is nothing comparable to the details contained in the state records for the broadly contemporary building of the Edwardian walled towns of North Wales in the 1280's. Nonetheless, much information may be derived from the murage measures granted to many Irish walled towns from the early thirteenth century.

PREPARATION   The New Ross poem places the building of a town wall, or at least its preparation, in a heroic light. This was probably not how it was normally viewed. It is the result of the literary device used, which may have been chosen for its suitability for propaganda purposes. This may have had something to do with the very strong commercial rivalry existing then between the new seignorial port at the northern head of the Barrow/Nore/Suir estuary and the much older royal port of Waterford on its western side. Yet, there is much in the poem that is factual and verifiable. It runs to 220 lines in all and it provides information too about the economic and social structure of New Ross. After a brief preamble, the implications of which will be discussed in the next chapter, the poem states the position simply—'They [the people in council] made a resolution thus: that a wall of stone and mortar they would build round the town . . . At Candlemas they began; to mark out the fosse they went; how the wall was to go the chief citizens went to mark it out . . . they summoned labourers directly; a hundred or more each day . . .'. There is in fact little hyperbole here except perhaps in the 'round' number and it may well recall a pattern of events that was repeated at many such towns about this time, before or after murage grants were acquired to help defray the cost. Financial matters are not referred to at all in the poem although labour costs alone are implied.

Possibly the only novelty of the New Ross situation was what ensued when local patience ran out with the labourers that had been employed. A co-operative plan was devised by the re-assembled council which required each guild or identifiable group to be responsible for digging a section of the fosse—'on Monday to begin with the vintners would go to the fosse, mercers, merchants and drapers along with the vintners. From day-break to the stroke of three they were to work at the fosse . . . a thousand or more, I tell you truly, go to work . . . with fine banners and insignia and flutes and tabors'. Whatever the truth of the numbers quoted the effect would to have been to triple at least the daily labour force. No trade or able-bodied section of the population was excluded—priests, particularly valued because of their 'youth' and thus their 'energy', seamen in port, and ladies on Sunday in countless numbers 'to heave the stone and carry it out of the fosse' are all specified.

The result of this great enterprise, which clearly acquired a carnival air, was the creation of a 'fosse twenty feet deep . . . and a full league' (6m x 4800m or c.3 miles). If it is assumed that 'deep' should be read as 'wide', this would suggest that it was similar in scale to the medieval fosse recently excavated at Carrickfergus but smaller than the one at seventeenth century Coleraine (Table 3.3). A league was a rather variable measurement and so too much emphasis should not be placed on the length given. In fact the landward circuit of New Ross was c.1575m and there was a further 750m of riverside, which would have given a maximum circuit of c.2325m. It is less easy to judge the truth of the contention that it was a plan 'as never was [put into effect] in England or France'. Equally, it is impossible to judge how common such a locally-based approach to town walling was in Ireland. It is hard to believe that such a co-operative approach to the first stage would have been widespread except perhaps in the very early stages of a settlement, when a simple and probably short earthen bank and fosse enclosure might have been made. There appear to be no early murage records for New Ross, the first known one dates from a century later. Yet such assistance may well have been acquired about this time because the real costs of town walling must have come with the stone work. Indeed, murage grants, which apparently started to become more widespread at this time, often specified a stone wall.

Before dealing with them in detail the question of the personnel involved, either as developers or experts, will be considered briefly. The murage records point to general sources of labour and to individual supervisors, whose role it was to ensure that the money was used for the proper purpose, but not to the actual craftsmen-builders as the Crown records for the North Wales towns do (Taylor 1974). The reason lies probably as much in the wider variety of controlling interest involved in the Irish towns, as in the comparative poverty of the Irish records. The matter is of more than passing interest because it concerns whether the stone walls, especially, were designed and built entirely locally or were the result of plans drawn up and supervised by experts who travelled from town to town. This would seem to have been the case at the French and Welsh bastides in the late thirteenth century (Beresford 1967, 3–13). Admittedly, the expertise there was largely in town-planning for the development of new towns, but town walls were often part of the overall plans. Town-walling did involve skills similar to those required by the builders of major stone castles of which there were many in Ireland. Indeed, the frequent presence of the same major landowners in Ireland and other areas of Western Europe linked to the English Crown would have facilitated such an interchange. Moreover, it is possible that, at this period in particular, with the Irish colony prospering but increasingly having to face security problems, there was much building activity at its towns. This might have taken the form of tower and gate strengthening, circuit extension or wall building for the first time, but it could have been on such a scale that the use of groups of peripatetic experts would have been feasible. New Ross would be an example of the last, while small-scale wall extension is known to have taken place at Dublin, *c.*1261, and the insertion of gates into existing walled circuits has been proved by the excavation at St. Martin's, Waterford.

Only a few named individuals are known to have been associated with town walling in Ireland. One was Brother Walter de Aqua who was sent with the official mission of inquiry following the Bruce invasion of 1315–18, 'to assist in the fortifying' of Dublin. The exact nature of his expertise is not known, but it seems more likely to have been administrative that technical, possibly concerned with the financial requirements. These were considerable to judge by the grants that were actually made later. At the technical level a so-far tenuous link can be established between a master carpenter or mason who was known as 'William of Drogheda'. He was a burgess of Caernarvon in 1298 and he may have worked at a number of the new Welsh towns on their castles or walled circuits. At an earlier date he may have been employed at some of the king's castles in Ireland (Taylor 1974, 1039–40). Parallels in style are noticeable between the round, seaward towers of Harlech castle and those of the St. Lawrence Gate barbican at Drogheda, which adds to the connection without necessarily proving it. As regards instigators, the walling of part of Kilkenny in 1400 (Stanihurst, 1586) is attributed to 'Robert Talbot' and that of Rosscarbery (list B) to 'a lady of that country' (Smith 1750). While nothing more is known of the latter and even the date is unclear, Talbot can be identified as a prominent citizen of Kilkenny. His actual role is not stated but there was a murage auditor in 1382 of that name. As such he might have been an administrator rather than an instigator. The walling of Cashel, 1317–26, has been associated with the current archbishop, fitzJohn (Leask n.d.) and the names of other lords are known from murage records. Some at least of these may have been instrumental in both the instigation and development of walled circuits at their own settlements.

FINANCING Murage is defined specifically as the 'right to levy a toll or tax in order to finance the building or repair of town walls' (*OED* 1938). As a term it may also be used more generally to cover other forms of funding for the same purpose, forms such as direct cash grants, the pardoning of debts, the use of fines—including those arising out of murage offences—and, most commonly, the partial remission of fee-farm rents. To avoid confusion the term 'murage charter' will be used to refer to the tax system because in such grants it was clearly written down which goods, coming into the town for sale, would be subject to tolls and at what rate. There are more than sixty listed in Table 4.1., the detailed provisions of which are known. They will be referred to here by the town's name and the date of the charter.

Whatever the form of the murage grant, the town requested and the king

Table 4.1: Murage Charters : detailed provisions known

DATE	TOWN	DURATION		REFERENCE IN YEARS
1221	Dublin	2	?	CDI I 1002
1223	Waterford	4		CDI I 1163
1233	Dublin	3	a	CDI I 2068
1234	Waterford	3	b	CDI I 2133
1234	Drogheda M + L	3		CDI I 2135
1237	Limerick	6	a	CDI I 2405
1243	Waterford	3	b	CDI I 2613
1250	Dublin	3		CDI I 3057
1275	Youghal	7	c	CDI II 1144
1278	Drogheda	3	c	CDI II 1517
1282	Kilkenny	3	d	CDI II 1913
1283	Kilkenny	4	d	CDI II 2136
1284	Dublin	7	e	CDI II 2181
1284	Cork	5		CDI II 2248
1286	Tralee, Mallow, Ard	7	f	CDI III 226
1289	Trim	7	f	CDI III 560
1291	Kilkenny	4	f	CDI III 912
1291	Waterford	4	f	CDI III 917
1291	Fethard	7	f	CDI III 1015
1295	Dublin	7	f	CDI IV 250
1295	Drogheda/Louth	7	f	CDI IV 251
1295	Castledermot	7	f	CDI IV 253
1296	Drogheda/Meath	7		CDI IV 311
1297	Dublin	5	e	CDI IV 435
1298	Clonmel	10	e	CDI IV 511
1300	Tipperary	10	e	CDI IV 752
1303	Emly	3	g	CPI 41
1303	N'cas. Mackinegan	5	g	CPI 41
1306	Kilkenny	5		CDI V 537
1308	Dublin	6		HMD 271-3

responded, generally, it would seem, in a positive manner. Royal towns such as Dublin and Waterford applied directly and other towns through their lord, the charter being granted to the lord himself as at Trim (1289), or to the town as in the case of Clonmel (1298). The grant was made by the king, or by the justiciar on his behalf and, in the fifteenth century in particular, the Irish parliament was also involved.

The fact that a request was made is in itself of interest, as well as the nature of the request, although this is rarely recorded directly and in detail. In one example from 1290, Waterford made out a particularly strong case, citing recent burnings of the city and poverty resulting from losses at sea, which made it 'impossible to manage without the king's aid'. To enhance the case further the city authorities also pointed out that fifty years had elapsed since the last murage grant (*CDI* III 622). Clearly, the granting of murage was not automatic even when a strong case was presented, for an inquiry was instituted into the 'state of the city' before a

DATE	TOWN	DURATION		REFERENCE IN YEARS
1310	Adare	3	h	CPI 42
1310	Croom	3	h	CPI 42
1310	Tipperary	3	h	CPI 43
1310	Athenry	3	h	CPI 43
1310	Leighlin	5	i	CPI 43-4
1310	Waterford	7	i	CPI 44
1312	Dublin	5		HMD 308-12
1318	Drogheda/Meath	5		HMD 413-7
1358	Youghal	5	j	Annals XXV-VI
1358	Caherconlish	20	k	CPI 61
1361	Galway	5	j	Hardiman 58
1364	Clonmel	10	l	CPI· 64
1374	Youghal	20	j	CPI 67
1374	New Ross	20	l	CPI 67
1374	Thomastown	20	j	CPI 68
1374	Kilmallock	10		CPI 68
1375	Kilkenny	7 j		CPI 70
1376	Ardee	10	m	CPI 73
1380	Drogheda	6	l	CPI 78
1381	Kilkenny	12	j	CPI 79-80
1385	Drogheda	12	l	CPI 82
1389	Ardee	10	m	CPI 87
1393	Trim	20	j	CPI 89
1394	Kilkenny	20	j	CPI 89
1396	Galway	perpetual		CPCR I 196-7
1404	Drogheda/Louth	?	n	CCR V 424-6
1408	Athboy	60		CPCR II 4541
1412	Dundalk	18	n	MCI 900
1437	Ardee	perpetual	m	MCI 668
1446	Athboy	60		CPCR 2 454-5
1469	Kells	?	k	MCI 181
1475	Siddan	?	n	SR Ed IV 367-8

The letters a, b, indicate similarity between charters; ? = period not stated.

new charter was granted in 1291. Indeed, the Limerick charter of 1237 contained the reproof that 'the citizens ought more liberally to contribute their own money'. The taking of murage tolls without royal permission was not lightly countenanced either, although Dublin, which was illegally taxing corn in 1316, was forgiven and even had the toll confirmed. The reasons given were the 'good service' of the mayor and citizens to the king, and the 'labour and expense' they were put to 'at his command, about the repair of the walls and the custody of the city' (*MCI* 4). No doubt the special circumstances of the Bruce invasion made all the difference then.

Murage, in whatever form, was essentially a financial provision arranged by central government for a major public work that would benefit both the town and its locality. The wording of early charters like Waterford (1234) made this very clear—'for [the town's] defence and that of neighbouring parts'. It was, therefore, similar to and often combined with grants for other major infra-structural projects, such as the building of bridges, quays and roads. Any of these projects might be located close to or within a town but, in addition to being beneficial to a wider community, they might also be of such a magnitude that they could legitimately be claimed to be beyond a town's own financial capabilities. Consequently, the murage charter may be seen as an attempt by central government to aid towns by broadening the financial base to include all who traded at the town whether they were locals or foreigners. The argument was that those who valued peaceful conditions, as traders usually did, should contribute to its costs but the loyalty of towns, which was highly regarded by feudal monarchs, was no doubt another factor. Yet it was clearly an inflation-inducing approach, and one that could also turn traders away from a town operating tolls, in favour of one not doing so. On the other hand, unlike most of the other types of murage grant, it did not involve a direct loss of revenue to the Crown and this was always an important consideration.

Murage measures requiring local labour services, grants of building materials or direct financial aid, date from Saxon times in England but, during the early thirteenth century, threats of invasion and experiments in taxation seem to have led to the appearance of murage charters as a new form (Turner 1970, 14; app. A+C). The first, to Shrewsbury in 1220, was followed almost immediately by ones to London and Dublin (1221). This emphasises both the closeness of the colony to developments at the centre and the key position of Dublin as the chief Crown bridgehead. In fact, the way in which concern for the defence of Dublin progressed up to 1220 may well illustrate how matters may have developed in England too. In 1204 the king 'commanded' the citizens of Dublin to 'attend to the fortifying of their city, everyone for his part'; in 1206–7 he involved the barons and knights of Meath in the same effort, apparently as the price of some favour which they had requested; and by 1214–15 Dublin was receiving a grant of 500 marks, more than twice the value of its annual fee-farm rent (*CDI* I 226, 315, 529, 597).

This new form of murage was similar in England and Ireland in terms of purpose, scale and duration. The purpose, already referred to and often stated in a charter's preamble, was to enhance the security of the town and the surrounding area by aiding the 'inclosure of the town'. The scale was small at this early stage, involving only a few items of trade. The duration was likewise limited, from two to four years, but it remained short for some time while the scale developed rapidly (Table 4.1, fig.4.a). Extensions could, however, increase the period over which murage was levied. A charter, granted to Drogheda in 1240 initially for three years, was extended in 1243 for a further two years (*CDI* I 2614—no details are given of the goods covered). Also other grants could co-exist with the charters. Dublin, for example, received a number of different grants in the aftermath of the Bruce invasion, 1315–18, as did Drogheda.

In England murage charters showed the same tendency towards increasing complexity (Turner app.A) and, incidentally, they now provide much information regarding the economic life of the feudal period (Orpen 1911 IV 274–5; MacNiocaill 1964 II 448–53; Lydon 1973, 14; Thomas 1986, 69–75). Such complexity may, in part, have been a response to another feature common to all forms of taxation, the growth of exemptions. Some of the early Irish charters,

MURAGE CHARTERS ~ COMMODITIES

	Early		Inter-mediate		Mature					
COMMODITIES SUBJECT TO TAX	DUBLIN 1221	WATERFORD 1223	DROGHEDA 1234 ★★	LIMERICK 1237	(A) WATERFORD 1243	(B) KILKENNY 1283	(D) TRIM 1289	(F) DROGHEDA 1296 ★★	(J) YOUGHAL 1358	(N) DUNDALK 1412
Wine	✻	✻	✻	✻	✻	✻	✻	✻	✻	✻
Wool	✻	✻	✻	✻	✻	✻	✻	✻	✻	✻
Hides	✻	✻	✻	✻	✻	✻	✻	✻	✻	✻
Honey			✻	✻	✻		✻	✻	✻	
Cloth			✻	✻	✻	✻	✻	✻	✻	✻
Iron		✻	✻	✻	✻	✻	✻	✻	✻	✻
Ships		✻	✻		✻	✻	✻	✻	✻	
Salt			✻	✻	✻	✻	✻	✻	✻	✻
Corn			✻	✻	✻	✻	✻	✻	✻	✻
Flour			✻				✻	✻		✻
Fish			✻	✻	✻	✻	✻	✻	✻	✻
Animals			✻	✻	✻	✻	✻	✻	✻	✻
Butter/Cheese			✻	✻	✻	✻	✻	✻	✻	✻
Animal fats			✻		✻	✻	✻	✻	✻	✻
Timber			✻		✻	✻	✻	✻	✻	✻
Woad			✻	✻	✻		✻	✻	✻	
Misc. Goods				✻		✻	✻	✻	✻	✻
Lead/Other Metals			✻	✻	✻	✻	✻	✻	✻	
Onions				✻		✻	✻	✻	✻	
Wax					✻	✻				✻
Alum/Mineral salts					✻	✻	✻			✻
Skins				✻	✻	✻	✻	✻	✻	✻
Fine Leather					✻		✻	✻	✻	

	Early		Inter-mediate		Mature					
COMMODITIES SUBJECT TO TAX	DUBLIN 1221	WATERFORD 1223	DROGHEDA 1234 ★★	LIMERICK 1237	(A) WATERFORD 1243	(B) KILKENNY 1283	(D) TRIM 1289	(F) DROGHEDA 1296 ★★	(J) YOUGHAL 1358	(N) DUNDALK 1412
Canvas/Linen					✻	✻	✻	✻	✻	✻
Coal/Firewood					✻	✻	✻	✻	✻	✻
Utensils					✻		✻	✻	✻	✻
Spices					✻	✻	✻			✻
Millstone					✻	✻	✻	✻		
Cinders/Ashes					✻	✻	✻	✻		
Heavy Woollen Goods					✻		✻	✻	✻	✻
Bricks/Lime					✻		✻	✻		
Pitch/Oil/Resin					✻		✻	✻		
Peas/Beans					✻		✻			✻
Foreign Foods					✻					✻
Horse-shoes/Nails etc.					✻	✻	✻	✻	✻	✻
Tan					✻	✻	✻			
Garlic					✻	✻	✻			
Meat					✻					
Seeds-Veg./Corn							✻	✻	✻	✻
Beer/Malt							✻	✻	✻	✻
Glass							✻	✻		
Ships' Tackling							✻	✻		
Apples & Nuts							✻			
Flax/Hemp									✻	
Olive Oil									✻	

Fig. 4.a

such as those to Drogheda (1234) and Waterford (1234 and 1243), stated clearly that the citizens or burgesses were to pay the taxes, but in time exemptions were acquired. This was particularly so with regard to residents but it applied to many different categories too. Goods entering the town for the personal use of residents were exempted early on and, as with all such arrangements, this was open to a range of interpretation. In fact, exemption from paying murage and similar tolls became yet another privilege that could be granted in return for loyalty. By 1327 the burgesses of Dublin were free of murage and other taxes 'throughout the king's dominions' (*MCI* 4) and the burgesses of Kilkenny and Callan had a similar privilege from their lord, the earl of Gloucester, also in the fourteenth century (*MCI* 533). Later, murage to certain towns in the Pale was granted with the proviso that 'it should not be prejudicial' to Dublin, Drogheda, Ardee and Skreen (*SR* III 1462, 25), and the murage grant to Kells in 1469 was similar. Such exemptions must have reduced the capacity of the charters to achieve their purpose and, consequently, must also have contributed considerably to the lengthening of the duration of most later charters. It will be clear from Table 4.1, and also figure 5.3, that from the mid-fourteenth century a duration of twenty years became increasingly common, while earlier one of ten years had been exceptional. In other words, Clonmel (1298) was atypical and Youghal (1374) or Trim (1393) almost standard. In addition, extensions to existing charters were frequently acquired, also for quite long periods. It is hardly surprising, therefore, that by the fifteenth century while only a few charters were apparently actually granted 'in perpetuity', notably Galway (1396) and Ardee (1437), there was a tendency for murage collection to become a habit for Irish towns. This, however, was clearly an abuse. Many charters contained the instruction that the customs should 'cease and be abolished at the end of' the stated term, whether that was a mere three years, as in the Dublin charter of 1233, or twenty in the New Ross one of 1374. Nonetheless, it was possible to deflect murage money to other purposes, providing permission was requested, just as it was possible to seek renewals and extensions of charters. A case in point was the prolongation of murage for a further three years allowed to Dublin in 1290, following the use of murage there to enclose the Exchequer, a task which had been carried out at the suggestion of the Treasurer of Ireland (*CDI* III 754).

Murage money, either from the charters or other grants, was open to other more obvious abuses such as embezzlement but this, too, was recognised in the provisions of the grants. In early charters, such as Limerick (1237), the justiciar and citizens were required to select 'two men of the city to collect the money' and to oversee its proper use. Arrangements were also made for accounting, usually under local supervision, with returns made yearly to the exchequer. The bishop, dean and parson of Cloyne provided the supervision at Youghal for the 1374 charter and the earl of Desmond at Dungarvan in 1463 (*MCI* 63). Fines were imposed for failure to comply with the regulations and these were sometimes added to the murage fund. In 1374, in a serious case, the provost and bailiffs of Galway were commanded to be distrained by their lands and chattels, until they should render an account of murage and pavage. Later on, however, as at Drogheda in 1404, towns were often discharged from rendering an account as a special privilege when times were difficult (*MCI* 807).

From the town archives of Kilkenny (*LPK*) there is evidence that the murage toll collection was farmed by the late thirteenth century, the names and the rates paid (£4 to £5 p.a.) being recorded on a yearly basis. In one year, 1384, the cost of maintaining 'keepers of the murage' at each of five gates amounted to 21*s*., the rate varying from 2*s*. to 4*s*. except at the internal gate with Irishtown, for which John Corviser was paid 8*s*. A century later, the gate keepers seem to have, in effect, become the murage farmers. They paid 2*s*. to 10*s*. in 1498 for the privilege, a total of about £3 for seven gates. Also recorded, there, were instances of murage theft by individuals. John Rothe, a butcher, was fined a cask of wine in 1384, valued at the apparently substantial amount of £6.13*s*.4*d*., for 'concealing money of murage' of unspecified amount but presumably considerable. In the same source there is a rare record of money spent on town-wall maintenance—four of the main gates were 'new-made and repaired' in 1500 at a cost in excess of £7.13*s*.1*d*. It is not clear whether this involved the gate houses or just the opening and shutting parts, probably the latter.

Unfortunately, despite a well established system of accounting centrally, few such records now exist and so it is impossible to compare the proceeds of murage charters, either between towns or throughout the period. Those that have survived, for Galway dated 1272–5 and 1278–80 and for Dunmore, Co. Galway,

	WATERFORD 1234	DROGHEDA 1234	KILKENNY 1282	CLONMEL 1364	DUNDALK 1412
Horse	1/2	1/2	1/2	(of 40sh value) 2	(of 40sh value) 2
Ox	1/2	1/2		1	1
Corn	weigh 1	crannock 1/4	seam 1/4	barrel 1/2 crannock 1	crannock 1
Herring	mease 1/4	mease 1/4	seam 1/4 last 2 1000 1/4	mease 1 barrel 4	mease 1/2 barrel 4
Other fish	100 1/2 or 1	horse-burden 1/4	seam 1 cartload 4	basket 1 1000 1	basket 1/2
Iron	cwt. weigh 1/2	band 1/2	garb 1/4 (steel)	band 1 100 pieces 2 100 Spanish 4	band 1/2 100 pieces 2 100 Spanish 4

Values in pence

MURAGE CHARTERS – TOLLS Fig. 4b

dated 1279–80, show how informative such records might have been (*rep DK* 1904/36, 47–8). In both the Galway accounts the money was underspent, indeed by almost one-third in the case of the later account, the total return for which amounted to about a 50% increase on a yearly basis. This may indicate that for Galway in the 1270s murage receipts were both increasing and more than adequate. The Dunmore account was of a different scale as befits what can only have been a much smaller settlement so far inland from Galway in march country. It amounted to less than one-tenth of the Galway account for 1278–80, but even so it was only marginally overspent. It is, in fact, the only reference to Dunmore having had town walls and a rare reference to its burgesses, four of whom are named in it as collectors of murage. However different this suggests the market potential of the two towns to have been, they both spent the proceeds in basically the same way, on burning lime and the wages of masons. In the later period the work at Galway was concentrated on a 'tower beyond the great [East] gate' and 'making walls towards the sea'. The details given indicate the work of both masons and carpenters, with labourers to assist them in breaking stones, carrying stones and wood. Lime was burnt closeby and iron was purchased for 'fabricating crows, pick-axes, nails and other tools', apparently on the spot.

In discussing murage charters it is necessary to consider, however imperfectly, the level of the taxes charged. This is complicated by the length of the Anglo-Norman period, over 250 years in this case, which must have allowed for considerable changes to develop in the value of the coinage. Differences between charters in the measurements used and even the obscurity of some of the weights add further difficulties. In figure 4.b five items common to most charters are compared very briefly. From these it seems clear that murage taxes were numerically small and generally fairly stable over long periods. Further evidence of the latter can be seen from a study of the three items—wool, wine and honey—which were basic to all murage charters. Usually a sack of wool was taxed at 3–4*d*., a hogshead of wine (52.5 gallons) at 2–3*d*. and a hogshead of honey, which started at 4–5*d*., stabilised at 2*d*. from the later thirteenth century. In respect of the first, comparison with customs duties shows that the murage taxes were also actually small. For the 'new custom' of 1275 a sack of wool was taxed at the rate of 6*s.* 8*d.*, but the comparable murage toll at Drogheda in 1278 was a mere 4*d.*, similar to general market tolls at Dublin in 1252 (Curtis 1938, 183; *HMD* 128–9). Comparison with the 'small new custom' of 1380 is less easy, due to differences in weights, but produces a similar pattern (*SR* I 479). A further comparison, between selling prices fixed by act of Parliament in 1470 on a range of goods and the Kells murage charter of 1469, shows that murage taxes were rarely set at a rate of more than 5% (Gale 1834, 14). Curiously, the murage rate tended to rise inversely with the value of the item; for example, fowl worth a matter of pence were taxed at about six times the rate for a cow.

The murage rates were probably kept low because some of the same goods were also subject to customs duties, a major source of Crown revenue, and some to local market tolls. But, the low rates must have contributed to the lengthening both of the lists of goods involved and of the duration of the charters. In fact, other sources of finance including customs duties, in particular the duty on the export of hides known as the 'cocket', were often remitted by the Crown for additional murage funds. This happened increasingly from the late fourteenth century. Waterford received such a grant in 1377, and at Youghal proceeds from the cocket were still making a contribution to murage funds in 1610. Low returns from murage charters, cited as the reason for transferring the funds at Leighlin (list B) in 1310 to castle building, could of course result from depressed economic conditions too. Another factor that arose later was the development of markets beyond the medieval 'land of peace', at Cavan and other centres in Gaelic dominated areas, at which no such toll system operated and so tended to draw trade away from the Pale towns in particular.

From the early fourteenth century murage charters sometimes specified a stone wall. Of the approximately fifty murage measures listed for the years 1310 to 1394 in the collection known as *Chartae, priviligia et immunitates* fifteen did so. They include the 1310–11 to Limerick for 'enclosing the suburb of Irishtown'. Some grants, particularly those to towns with well established walls, also indicated that the grant was for particular types of work or structures. Again, Limerick provides examples with grants in 1320 for 'amending' the wall and in 1375 for 'repairing' it. Waterford's 1310 charter refers to 'defective walls, towers and gates', and the one granted in 1380 to Drogheda '*extraque parte aquae*' mentions a tower near the quay as well as the bridge which needed repair. Earlier charters to Drogheda Louth, in 1316 and 1319, referred to additional works of 'new construction', which suggests extension of the system, and one for 1325 specified 'new towers'. This might have involved the addition of new ones to an old stretch of wall, to improve it, or the construction of towers in conjunction with a new extension to the circuit. The southern gate of Clonmel, also its bridge gate, was mentioned in a grant of 1463 but these references do tend to be exceptional and many charters, unfortunately, are quite general in their wording.

Some of the Dublin grants are usefully specific and further illustrate the system. The request for one made in 1308 for aid to 'build the towers of the new gate, lately fallen' makes it clear that the result was sometimes less than that desired. A charter for ten years was applied for but only a four-year one was granted. Again, in 1311–12, a request for help with repairing Isold's tower and the quay there was delayed, pending auditing of the accounts. Clearly, murage grants were far from automatic or else Dublin suffered undue scrutiny due to having government officials on the spot. Murage to an individual, a former mayor, is also recorded at Dublin in the early fourteenth century and may have been common elsewhere, although no instances are known. It is probably not just the better preserved records that put Dublin ahead of any other town in the variety and continuity of its murage. As the capital or administrative centre of the feudal lordship its defence was crucial. By the end of the sixteenth century it was also following the pattern, then well established in England, of imposing a local cess or tax on inhabitants instead of murage tolls.

Occasionally, instances are recorded of murage going to structures not apparently part of a circuit. For example, the 1375 murage charter to Jerpoint (list B app.) appears to have been specifically intended for the defence of the Nore bridge, by means of one tower and a gate on the southern end. Beyond there a new town had been built which later became deserted, possibly to some extent because it lacked a circuit of its own. The transfer of murage funds to castle building has been noted already for Leighlin in 1310–11. This may often have been the fate of money raised by charters granted to small settlements at which strong castles already existed. Examples here are places like Croom, Co. Limerick, and Mora, Co. Cork, both list B and settlements at castles for which the only evidence of town walling is a single murage grant, of 1310 and 1317–8 respectively. A slightly different instance is that recorded for Galway in 1427 when the local lord, de Burgh, received funds from the town's murage 'to subdue the Irish'.

Co-operative measures between adjacent or associated towns, and between towns and the area around them usually up to the county level, were common from the late fourteenth century. The 1376–7 murage charter to Ardee required that tolls, being taken there for the lord's other 'town' of Roche, should cease. This is the only hint that Castleroche (list B) might have been walled but possibly, as at Mora, money was concentrated on its castle. The 1393 charter to Trim allowed for tolls to be taken also in Athboy, Skreen and Navan, the refuge roll of Trim being high-lighted by the phrase 'where all the *fideles* of county Meath congregate'. By 1423 Navan and Athboy, which as walled towns also received murage in their own right, were replaced by the minor settlements of Slane, Dunboyne, Greenogue and Dunshaughlin (*MCI* 7). Such urban-based murage collection seems to have been a feature especially of the Pale but more rural-based funding was probably very common. In 1449, for example, the 'inhabitants of Ulster' were required to pay £40 annually for five years towards the murage of Newtown Blathewyc (list B), and those of 'county Kilkenny' £20 (p.a.) for four years for the repair of Thomastown's walls. Similar provisions were made for Fethard in Co. Tipperary, also in 1449, and for Naas in 1467–8, when the 'lords and commons of Kildare' shared the burden equally over a ten year period. At Dundalk in 1458 labour services were involved. Two men from every ploughland in the county (of Louth) were required for two days' work annually 'to fill the moat with sea water'.

In the post-medieval period, murage tolls continued to be included in most of the governing charters of the new towns of the Tudor and Stuart re-colonisations, but other forms, such as grants and fines on undertakers or local taxes, were also used, especially at Jamestown and Bandon. The interest of the seventeenth century walled towns lies chiefly in the costs that are known to have been involved in the building of their defences which, being contemporary over a short period, can more easily be compared. In addition, they may be related back to the medieval period as far as they indicate the relative costs of the various parts of the circuit. Despite obvious differences in style, due to advances in the technology of warfare, the common features of murage funding and the refuge role for the newly settled hinterland makes such extrapolation legitimate.

BUILDING IN PROGRESS   From the post-medieval period too there is more direct evidence from other sources of how murage money was used or responsibility was divided, and of work in progress. At Dungarvan in 1537 the constable of the castle paid the masons for repair work on the town wall, while the burgesses fed them, the commons provided workmen to make mortar and carry stone, and the lord supplied a boat for carrying stone and horses for transporting it from the boat. These details seem to echo both the New Ross poem in its picture of all sections of the town playing a part, and the Galway/Dunmore murage accounts, the only medieval documents to indicate how financial provisions were translated into work on the circuit. Work in progress on the walling of Loughrea in 1574, but not its management, was also described in a contemporary report—'the town is well ditched and trenched, and fair walls begun but not finished, having three fair strong gates made like castles. . .'. One of these may be the surviving gate house.

The Kilkenny town records, also for the sixteenth century, show in detail how a town kept its wall in repair and modernised it. In 1506 a bulwark was made at the town's expense 'without the outer gate of St. John', the bridge-head suburb on the opposite bank. The wall in the same area required lime, stone, slate, lath and 'pyn' in 1570 and the maintenance of a house (?gate) and turret was also mentioned. It is not clear whether the supplies were required for repair work on a stone wall or for the upgrading of an earth-and-ditch type of enclosure. In 1580 the gate house at the Hightown or western end of the bridge was to be 'built up in height with lime and stone, to agree with the height of the old work and battle-ments'. Similar measures financed by murage or general town funds must have been common at most towns throughout the colonised area where circuits still survived.

At Carrickfergus a picture of work in progress can sometimes be glimpsed that is generally missing for other towns and may be typical in many respects. The constable of the Queen's castle, Capt. W. Piers, took a keen interest and may have been responsible for beginning the stone wall by the sea on either side of the castle in 1575. In 1581–3 men were reported to be 'working on the wall', which was also said to be 'not half-finished'. Landowners affected were to be compensated for loss of ground, at the rate of about 20p per metre, whereas previously they had been responsible for 'backside' defence, a considerable change in attitude. In 1611, according to a report of the Plantation commissioners, men were at work thus—'masons and labourers' at the walls; 'sundry quarry men and labourers' at quarries close by for rough stones; and at some distance for specialist 'limestone and freestone' cutting. Also in use were 'ox and horse teams and many garrons' for carriage; 'four lime kilns on fire'; a 'boat of 8 tons' and a 'barge of 15 tons, which was purposely made and continually employed' for the long distance transport of stone; and 'a good store of coal ready' for burning the lime. Charcoal and its source, cut-wood, may be substituted to turn this eye-witness account for Carrickfergus in 1611 into a picture of any earlier Irish town wall being built. It is but a dry prose equivalent of the scene set more eloquently in the New Ross poem of 1265.

For the three main Plantation towns the names of the experts involved are known rather than just those of the instigators. Many were military men and so a good deal is known about them (Loeber 1977, 32–313). At Bandon the project was supervised by Capt. Richard Croft (fl. 1597–1629), who had been at Carrickfergus earlier. By 1612 he was one of the original burgesses of Bandon and later its provost. Like many of the others, he may have come from England and so the tradition of operating on both islands, possibly begun by medieval experts such of Master William of Drogheda, continued. Croft appears to have supervised the wall building at Bandon in 1620–2, after which he was replaced by the mason, J. Lodden. This suggests that Croft, the military expert, may have been employed chiefly to translate the plan onto the ground, with the actual building up of the wall being taken over by a different type of expert. Again, a procedure such as this may have been common earlier. The original plan, 1613, for a walled town at Bandon, on the north bank only, was drawn by C. Jefford but the identity of the author of the later plans, *c.*1620, is not known. These required the building of similar but not identical walled towns on both banks of the River Bandon. They may have been the work of Crofts or drawn to his specifications.

The town defences of Coleraine were possibly designed by Sir J. Bodley (fl.1550–1617), a Director-General of Fortifications in Ireland. His connection seems to have been slight but did include an inspection. His 1614 report complained of 'modifications for the sake of economy' but did not claim that these actually involved a change from a stone to earthen wall. He described the walls as weak because the proportions had been reduced, and stated that the ramparts needed to be thicker and higher, the ditch deeper and the gates of stone rather than wood. Such judgements might have had a familiar ring to the ears of town authorities in the Middle Ages.

The Londonderry town wall also appears to have had a military-based design. It is attributed to Capt. Sir E. Doddington (fl.1602–19) who later became constable of Dungiven castle in Co. Londonderry. It was organised on the ground by Capt. T. Raven (fl.1572–1640, *D of S* 212) who was an alderman of Coleraine, and is thought to have drawn the fine maps of the two towns for the Phillips and Hadsor investigation of 1622. The actual wall building was the responsibility of P. Benson, who was a bricklayer and tiler from London and later became a major landowner in Co. Donegal. He was involved as early as 1614 when he provided tenders to the London authorities, having been promised the job 'if his costing was the lowest' (*Phillips MSS* 45).

Bodley in his official capacity had inspected the site in 1608 after a major attack. He probably also tended the advice, later cited by the Lord Deputy's report, 'that Derry must be walled and fortified'—the repairs of 1608–9 being 'unsatisfactory' because made of 'earth and sod' and so subject to rapid decay. He inspected again in 1614 and complained that the surviving forts had not been put to use. The Irish Society reports indicate the work in progress as well as the assessment of the results. Their agent in Derry was requested in 1612 to 'take advice of the servitors regarding the height and thickness' of the projected wall and to 'avoid errors made at Coleraine'. At this stage Sir J. Vaughan was involved as an advisor. In 1613–14 it was reported that the ground was 'trod out', as at New Ross, and the plan worked out with the advice of Capt. Panton, a military engineer. Problems with the builders were resolved and 500 tons of lime 'of superior quality' provided. In 1615 Raven was 'continued' as surveyor for two years—'for measuring and setting out the fortifications'. By 1616 the walls were 'half-finished', apparently satisfactorily—'two drawbridges and one gate erected' and the ditch dug where necessary. By 1618–19 the walls were completed. Therefore, the Londonderry circuit, in marked contrast to the Carrickfergus, was built rapidly, probably within only six years. In that time the wall was brought to full height, as were the four battlemented gates, although access to two was 'not yet ready'. This meant no leaves (gates or doors) but two had portcullises and the others drawbridges. Still required, according to Pynnar, was a guard house and more inhabitants because there were not enough 'to man the walls'. Again, analogous reports and comparable situations may have existed in medieval times, with man-power shortages being a problem then too at some new settlements or at those in decline.

At Londonderry, there ensued much careful, but not necessarily sympathetic, inspection. Prominent in this was Capt. Sir T. Phillips, who had originally started the development of Coleraine and who had later acted as the Irish Society's advisor for the area generally. The deficiences of the Coleraine wall seem to have been the starting point for his and other critical reports. Apart from complaints regarding the provisions for ordnance and men at Londonderry, the chief criticism there was of the site. In 1627 Phillips described it as 'so ill situated that both walls, houses and streets lie open to the command of shipping that shall come to the harbour, and also to the divers hills about the town'. Various additional and extramural devices were recommended, including the construction of a block-house on a new quay to keep the river approach clear. Further, the age-old dilemma was raised—if the town was worth defending it was also worth taking and so the defence had to be sufficient, or at least to look sufficient to make such an attempt likely to be costly. The report expressed it thus 'if Your Majesty do not intend to have it made a town of war . . . then we think it fit not to have any store of ordnance, victuals or munition at all, for it would be too great a bait for an enemy that should sit down before it, and the city once lost would be the overthrow of the whole British Plantation'. The last comment returns to the need for walled towns as the ultimate refuges of a colonisation, a policy operated by the early Anglo-Normans by their acquiring and improving the few Hiberno-Norse walled towns, and later emphasised in the preambles to many murage charters.

By the end of the seventeenth century Londonderry was being described variously as a place of 'great strength' and as one of 'no strength'. Certainly, it performed successfully its role as a refuge for the plantation in 1689, but missiles from the armies besieging it did over-fly the walls as predicted and caused much damage and casualty within. Moreover, it held out only just long enough to be relieved by sea, and this was perhaps the best that any of the walled towns could hope for at any period. Even the most effectively walled towns needed such a life-line when surrounded by determined besiegers rather than attackers aiming at a quick result. Then a walled town could become a trap as well as a refuge, as the increasingly starving inhabitants of Londonderry found with the passing months.

COSTS   The reality of the medieval murage funding is only rarely visible. The significance of the Galway/Dunmore murage accounts is not that they were balanced at the time, because this may be purely technical, but how much detailed information has been lost because they are the only survivors. Many of the other varied murage grants, as opposed to charters, refer to specific sums— half the fee-farm rent for five years, a grant of 100 marks etc.—which in theory could be computed. They would still provide only part of the picture because the returns from murage tolls could not be added or other toll grants, such as the 'cocket', which were often also allowed for murage purposes. Further, there is the problem of currency fluctuations. Perhaps the most realistic picture is that derived from the flurry of murage funding post-1318. The Drogheda authorities claimed that they had expended 'beyond the receipts of their murage' more than £1000 of their own. At Dublin near panic had existed in 1315–6, presumably because of the open riverside and extensive suburbs. The former was apparently hastily walled but the latter had to be burnt, and the resulting costs were put at over £10,000. Payment of the fee-farm rent of 200 marks (£130) was deferred for Dublin. In Drogheda's case they were allowed to pay a fine on a technicality related to murage accounting. Neither of these concessions seems especially generous but they have to be placed in the context of subsequent new murage measures—a five-year charter and cash grants worth £440 for Drogheda and similar but greater measures for Dublin (*HMD* 393–420).

No costs are apparently available for the new towns of the Tudor recolonisation— Maryborough, Philipstown or Roscommon—but there is an estimate for work at Athenry in 1576. This involved the building of a new wall of *c*.500m at a cost of £2000, a rate of *c*.£4 per metre, to be levied on the county. The purpose was to reduce the large walled area to one more commensurate with the actual population. This seems to have been a unique project and the opposite to some extent of what happened at Carrickfergus, although the extension of the wall there, as it was upgraded, produced an area still not quite the size of the reduced one at Athenry. The later sixteenth century saw a stream of projects and estimates at Carrickfergus, including £1000 in 1571 and £1500 in 1594, none of which can be tied down precisely to actual work. By 1605 Carrickfergus was still reckoned to require £4000 for the work to be finally completed. This figure, like some of the earlier, may include work on the castle and pier, which are also mentioned as in 'need of attention'. If the landward circuit, which had two gates in its enlarged and modernised form, was only concerned the rate would have been c.£5 per metre. Similarly protracted efforts were made at Athlone in the early seventeenth century on behalf of the old medieval walled town on the east and, later, the settlement around the castle on the west. A figure of £5000 was estimated for the east in 1618–19 and was said to have been doubled as the work of modernisation progressed (Murtagh 1980, 94–5). This would give a rate of c.£10 per metre.

This work was contemporary with the building of the new Stuart plantation towns of Londonderry, Coleraine, Bandon and Jamestown for which more comprehensive costs are available. In these cases private investors were involved although not necessarily very generously except, perhaps, in the case of Boyle at Bandon. The right to charge murage tolls was still enshrined in the Ulster charters of incorporation but the costs were borne by the London Companies. Both Bandon and Jamestown were to be financed by local levies but the collecting of these was not found to be easy at Bandon at least. As was probably true earlier, too, people were readier to request, and even to use, a refuge centre than to pay for it. The costs of Bandon and Jamestown were estimated at quite different rates, both for wall and gates, three in each case (Table 4.2). The differences may lie in the nature of the structures, the Bandon wall being simpler and apparently unramparted, more like a medieval wall with elaborate gates, and the Jamestown probably being heavily ramparted, like Londonderry's. Hence, Bandon was estimated to cost £7 per perch and Jamestown £18 per perch. By contrast, the Jamestown gates were to cost a mere twentieth of the Bandon. This may confirm as original the gateway aspect of the North Gate of Jamestown, which survived until recently, because being more an integral part of the wall than a gate house much of the cost would have been born by the wall. It is possibly significant that the Jamestown estimated costs exactly totalled the projected murage revenue of £3000. Coote took out a recognisance for nearly twice that amount which may indicate that the plans were altered. What actually happened there is not known, but Boyle claimed that he spent £14,000 altogether at Bandon, more than twice his estimate. It is difficult to be sure of Boyle's figures because he was given to exaggeration, especially when he wished to display his efforts as comparable to that of the Londoners' best.

Overall, the costs per metre of circuit at Jamestown seem to have been about £4, the same as the estimated costs at Bandon but under half the actual. The final total at Bandon was comparable to that for Londonderry, where over £12,000 was spent on a shorter but differently styled circuit, giving a rate of £9 per metre. What is probably more interesting is that the earthen circuit at Coleraine was not significantly cheaper, at least in the long run. Clearly, the objections to its struc-

Table 4.2: Cost of Town Walling

LONDONDERRY 1609-29

Circuit 1375 m
Rate = £8 per metre
Building Period = 5 years

£ 8357	´Town Wall
2000	Ditch + Rampart
400	Gates (4)
300	Platforms for Bulwarks
40	Carriages for Ordnance
50	Guard House

£11147   Total + lime kilns £120, quays £170, paving £800, some of which may have been associated (£1090).

COLERAINE 1609-29

Circuit 1100 m
Rate = £8 per metre
Building Period = 3 years

£8511   Total

(estimate 1613 = £4500)

BANDON 1620-7 +

Circuit *c*.1500 m
Rate = £4-10 per metre
Building Period = 7 years

£14000   Total

(estimate = £6000 incl. £2500 for 3 gate houses
       + £2534 for 362 perches of wall [1800m] @ £7 per perch)

JAMESTOWN 1622-8

Circuit 750 m
Rate = £4 per metre
Building Period = 6 years

£2880	Town Wall (£18 per perch)
120	Gates 3
£3000	Total (£5000 Coote recognisance)

Sources: listed in gazetteer entries

ture were soundly based in that repair and improvements to it seem to have doubled the estimated cost, from £4 to £8 per metre. It may be for similar reasons that some medieval town walls did not apparently materialise. When the funding could not be predicted and depended ultimately on something as fickle as market-trading, there must have been real difficulties in continuing with capital intensive projects such as a stone wall. Consequently, the temptation to economise in the short-term might often have been compelling. The resulting wall, structurally comparable to Coleraine's, would have had but a short life, particularly if funding became more, rather than less, difficult making the constant repair that would have been necessary, impossible.

The Londonderry account is detailed and shows that three-quarters of the money was spent on the wall, and even more when the cost of the ditch and ramparts are included. The costs of the gates was, as at Jamestown, minimal but may refer only to the actual shutting gates, as well as to the stated portcullis and drawbridges. In contrast, the Bandon gates were estimated originally to cost almost as much as the walls. They were definitely substantial by comparison with the wall, to judge by the maps and surviving plans, but it is not clear how they fitted into the final total. Such initial relative costs would not seem unreasonable for medieval towns in view of the surviving structures and excavation evidence. It emphasises the vulnerability of the openings in a circuit, and the capacity to turn such weak points into impressive entries which could also draw attention away from the quality of the rest of the circuit. There the extra costs could be unobtrusively recouped if necessary. Then, as always, there was no ultimate security; a town wall was in the first place essentially a bluff, a means of protecting by deterrence.

TIME   It will be seen from Table 4.2 that the circuits of the plantation towns were all built within ten years of work commencing, some in considerably less time. Coleraine's was the fastest, *c.*1610–12, but the least satisfactory. There may well have been a connection and, while matters of economy may have dominated, it is possible that other factors were involved too. Progress was slow at Londonderry, the other town developed by the London companies, and so they may have felt it desirable to have one urban settlement, at least, secured quickly. Such a motive could well have been strong in medieval times too, leading to rapid but inferior construction which later soon decayed naturally and/or was easily overwhelmed.

One of the Bandon maps, unfortunately undated, is almost a progress report with indications of which gate and section of wall was by then completed (TCD MS 1209/41). In all that circuit took seven years and Londonderry's was completed within six. No doubt there was still much that remained to be done, particularly with regard to detail, but the reports make it clear that at Londonderry the settlement area was enclosed—by a strong stone wall with some gates working. Therefore, the circuit was capable of being used as a means of defence. In addition, the rampart was in place with nine bulwarks and two half-bulwarks. Looking at the Londonderry wall today such completion within six years does seem a very considerable achievement, but it was virtually repeated at Bandon and Jamestown and so it was not unique, although the circuits were rather different in style or scale. In contrast to these new towns where settlement developed with the walling, like the Edwardian towns of medieval North Wales which were also generally enclosed within a ten year period, progress at the other Irish towns walled in the sixteenth-seventeenth centuries, Athlone East and Carrickfergus, was painfully slow. Both of these seem to have had a medieval wall, the nature of the latter was earthen and unsatisfactory and of the former unknown. It took at least thirty-seven years to upgrade and extend the Carrickfergus circuit and twenty-six years to modernise the Athlone, that is in addition to periods of forty years for each during which projects were planned and abandoned, or only half-fulfilled, generally for want of funds.

The medieval parallels may, more often, have been with Athlone and Carrickfergus than with Londonderry and Bandon, but there is no reason why they should have been exclusively so. As already indicated, a partial circuit was a nonsense from a defensive point of view and so, when periods of a century and more are suggested, as noted in chapter 3, it must be presumed that matters of detail rather than substance were involved. This does not rule out the possibility that some, possibly even many, circuits may have been very mixed in terms of structural quality in the early stages and even for long periods or, in rare cases such as Gowran and Callan, always. They may often too have been non-existent alongside waterfronts and even by quite small streams, earthen on naturally defensive slopes, and if stone, only apparently strong. Much time might be spent improving a minimum grade of circuit, but if it did not at least seem to be a serious obstacle and if it was not capable of serving as a defence mechanism it would have been virtually useless.

Time could influence the effectiveness of a town wall in two ways. Firstly, it could provide the scope for increasing the sophistication of a minimum-style circuit, but secondly, it could also enhance the capacity for deterioration, particularly of a poorly constructed circuit. Work in progress on the Athenry circuit in the late 16th century was halted and its results largely ruined by attacks and this may have been a common problem earlier. The murage and other evidence for medieval Ireland is not sufficient to indicate how long it took to complete a circuit, either to an effective minimum or a desirable maximum. Clearly, some may never have reached the latter and some degree of work was probably always on-going at many, if not most, medieval walls. But the evidence of the seventeenth century points to rapid rather than protracted enclosure, even at Carrickfergus, once the will and/or the funds was present.

USE

The primary purpose of a town wall was the defence of the town and its surrounding area. This is made very clear in the medieval murage grants described earlier. In a sense the town wall was a very visible insurance policy but its various parts—fosse, wall, rampart, gates and towers—could also be put to other uses. These will be considered later, followed by sections on the removal or demise of the system and on the influence of the circuit on the development of a town, particularly of its street pattern.

DEFENCE   The attraction of the walled Hiberno-Norse towns for the first Anglo-Norman invaders is very striking. Having landed at the relatively obscure and therefore undefended part of Co. Wexford, Bannow Bay, they headed first for Wexford and later for Waterford, both walled towns which required the use of siege tactics before they could be taken. The riches of these urban centres were no doubt a factor, but so must the strategic and, in the longer term, the economic value of holding such well-established and defended ports. They could and did act as firm bridge-heads for the development of Leinster generally. For the same reasons the king soon saw to it that Dublin, Waterford and a scatter of other ports from Limerick around the south and east coasts to Carrickfergus were reserved to him, and defended by castles and/or town walls.

For the many settlements which developed, or were intended to develop, as towns in the hinterlands of these key centres defence may have been a less pressing consideration initially, particularly as the Anglo-Normans were not systematically opposed. The New Ross poem makes it clear that the walling of this, seignorial-founded, new port should be seen in the context of specific security problems in the area. These resulted from infighting amongst the resident Anglo-Norman lords, which was related to the Barons' War then in progress in England (1264–5). The poem says 'they were fearful of a war . . . between . . . lord Maurice and lord Walter . . . What they feared was that they had no town walls'. There was no castle at the town either, except across the wide river at Rosbercon, because New Ross was founded, *c.*1207–11, away from the inland Marshall manorial centre of Old Ross to act as a port for their extensive Leinster lands. If there was a simple earthen bank-and-ditch boundary to the settlement it is not mentioned in the poem. The only reference to existing defensive measures is that 'once the circuit is complete there will be no need to have a watch'.

From the middle of the thirteenth century war, either provoked as in this case by Anglo-Norman or in others by Gaelic magnates, showed signs of becoming endemic in Ireland. The murage measures alone provide evidence of actual attacks on towns. The usual phrase is that the town was 'burnt', for example Athy in 1308, Adare in 1376 and Carrickfergus in 1402. It is difficult to know now how to assess this. Where walls existed it might have involved a 'hit and run' attack on the suburbs, but a record for Waterford suggests that the walled area was actually attacked there in 1290 (*CDI* III 622). Given that most urban buildings would have been made of wood and thatch, the effects of even a small-scale attack, such as lobbing a burning missile over the walls or through an open gateway, could have been devastating. The 'town burnt' might have been an accurate description but neither can an element of exaggeration be ruled out.

The Bruce invasion of 1315–18 provides the first evidence of sustained attacks on individual towns and, perhaps as important, the level of fear that these attacks produced at others. Dundalk, a new manorial town apparently walled by then, was burnt and taken at an early stage. Carrickfergus succumbed in late 1316 after a long siege, the government failing to relieve it because the Scots held the northern Irish Sea. An attack on strongly walled Drogheda Louth proved unsuccessful and, having taken a look at a hastily strengthened Dublin but unaware that inside the walls an atmosphere close to panic existed, the Scots moved on. They concentrated then on ranging far and wide in the countryside of central and eastern Ireland, where they caused serious devastation and long term damage to the colony because much of its economic strength lay in the produce of the countryside. The murage records for the succeeding years tell of the measures taken at Dublin—the walls strengthened, tolls levied without licence, suburbs prostrated to avoid them falling into the Scots' hands, a church tower pulled down for its stone-work, closure of the east gate (Dame's) causing disruption and loss to the mills beyond it (*HMD* 402–12, 441–6). It is likely that a new wall was hastily built along the River Liffey at this time to enclose the reclaimed riverside and quay area which, until then, was only walled on its landward sides. The impact on Drogheda was described thus—'from the first arrival of the Scots in Ireland until the death of Edward Bruce near Dundalk [35km to the north], they were daily occupied with the works of their walls, towers and enclosure of the town, for the defence of themselves and adjacent parts' (*HMD* 417–20). By then the town wall there was at least in part over eighty years old and probably no longer entirely fit to be put to the test. Other towns on the path of the rampaging Scots and their allies in Ireland probably gave similar attention to their town walls and were the safer for it.

In the later fourteenth century the Irish walled towns were tested often by Gaelic attacks from fastnesses which were emerging as increasingly significant areas within or just beyond the colony. Caherconlish was described as a town in the 'march' in 1358. So were many others including those on the edge of the area subsequently known as the Pale and some in the south-east, such as Thomastown in 1374. Caherconlish was said to have been 'destroyed by Irish and other malefactors' and the nearby, but probably more formidable, Kilmallock was described as 'destroyed and burnt' in 1375. New Ross, despite its town wall, was taken in 1394 by forces from upland Wexford but Carlow held off persistent attacks during the years 1370–1400. Even Waterford was by then often subject to lightning-type attacks from the Decies area close to it. At nearby Dungarvan insufficient 'walls and trenches' were listed as a factor in 1463, in what were described as 'frequent' attacks by 'English rebels and Irish enemies', a common combination and source of trouble. Dublin, too, was increasingly vulnerable to attack due to the proximity of the Wicklow mountains, but generally it was its suburbs and the surrounding villages or small towns that suffered most. It has been suggested (Lydon 1979, 5–15) that Waterford in particular, but also walled towns generally, became rather adept at 'crying wolf', using the occasional instance to gain the maximum financial assistance. Waterford was accused in 1399 of doing little to improve its defences despite having received many grants (*IHD* 68) and so the possibility of over-exaggeration was recognised at the time. On the other hand the 'ageing' factor would have been an increasing problem for the fabric of the walls at a time when lower returns were being received from murage tolls. This was in part due to the increase in exemptions from the payment of murage and to economic depression resulting from the periods of political instability which became endemic in late medieval Ireland. Town walls would, therefore, have needed more or less constant attention. The fear of attack was doubtless as potent a force then, as it is known to have been earlier. Indeed, it may have been greater because the population of the lordship had shrunk in the aftermath of the Bruce invasion and the Black Death. Depopulation of the countryside must have led to an increasing sense of isolation in the towns, particularly in those beyond the south-east. In these circumstances the towns can hardly be blamed for making the strongest possible case. Carrick-on-Suir did so in 1450 in a request for murage assistance. The fact that it had been twice 'entirely burnt' in the last 14 years was emphasised and attention drawn to its wider strategic importance as a key stopping place on the inland route from Waterford towards Limerick.

For England and Wales, Turner (1970, 76–9) also notes that towns (and castles) were 'burnt' with 'monotonous frequency' in the medieval period, but suggests that the effects were probably slight. Specifically, Winchester was entered and burnt in 1264 during the Barons' War, despite good town defences. The town of Gloucester was taken the next year, the castle holding out a few days longer than the walled town. Both these towns were receiving murage grants intermittently post-1225. At Northampton besiegers were shown a weak spot in the walls, but in London iron chains stretched across streets were used within the walls to add to the defence. These incidents were contemporary with the 'walling' of New Ross as related in the poem. The problem of the march in Ireland had its parallels in England too, along the Welsh and Scottish frontiers, the extreme case being Berwick which, despite many improvements to its circuit, changed hands thirteen times during the years 1174–1482. Thereafter it was reduced in area like Athenry, and rewalled in a bastioned style (Beresford and St. Joseph 1958, 178). The vulnerability of attack from the sea was felt alike along the south coasts of both islands, at Southampton as much as at Waterford. A detailed account has survived of the unsuccessful 1315 siege of Carlisle. Its defence was generally similar to that in operation earlier at Hiberno-Norse Wexford, but the means of attack had advanced technically. It involved machinery for damaging gates, towers or the curtain wall by projectiles, as well as mining devices, long ladders and mobile wooden towers which were higher than the wall. Some of the machinery did not fulfill its promise, apparently sinking into the ground. This would have been a problem at many sites in Ireland too, but no Irish accounts are known of such devices in operation.

Walled towns seem to have featured most strongly in the wars of the mid and late-seventeenth century but this may be a reflection of fuller records. Two scenarios are illustrated by the sieges of 1641–2, 1649–50 and 1689–91. Firstly, relief by sea was crucial in raising a prolonged siege, for example at Londonderry in 1689 and, less spectacularly, at Coleraine in 1641. Secondly, no medieval stone town wall could withstand heavy and concentrated bombardment despite being reinforced. Cromwell's attacks on Drogheda and Wexford demonstrated that all too well. The other towns to which his army laid siege and forced to surrender— New Ross, Kilkenny, Limerick and Galway—did so out of fear of the consequences of holding out unsuccessfully, as illustrated by the Drogheda and Wexford massacres that followed his capture of those towns. In other cases the results were more finely balanced. In 1601 the Spaniards could have held Kinsale longer if their reinforcements from the sea had been maintained, whereas the success at Londonderry in 1689 came only at the eleventh hour when the sea link was re-established. The ridge site, surrounded on two sides by the river and on one by the bog, made Londonderry difficult to get close to and so, in that respect, its walls were not physically tested. However, the problem of higher ground close enough to be used by opposing forces, raised as a fault in some of the earlier inquiries, did manifest itself and the town, if not the walls, was severely bombarded. This was a serious defect because, while the circuit provided one type of security, that of a strong refuge, it gave the opposition the opportunity to destroy those concentrated within. It would have been a better site in the medieval period when over-passing a wall would have been less easy. In fact, if the bombardment had been concentrated only on the area within the walls it might well have been successful, in which case it would have rendered the wall largely irrelevant.

An external factor which sometimes helped towns under siege was the onset of winter. In effect it gave a hard pressed town a breathing spell and time to strengthen the circuit. For this reason Cromwell was forced to turn away from Clonmel, and the 1690 siege of Limerick was raised temporarily, although the walls had actually been breached. When it was resumed the following year it · followed on from the surrender of Athlone, also after a second siege. In view of this Limerick, although once more intact defensively, decided to surrender. The fall of Athlone, then heavily walled on both sides of the River Shannon, again illustrates the advantages and disadvantages of such defences. The one side could help to defend the other but the taking of one, without being able to take the other, could prove self-defeating, given that the opposing forces had rough equality of fire-power. Total encirclement was the answer for the assailant, if an expensive or long term one. In this particular case the defences on the west side were, if anything, too intensive and it fell to sustained physical attack from the east side because sufficient reinforcements could not be moved in efficiently.

There are some glimpses, often graphic, of the actual mechanism of a siege and defence, especially from Cromwell's papers. In the absence of contemporary material these must serve for the medieval period too. He described how at Inistioge the defenders 'vapoured over the wall' to safety within it, but fled by boat once his forces 'set fire to the gates' and prepared to enter—the refuge/trap dilemma. At Carrick-on-Suir the defenders attempted to dig under the walls while his forces blockaded the gates. Entrance to Drogheda was achieved by bombardment of the SE corner from beyond the deep ravine which provided a natural fosse there. A medieval wall was not designed to withstand a physical force of such strength and even attempts made towards the southern gate to strengthen the wall by outworks were unsuccessful. A fundamental change had occurred in favour of determined besiegers. The earlier unsuccessful siege of Drogheda in 1641 provides the contrast in the much more medieval picture that it provides—ladders used to scale the walls and guards posted to watch out for them and for those attempting to gain access from the river.

There is very little difference between this account and the descriptions by which Gerald of Wales recalled the Anglo-Norman attacks on the Hiberno-Norse towns—at Wexford the defenders 'burnt their suburbs' and harried the assailing Anglo-Normans by throwing objects at them from the walls. Then, as later, arrows from archers and less mechanical weapons such as blocks of wood and stone from the citizenry were used, but ultimately to no avail there, or at Limerick in 1175. But at Waterford in 1170, a weak point in the defences is said to have proved the downfall of the Hiberno-Norse town—a small building sitting over the wall and supported externally by a beam, was removed and the wall collapsed along with it, making entry possible. Such alteration or adaptation of town walls, as well as poor building practices, was always a possible hazard. The gradual in-filling of a fosse during a long period of peace was a common activity, too, that could reduce the defensiveness of the circuit. At Dublin in 1558 people were to be fined for 'putting dung or filth' in the city's fosse. Also then, unofficial doors or posterns, or actual breaches in the wall, were to be 'closed up with lime and stone' by a certain date or the individual concerned risked being fined £10. In 1580 houses and other buildings 'within 20 yards of the town wall, which may be injurious to defence' were to be removed and the walls to be rampired. At Cork, even in the early eighteenth century, access to the walls was to be maintained and rubbish dumped there to be removed. The actual opening of a gate by sympathisers happened at Clonmel in 1641. When this occured it mattered little how strong the town wall was. During the same conflict it was said that the generally decayed state of Dundalk's town wall had contributed to its capture, and that Ardee's heavily reinforced Bridge Gate was side-stepped by the use of a ford. There the small river may have proved no substitute for a town wall. Gate houses thatched with straw were also an invitation to attackers, as Carrick-on-Suir and Callan found as late as the Cromwellian period. Similar gates may have featured prominently in the records of towns being burnt in the medieval period. Many may even have been built partly of wood too, as those at Coleraine were originally in the seventeenth century.

The later murage grants indicate much maintenance activity, either in anticipation of trouble or after it. The greatest anticipatory attention in the fifteenth century seems to have been given to the towns of the Pale march, yet Navan was so seriously damaged by the Irish in 1539 that the wall required 'rebuilding'. In 1577 Naas was described as 'open on all sides, gates not shut nor watch kept'. Perhaps by then the danger, perceived locally there as opposed to nationally, did not seem so great. However, Gowran about the same time used the idea of the walled town as a garrison point to argue in favour of more murage finance. Manpower, or the lack of it, may also have been a factor as the population declined due to the ravages of plague, famine and emigration in the later Middle Ages. It undoubtedly was a factor in the reducing of the walled area at Athenry in 1576 but there had been no such problem at New Ross in its heyday. The poem makes it clear that both men and armament were there in abundance. The scheme at Athenry was pre-empted by the attackers who returned, setting fire to a new gate and driving off the masons at work on the wall. By 1598 Athenry was still a sorry sight 'all ruined save the wall'. It was a conspicuous case of a town requiring more than a wall, and a castle, to ensure its safety even when the government had taken a direct, but possibly not a sufficiently sustained, interest. In a rare specific record the walls of Kilmallock were said to have been 'heightened' in 1583, following official interest there on the part of Sir Henry Sidney. His accounts, made during much travel in Ireland as Lord Deputy, provide a valuable picture of the walled towns in the post-medieval period. His description of Carlow in 1577 was not encouraging—'large . . . the walls ruined and down at many places'. It was in a vulnerable position but one that was crucial for the route to Waterford. There is a rare medieval document for the period in the late fourteenth century when Carlow was briefly the seat of the colony's Exchequer, which suggested a means of arming its guards—'a master smith to dwell there in the king's service for three months for the purpose of making guns, harness, and other articles for the defence of the place against the Irish' of Wicklow/Wexford.

In the aftermath of the Fitzgerald-led attack on Dublin in 1536 the king required the placing of a falcon or small cannon on each of the six gates (*CSPI* III 27). Regulations for guarding or manning the defences survive for both the medieval period and later. In 1305, three watchmen and three assistants were to be appointed for each of three sections—the old walled area was divided into two (perhaps the Hiberno-Norse original and the extension) and the third was the newer riverside area. The surviving 'inner' town wall no doubt aided this task. At the very end of the sixteenth century two men were assigned to each of the six main gates 'in time of danger' with instructions, during an emergency, to let women and children from the suburbs in via the wicket of the gate but not men, who were to stay and defend the suburbs. Under normal conditions the gates were to be shut at 8p.m. but the wickets to remain open for a further hour, when they should be guarded. Thereafter, an additional six guards were to 'roam' the town. Arms etc. were not to be allowed out of the city nor strange beggars in, both probably rather difficult regulations to police. At Limerick in 1680–1, under normal conditions the gates were shut at 9 in the evening in winter and at 10 in summer. Opening took place at 7 in the morning in winter and 4 in summer and the keys were kept under guard over-night. The locking of gates during church services on Sunday is recorded for the seventeenth century, particularly in the ports towns of Munster, for example at Youghal in 1673.

In the records of other towns the following arrangements are noted and probably were often to be found at most walled towns. At Kilkenny the watch at the seven main gates consisted of two or four men in 1641. The reason for the distinction is not given but probably had something to do with the size of the gate and/or the number of wickets attached to it, or its relative commercial importance. The western gates had two guards and the Castle, Bridge and Irishtown gates four each. When private postern gates were allowed, as they were increasingly in the modern period, their keys had to be deposited with the mayor but the owner was responsible for the gate's security, for example at Cork 1701. The shutting of the gates by night remained a memory at Galway as late as 1824. Also for there the use of chains hung across the streets as a secondary defence against horsemen is recorded, perhaps to keep them out while pedestrians were still being admitted, and even earlier, in 1557, the movement of fishing boats through a postern gate, had been forbidden outside normal opening hours. An examination of the Galway town wall in 1747 resulted in the recommendation that twenty-four sentinel boxes of brick and stone be built 'for the security of the town, the protection of H.M. revenues and the preservation of the wall from unofficial breaches'. The manpower required was listed as 2 per gate (5 gates) and 10 around the walls (varying from 5 to 2 depending on the distance involved, an average of 1:100m). A further 8 were required for the citadel and seven bastions, 4 in the main guard and 1 each in the three main gates, and 12 others, presumably to wander around inside the town—a total of 47 men. It is not known if this arrangement was put into effect on this scale but something like it would have been normal practice. Rather more modest measures had been provided for at Cashel, 1683–90—7 men, 4 English and 3 Irish were to be used 'within the gate' and 'fit persons to wait and watch at the upper and lower gates'. The ethnic distinctions provides an interest here but its significance is not clear.

OTHER USES   Other uses for all or part of a town wall system were essentially evolutionary. They represent developments of an existing system, often for reasons of convenience and generally unconnected with the original and main purpose which was defence. It was probably only in the eighteenth century that other uses came to real predominance and, even then, town authorities usually tried to see that they operated within the framework of a defensive potential. There were still occasional, brief periods of alarm, such as during the 1745 Jacobite rebellion in Scotland, or when the fear of invasion or uprising arose in different parts of Ireland. Even in the nineteenth century parts of town walls could still be rented, although the main defensive role no longer existed and almost everywhere the circuits as a whole were neglected.

Basically, other uses arose, firstly, from the structural nature of the system, especially of the gate houses and towers, but also of the curtain wall and the fosse; and, secondly, from the boundary capability provided by the physical presence of the wall. The money raised from the commercial letting of parts of the circuit could be used to defray the cost of upkeep of the system, helping to make it self-financing at least in respect of maintenance, or it could be put to other town needs. Rents are recorded for Kilkenny, 1596–1600, for rooms over the seven gates of Hightown, and Kilbryde's tower, as well as for encroachments on the town ditch, presumably either by buildings or allotments. Only one instance is known of a chapel in a gate—at Limerick's Thomond Gate in 1677 (a chapel still survives over a gate at Warwick)—but gate houses and towers were often leased for use as meeting places, private residences or stores. Two of Waterford's towers were used as ammunition stores in later periods. A good deal is known regarding the uses of the buildings along the Dublin circuit (Healy 1973). By 1585 many towers there were known by personal names—Genevel's, Usher's etc. (fig. 3.d)—which may relate to current or former users. Leases of both gates and towers were made at different times to individuals or groups, like the 'Corporation of Barber Churgeons' in 1661 at Pole Gate, Dublin, and the Taylors at a Drogheda tower. The portcullis room was reserved 'in time of danger' and similar restrictions must have been written into most leases of gates or towers, particularly with regard to keys for the gates and access to the structures. The 1816 rental of Dublin included the items—'tower over St. Audeon's Arch' (£1.5s.0d.) and part of the town wall and ditch near Werburg's Gate (£5). Similarly, at Kinsale in the seventeenth and eighteenth centuries, there were leases of a 'castle or tower on the town wall [above High Fisher Street], the common strand rampier at the quay, the castle or old blockhouse, holdings on the rampart, part of the town ditch, a piece of town wall, a passage through the town wall, a door through the town wall (6d.), Fryer's Gate (£10), Cork Gate

(£6.10s.0d.)'—rents charged in 1731. At Londonderry, houses that were built officially in the fosse area below the south-east side during the eighteenth century were said in 1814 to be very dilapidated. Not long afterwards the use of Hangman's Bastion 'for a garden' was approved. There are many such instances listed for Londonderry (Milligan II 1948–50) and, of course, the walls became a popular promenade with trees planted to improve the aesthetic quality. The same happened at Limerick Irishtown, Galway and elsewhere. However, the comparison of the Londonderry wall-walk with that of Padua, which was made by the future bishop Berkeley in 1724, is difficult to evaluate as is an earlier comparison of Carrick-on-Suir's wall-walk with that of Chester. If they were reasonable they high-light the loss to Ireland that the early decay of its walled circuits has achieved.

Yet, the problems of such old structures must have become increasingly burdensome in modern times, as the history of one Cashel gate house shows. In 1667–8 'a house over the gate in Conafoy' was rented; in 1680 the 'proprietor of the house fallen down over Canafie Gate' had to 'clear the stone and rubbish fallen down from the town wall and build it up again; by 1732 compensation was to be paid 'so as not to build over Cannafie Gate but to leave it as an open passage, the full width of the street'. The dangers and inconveniences of a system that had out-lived its original purpose are also indicated by the Dublin records. It was claimed in 1704 that 'the town wall without New Gate is ruinous and ready to drop on a malt house in Lamb Lane'. Permission was sought to take it down and rebuild, and possibly for this reason it remains one area where Dublin's wall still stands. Also, in 1722, it was recorded that the 'city wall fell on a stables' and costs for the resulting damage was requested. The actual gates, whether of reinforced wood or iron and the portcullis must also have been of use. There is only one record, from Coleraine for 1710, of the gates being used—to make horse shoes. It was denied. The use of the Maiden Tower, 'so much as may be conveniently pulled down', was recorded at New Ross in 1713 for 'building up' the south aisle of the parish church, the opposite of the use of a church tower's stonework at Dublin in 1317 to complete the town wall. As late as 1885, the town wall formed 'part of a house' at Wexford while earlier, in 1852, a large square tower had been removed to 'give light' to the chancel of a church, and the 'old rampart' had been terraced to add to the gardens ending at it. At Youghal, where the main gates were rebuilt in the eighteenth century, one of these, the Inner North Gate, was put up for sale in 1761, the implication being that land close to it was available for building a house on, and that the gate itself was a source of re-usable stone. At the same time, building 'against the town wall' was allowed near the southern gate, which still survives at Youghal, and earlier, in 1721, probably as the result of a similar project, 'to break windows in the town wall' was permitted. The same had happened at Drogheda in the late thirteenth-fourteenth centuries so that the Franciscan friary church could have a window where it abutted the town wall. In Dublin by 1681 the city wall from the new east gate, Essex, towards the river was so much decayed that it 'only stood because houses were built onto it', but usually the complaint was that adjacent buildings prevented access to the town wall.

It is clear from the Galway and Waterford town records that permission to use parts of the curtain wall was carefully considered, although it is equally clear that there was much unauthorised use. The making of unofficial openings was probably the most common practice, either by cutting small door-ways or by allowing sections of the wall to collapse. The 1747 Eyre report on the condition of Galway's wall notes all such breaches and the 'back yards' made around them, possibly with stone from the wall itself, also the removal of the rampart for use in gardens. This last, by laying bare the relatively thin and mostly very old medieval curtain wall, made its collapse even more likely. At Waterford in 1670, surveyors had been ordered to 'view the wall near the Ring Tower and if they judge that building will not prejudice the wall nor passage thereon . . . they should give liberty to build to the said wall, leaving the same way and passage on the wall as now is'. Likewise, permission 'to break the city wall' at a certain point in 1694 is recorded there, but 'breaches in the wall to press herrings' were disallowed in 1698–9, a rather unusual use and probably not a very pleasant one.

Such seventeenth and eighteenth century concern for the integrity of the defensive system cannot have been new. It must have been a continuation of procedures and practices that developed along with the medieval and later town walls themselves. Even the defence against toll evasion, which was behind much of the later Galway concern, would not have been new because the use of the circuit to collect tolls effectively was essential to the early murage measures. However, the areas of responsibility are outlined most clearly in the later Cork city records. A 1610 jury inquired into the 'king's walls of the city of Cork' and in 1717 it was stated more explicitly—the 'walls belong to the Crown . . . the City is obliged to repair them . . . the ground on which they are built belongs to the Corporation'. Thus, the city could make 99-year leases of 'two-foot walls on the inside of the town wall' but these were subject to annulment, should the corporation be 'obliged to repair the wall'. In the same vein, at Youghal in 1629, the mayor was admonished by the Lord Admiral of Customs because of the poor state of the wall along the sea, where goods were able to come and go through gaps without paying customs—'in all sea towns of good government there has ever been a special and continual care required that their walls should be sufficiently repaired, maintained and kept from time to time for his majesty's services'.

It is hardly surprising that, on a site so confined as Cork's, encroachments upon the city wall were many and varied, both in medieval times and later. The following were recorded in the 1733 survey—6 houses with gable ends using the wall; 36 houses built on the foundation of the town wall (probably a more recent development as the wall decayed and was not repaired so frequently); 4 summer houses on top of the wall or a tower; 2 gardens and quays outside the town wall with access by bridges to the suburbs; 15 private gates, passages or slips through the town wall. Previously at Cork, in 1713, part of a house was to be taken down because it had been built against the town wall and in 1624, repairs to the wall were required to make it 'look like the rest'. Archaeological investigation of the medieval walls has indicated recently, both at Cork and Wexford, that this was certainly a procedure with a long lineage and some of the few medieval records for Cork also show permission being sought from the Crown to 'break' the wall temporarily, in 1286 and 1291. In the later instance the reason was the need to 'convey a ship' out of the city and the cost of rebuilding was placed on the applicant, in addition to a fine. Similarly there in 1733, if less urgently, 'all persons who have made use of the town walls' were 'to promise in writing to rebuild if required', and 'to pay an acknowledging fee'.

The primary, defensive, and subsidiary, communal, uses of the system are seen together in the leasing of the Marine Gate at Cork in 1627 for £6 annually—'the water bailliwick' was to be possessed by a merchant provided he 'builds a new, substantial Marine Gate at his own charge and leaves the key with the mayor'. Such 'privatisation' may have become increasingly common as the primary use waned in importance. There are many instances recorded of the use of gates for toll collection. This need not only have been for murage purposes but for general market tolls and also harbour and customs dues, as recorded for Youghal above, because the gates provided ready-built control points. There are also references to 'porters' of the gates, for example at Youghal in 1643 and Kinsale in 1658–9, which may indicate that large wagons had to stop outside so that porters with hand-carts could ferry their goods to the market after the tolls had been paid. It is possible that the need for efficient collection of market tolls did more to keep town walls in repair in the eighteenth century than concern for the town's defence. Certainly the Galway evidence, already quoted, suggests that the infiltration of goods through the many gaps in the circuit was the prime worry. Yet, the early nineteenth century agitation against the toll system generally did not, apparently, result in attacks on town walls. This was probably because by then they were largely un-used, having been allowed to decay in favour of cheaper policing measures such as toll booths set up at any convenient point on streets leading to the market. Nonetheless, tolls for the upkeep of town walls were still claimed wherever possible until they were abolished in municipal reform measures post-1835.

The limited access points provided by the gates of an intact circuit could also be used to enforce other urban regulations, including those to do with transport, health and social policy. Undesirable aliens, beggars, vagabonds or people suffering from diseases such as leprosy could easily be turned back at the gates, as could those who were not residents. This may have led to the development of the many 'Irishtowns' which appeared particularly in the seventeenth century outside gates, for example at Clonmel's West Gate and Athlone's Dublin Gate. Their inhabitants may have provided services connected with the gate as a toll point, such as porterage and the care of wagons and horses. At Kinsale in 1690 'Irish papists' were to be enlisted to repair a breach in the wall, possibly from an Irishtown nearby. The Irishtowns that were walled at Kilkenny and Limerick in the Middle Ages may be rather different cases. The former was an independent urban settlement belonging to the bishop and older than the Hightown of Kilkenny. The latter was a suburb of Limerick and probably not so named until long after it was walled.

The visible boundary aspect of the town wall provided a convenient marker. This was not a strictly legal one as the earliest charters to Dublin and Waterford show—'tenures both within and without the walls' were covered by their provisions. Suburban development was, therefore, an expected feature and a town's lands were much greater in size than its defended area, but special rules could be made to apply there more easily because the wall could be cited simply as the limit or boundary. To some extent these were all the more necessary because of the greater intensity of settlement that the wall might induce; for example, the more rapid spread of fire or disease through close contact. At Coleraine new leases from 1715 forbade 'thatched houses or cabins within the walls, or houses rendering tallow, making soap or slaughtering animals' because of fire danger and nuisance. Galway c.1800 was said to have been very subject to contagious diseases 'before the wall was demolished'. The lack of space, again at Galway, may have resulted in the 'burying of dead without the walls', said in 1579 to have been an ancient custom there. Some of the provisions were made necessary by the need to keep the walls in a defensive condition; for example, the prohibition on building or repairing any 'straw or thatch house' within four metres of the Galway wall in 1521. More often than not such by-laws seem to have been ignored until an emergency occurred, or the rules were reviewed. At Dublin in the late sixteenth century houses and other buildings within 18 metres of the wall were to be removed, possibly a considerable undertaking and equally possibly not always carried out as their continued existence in some areas at the time of the 1585 survey suggests (figure 3.d).

The mid-seventeenth century Civil Survey shows just how convenient a boundary the town wall could be, even if property was not meant to end at it literally. This applied equally to properties without or within. Thus, properties were described at Kilkenny as an orchard near the castle joined 'without the town wall', while within one had a summer house 'next to the town wall'; and at Kilmallock as a waste plot 'mearing with the town wall north and east and with the street west', and a garden 'without the town wall opposite and east' of the former. Corner sites such as this last could be the most precise but descriptions such as 'without St. John's Gate', also at Kilmallock, are no longer so useful although at the time they may have been more precise.

At Cork, especially, this survey of 1654–6 emphasises the ever visible presence of the town wall, although perhaps only accidentally and because of the lack of depth peculiar to that site. Very many properties are described as having a 'backside and all lands from thence, extending to the city walls'; 'large stable with plot of waste land, extending to the city walls'; 'front house near the South Gate, garden extending to the town walls'. If this gives a complete and even a cosy view, so it should because the walls were in the first case meant to protect the settlement. However, they may have had side-effects too. The visible boundary of the curtain wall may have had psychological implications in terms of urban pride, exclusiveness and restrictiveness, at which we can only guess now. Many centuries on, the spread of Limerick post-1760 beyond the walls was seen as a liberation. The city 'began to show much better than it had hitherto done, and to have a wholesome air circulating in it' was the description used (Lenihan 1866, 348). This seems to hint at the confining or restrictive nature of a walled town, on the state of mind as well as on its areal development. Nonetheless, the practical use of the town wall as a property boundary was, and still is, very marked at both medieval and later walled towns. Examples range from the earliest—Dublin, Limerick and Waterford—through the later medieval—Athenry, Clonmel and Kells—to the Stuart towns such as Coleraine and Londonderry. This use often outlived the fabric of the wall which sets it apart from the others just discussed. It will be referred to again below (Influence).

REMOVAL   In the first official review of the state of corporate towns in Ireland, which included most studied here, the report stated that 'the considerations for which they [murage charters] were given have been almost everywhere neglected, some long unperformed, some imperfectly attended to; the ancient walls and for- tifications are generally razed or fallen into decay'(*MCI* 1835–6, 36). Although some town walls were little more than two hundred years old, many stretched back to the early murage charters of the thirteenth and fourteenth centuries, and a few, at the Hiberno-Norse walled towns, were even older. It is clear from the foregoing section that the care and upkeep of these town defences was at best intermittent, probably often undertaken in the face of impending calamity, fol- lowing on from it or arising from the fear engendered by the experience of others. It is also clear that the abandonment listed by the report was, despite appearances, a relatively recent phenomenon, to judge from the interest still taken in the walls in the eighteenth century. Of course, many of the resolutions and reports noted above may not have been acted upon, but corporate bodies would hardly have wasted their time on them if they were not regarded with some degree of impor- tance. As the eighteenth century wore on major changes arose. Firstly, the memory of war and the general lawlessness which had resulted in attacks on towns receded, making the town walls seem pointless. Secondly, many of the smaller towns passed into the control of individual landowners, for example Kilmallock in 1776 went to Oliver and later, by sale, to Gascoigne (*MCI* 71). Thirdly, partly allied to such changes and partly resulting from a growing sense of civil liberties, the collection of tolls, usually at the town gates, became difficult and counter- productive in that the cost came to outweigh the profit. The report is dotted with comments such as that for Youghal—'gateage and market tolls not collected for some time because of local opposition'; or that for Athboy—'tolls and customs collected up to 1828 by the Darnley family but abandoned because of opposi- tion'(*MCI* 113; 121). Fourthly, developments in road transport improved it dramatically, putting pressure on narrow streets or points such as gateways, whose heights might also be a restriction. Fifthly, the growing prosperity of the island led to new streets being developed at towns, often to house professional people whose numbers were growing and whose ideas on town planning were influenced by the spacious new 'planned' estate towns and new housing ideas generally. The buildings on St. Lawrence and Fair Streets in the large walled area of Drogheda Louth were redesigned within the walled town, but elsewhere a breaking out of the walled area was more common. The most spectacular examples were to be found at Dublin, Cork and Limerick, while at Waterford

133

redevelopment took place both within and without alongside the town walls, and at Galway more modestly outside.

Clearly, the reaction to the surviving town wall might vary considerably, even within any one town. The eighteenth century documents already quoted illustrate the adaptive side of the process—the town wall being built against or its foundations being used and thus being built 'on'; the stone-work of towers or gates being available for other purposes; and the curtain wall stonework succumbing, too, in small scale and probably surreptitious pilfering, for the building of cottages or garden walls. Gates continued to have a useful role as toll collecting points but they were very vulnerable because they restricted the road way. Anyhow toll collection could be operated from nearby buildings just as well and simpler, wider gates could be erected. At some towns gateways were initially widened, for example at Navan in 1786 and in 1796, before being ultimately removed. In the same way the Londonderry gate houses were taken down and wider gateways rebuilt in the late eighteenth and nineteenth centuries. Stretches of the curtain wall and its associated towers, which were inaccessible except from private gardens within a town, were also at risk, particularly if they were already undermined by sieges of the seventeenth century and/or normal weathering. As is clear from the section above, the earthen rampart made good gardening material, and the stones of the wall-walk could be utilised at least in part while the curtain wall still appeared untouched from the outside. Private gardens or back-sides ended at the town wall of most Irish towns in effect, even if a space was meant to be kept free, and so it must have been tempting to regard the wall as one's own. There are very few instances of streets surviving inside the wall, although the early maps suggest that they existed once and there are references to such areas being cleared during emergencies.

Piecemeal removal, therefore, seems to have been the norm and it was often allied to an ignoring of the structures where redevelopment was not an issue. This was probably the most benign fate that could befall a town wall except discreet and informed preservation. There seems to have been only one case of a campaign for the preservation of a circuit, at Londonderry, and it was motivated by the town wall being the very visible symbol of the famous victory (Milligan 1948–50 II 96). Londonderry's southern rival, Bandon, lost its walls soon after welcoming James II. They were demolished, not quite entirely, so that the town could not be held against him in the future, if the inhabitants changed their allegiance. The condition of the walls had been reported as 'deteriorating' by 1678. The river had undermined parts during heavy flooding; the platforms, probably wooden, in the towers were said to be decaying and munitions were inadequate. This state of affairs at a newly walled town, perhaps more than anything, shows the equivocal interest towns took in their walls. It may also have contributed to the decision on the part of the Protestant planters to welcome, rather than resist, James II.

The development of a new town centre to the west and south of Limerick Irishtown at the end of the eighteenth century brought some removal of the wall and gates there but still only in a partial manner. Unfortunately, the fine West

Water Gate was demolished. Yet, near its site a stretch of town wall still survives almost to full height and acts as a property boundary to buildings as well as land. This particular 'other use' may have been the most active preservation force in most towns. The commercial centre of Limerick moved into the new town, especially from the older walled area, Englishtown. There, apart from the harbour area which was reclaimed, benign neglect set in along the walls so that, as in Irishtown, short stretches and the occasional tower still survive. Even more of the shape of the walls of Englishtown remains because a street was built along much of the eastern fosse. The same processes have resulted in the survival of little used gates in Dublin and Drogheda or a stretch of curtain wall complete with towers in Waterford. In the same way, too, more structures, again especially gates, survive in towns such as Kilmallock and Athenry, which did not share in the nineteenth century expansion characteristic of those that were regional centres, like nearby Limerick and Galway.

There is at least one example of the wholesale removal of the walls and there may have been more. The town walls of Dundalk were removed *c*.1720–50 by a local 'improving' landlord who used the stone for harbour development. The harbour there was almost an outport in the area beyond the extra-mural friaries, known as Seatown. Elsewhere harbours were more often adjacent to the town and their development was one of the most potent forces in the removal of town walls. It has already been noted how the outer riverside wall at Dublin, probably only built during the 1317 emergency, had disappeared by 1585. At Youghal and Clonmel it is known to have survived into the eighteenth century but then to have given way to developments along the riverside. Likewise at Waterford, the quay was open in the fourteenth century and that stretch of the town wall disappeared first, although its gates, or some of them, survived longer as toll points.

It was inevitable that town walls would be removed or allowed to decay, once their prime purpose ceased to exist, and the importance of secondary uses, such as boundary lines or toll services, gave way to the need to expand and/or rebuild. Civic pride, which may have had a role in their development or, rather more likely, in their embellishment, may well have aided their demise. The relief, noted above, that was expressed at Galway and Limerick when the walls were removed or escaped from is almost palpable. There was certainly a feeling that they fitted ill with a progressive town, giving it a dingy, old-fashioned air. At Drogheda in 1820 the walls were described as 'high but antiquated' by the travel writer T. Cromwell. By 1835 the town wall was recorded by the Ordnance surveyors as 'almost disappeared . . . seven gates all gone except Lawrence's'. There must, therefore, have been much active removal work in the intervening period, both on the part of individuals and of the town authorities, the latter with reference to the gates in particular. There may have been some feelings of sentiment for individual structures so long part of the local scene but, if they also caused traffic problems or inhibited development of one's own property, such feelings were probably easily overcome. A sense of heritage, now so widespread but not so very strong when put to the test, as shown at Dublin recently during Wood Quay controversy, was only beginning to develop in the early nineteenth century. It can be seen in the writings of Crofton Croker about Kilmallock but it did not lead to the survival of both the gates he described in 1824, although one still stands.

It would be ridiculous to complain of the decay and partial removal of town walls in the last two hundred years, given that they were clearly largely useless relics and often inhibiting ones too. Yet, descriptions such as that of Luckombe for Kilkenny in 1779 must cause some regret—'nine gates still standing'. If only the best had been kept for their architectural interest alone and a way had been found to develop around them, they would have added so much to the riches of the city. Of the nine a poor arched gateway, the friary postern, is all that Kilkenny now has, in addition to short stretches of the curtain wall alongside a few towers in tolerable repair. These can be found on back streets, at the ends of gardens or glimpsed through yards when gates are left open. They can now be retrieved as 'heritage', but they are needlessly poor compared with what survives at York or Chester, Conway or Caernarvon, and countless towns both large and small in mainland Europe. However, it is at least unlikely now that those which still survive as partial ruins and as rebuilt gates, will in the future go the way of the majority.

INFLUENCE ON TOWN PLAN: *Reference should be made to the maps for the individual towns in the gazetteer where the basic elements of the street patterns are indicated.* The degree of influence exerted by a town wall on the development of a town, and particularly on the form of its street pattern, must always be a variable quantity. It will depend on the relative sizes of the area walled and the area settled, and their temporal relationship—whether they were developed more or less together initially, or whether the wall came much later. Given the long period from Hiberno-Norse to late Stuart times, there is much scope for variety, especially at sites where urban growth has been most vigorous. Dublin is a prime example of this, although its town wall was not extended in post-medieval times. At the other end of the scale there is Jamestown which today does not fully occupy its small seventeenth century walled area, although it does over-flow it slightly on one end.

It is not proposed here to trace in depth the varying relationship at individual sites through the centuries, but to concentrate on the present town plans. In so doing, some of the stages passed through at the more developed sites will in fact be covered at other sites. It should also be acknowledged that steady growth has not been the fate of all towns, or even of most. There have been at least two major events which reduced population levels severely and must have had some effect on the extent of the settled areas of towns—the Black Death, 1348, and the Great Famine, 1845–8. More locally-based events, such as the destruction resulting from a successful siege, could have a major impact, while, less dramatically, towns have declined too through the emigration of individuals concerned by changes developing in a wider area. This might be sparked off by the emigration of significant individuals such as the resident medieval magnate; the Butler withdrawal from Nenagh to Gowran in the mid-fourteenth century is a case in point. It doubtless affected both towns but in different ways.

The influence of a town wall was derived in the first place from its physical presence. This provided constraints chiefly on the lateral spread of the settlement and on movement to and from it. The former was associated with the circuit as a whole and the latter largely with the openings or gates within it. Neither were unalterable structures but considerable expense and time would have been involved in extending even part of a circuit. This would have depended to some extent on the fabric of the wall. It would, for example, have been relatively easy to alter the earth and sod medieval wall of Carrickfergus. Small alterations are recorded for Callan's wall in 1583, which also may not have been made of stone. Yet, many Irish stone circuits were extended officially and considerably once and, occasionally, more often. On the other hand, a new gate could be provided more easily, although its insertion could have implications for the defensive integrity of the system, and so it would not be done without due consideration. The history of the development of new gates in the northern part of the Londonderry circuit in the nineteenth century shows how protracted a process this could be. In the end only two new gates were made, while a gap for foot traffic sufficed at a third point. The only substantial interruption of the circuit, for a new road, was made later. In addition, there always was available the compromise of a postern gate, privately operated or occasionally opened to serve a particular purpose, but this too could compromise the town's defence.

The simplest scenario is that of a linear town sitting astride a through-route, with a basically rectangular wall. The single main street would join the two main gates on the short walls, and properties lining this street would run back towards the long sides of the town wall. There could be a sub-mural street between the back ends of these properties and the wall, giving access to both. This would have advantages for defence and for deflecting farm and other awkward local traffic away from the main street to an internal circulatory system. Additional streets could also develop along the line of the properties and lead to the development later of postern gates in the long walls. In time these could become main gates and a cruciform or grid street pattern could arise. Jamestown is an example of such a simple case in its earliest stages, and Ardee seems to show signs of having had a similar structure originally. There, the properties facing on to the west side of the long main street end, for the most part, at the town wall line or at the remains of the sub-mural street, while their opposite numbers on the east side have as much as two large fields between their ends and the line of the town wall. In other words, the area occupied by the main street properties is only half that once walled, and is located asymmetrically within the circuit.

There is only a little evidence at either of these towns for a sub-mural street, that is one lying along the wall on the inside. Such a street was part of the original plan at Londonderry, Coleraine and Bandon. At the last it was intended for most of the circuit of the initial plan but only for parts of the two circuits of the later. The early maps for towns walled in the medieval period tend to show short stretches of sub-mural streets, presumably remnants of a once generally complete system. Examples survive in parts of Kilkenny, Kilmallock and Drogheda. Sub-mural streets lead usually alongside the wall from a gate on the main street towards a side street, which might or might not also have a gate associated with it. The late sixteenth century *Pacata Hibernia* maps for Cork, Limerick and Youghal all show building blocks set well back from the circuits and this is confirmed by other maps. Speed's 1610 maps for the same and other towns give a more mixed picture. The 1585 survey for Dublin does not refer to a sub-mural street, which may not be significant, but does note on three occasions that houses 'join close' to the wall (on the west side). As the most developed town it may have been displaying evidence then of sub-mural streets being colonised, or otherwise disappearing under pressure of urban development.

The sub-mural street can be seen as a direct result of a town wall, although it is similar to back-lane development at villages or other towns. Nonetheless, it is one of the main means by which the wall may continue to have an impact on the town plan long after it has actually disappeared. This event, whether it occurred suddenly or protractedly, also gave scope for street development. It could have a similar effect to that just described, providing a circulatory post-mural street which, if combined with a sub-mural street, could form a broad 'ring' road. It may be an inner or outer ring-road now. In many ways is a most useful legacy which incidentally preserves the imprint of the walled circuit. On mainland Europe, many towns and cities were walled well into the nineteenth century, with elaborate sixteenth or seventeenth century circuits enclosing the original medieval ones. The later walls now provide sites for dual-carriage ring-roads close to the urban core of large cities without involving other forms of urban clearance. Brussels and Vienna are good examples. At the latter, in particular, the site of the later circuit provided such a broad zone for development that it was also made into a focus for major public building projects such as the new parliament house, town hall, major museums and theatres. It remains one of the most impressive parts of the city and a vital link in the transport system. On a much more limited scale in Ireland a post-mural ring-road has developed to a large extent at Drogheda Louth, Cork and New Ross and to a lesser extent at Limerick, Waterford, Galway and Belfast.

The site of the fosse alone often led to the development of an extra-mural street similar to the internal sub-mural one. This has happened almost completely at Londonderry but, for the most part, at the base of the ridge rather than directly beside the town wall. More often such a street arose parallel to but beyond the fosse, as it has along the western part of Youghal, and partially so on the west sides of Wexford and Kilkenny Hightown. These are essentially streets guided by the dominant morphological feature, the long line of the town wall. They may also have arisen in an *ad hoc*, evolutionary way as links between pairs of streets leading to gates in the circuit there, rather than more directly by design. So long as the wall remained an active defence such extra-mural streets would have helped an attacker just as effectively as sub-mural streets would have aided the defenders. Except at Londonderry, too little remains of Irish town walls, especially of the fosse and rampart, to provide the slight but pleasant green line that is found still at Conway and York. The extra-mural road runs alongside it in both cases and makes a visually pleasant approach to the present town centres within the surviving walls. At Visby, a small town in Sweden, the walls and fosse provide an extensive parkland divide between the town core and the outer residential areas, but this, too, is missing in Ireland although it could be developed at a town such as Athenry.

Probably the most spectacular and complete case of post-mural street development is found at Dungarvan where a grid of streets replaced the town walls when they were partly removed in the early nineteenth century. A new, landlord-inspired town was also built to the only landward side of the walled town, effectively doubling the developed urban area. On two sides the town wall gave way to open quay development. Of course, it was along waterfronts, whether sea or riverside, that towns seem to have been walled for the shortest time. Consequently, quays are probably the most common post-mural streets, although sometimes they have been there so long that their 'mural' phase is not known for certain. Convenience for the town's commercial life, often leading to its increase, was the powerful force at work there. Additionally, the fabric of the wall could be re-used in a widening of the quay-side or the development of projecting jetties. At the same time the gates could be kept both for defence and as toll points. Wharf buildings could, to a large extent, replace the wall as a means of preventing uninterrupted access from the water, an area of access which was inherently more difficult than by land anyway. Quay-side street building could also involve extension of the town by reclamation. This happened quite extensively at Youghal and, in a more limited way, at Limerick Englishtown. There, the external harbour was filled in and a sub-mural street widened.

The transformation of Cork's circuit involved most of the possible stages of waterfront development. At the north-east corner a sand-spit type feature provided the only extra-mural area not requiring reclamation. It was probably used initially for beaching boats and later it was built on, concealing the wall and giving a curious angle to the subsequent extra-mural street. Elsewhere, extra-mural quay/street development had begun by the 1690s to the south-east, using the river fosse there as a waterway. This must have involved reclamation just outside the wall and deepening of the fosse beyond, causing some lateral displacement of it. A similar but post-mural, development took place as the old central and internal harbour on the east side was filled in and built on. On either side of the North Gate quays also developed at one of the main branches of the river Lee, initially outside the line of the wall. In time the wall tended to disappear behind and below new buildings, as it did also in the south-east. There, the second stage was to infill the river fosse and use it to replace the quays by a much wider street. This then became one of the new main streets and the quays were pushed further downstream, as the marsh area beyond the walled town was also reclaimed and developed into the 'new town' or city centre. A similar pattern of quays at the fosse, followed by infill and a wider street occurred along the northern part of the west side. Only in the south-west, where the other main branch of the Lee bends alongside the town wall as a fosse, have no new streets arisen and the ring road of streets is interrupted.

The imprint of the town walls survives, therefore, in the street pattern of Cork.

Because the walled area was vacated rather than maintained as the centre of the fast-growing modern city, the medieval street pattern has been largely unaffected, as at Limerick. In outline the walled town survives but as a functional town centre it is, as it were, in semi-retirement. With the vertical presence of the walls gone it does not have the choice of full-retirement as an open-air museum piece. This, of course, is a choice which still remains for Londonderry whose walled area is of a similar size. There, however, the commercial core continues to be partly within the walls on the north side, from where it overflows into the quay area.

Yet, in both these cases the influence of the shape of the walls was not crucial but was itself derived from major topographic features. These served to enhance the defence of the site—for Cork the islands between branches of the Lee, and for Londonderry the pronounced ridge surrounded on three sides by the bog and the River Foyle. In the latter case the ring-road at the base of the scarp would probably have occurred anyway, whether the walls were above it or not. Likewise, towns which developed along straight stretches of riverbank, such as Kilkenny, or by the sea, such as Youghal and Wexford, tend to have a linear shape to their street pattern which was also true of their walled area, but this too is basically due to the under-lying topography. Such a potential shape could, however, be deflected by a dominant through-route which could draw the line of settlement back from the waterfront. This seems to have happened at towns on minor rivers such as Ardee, but it can be seen also to some extent at Trim, Coleraine and probably Thurles. The highly linear shape of Dundalk might seem to be another example but it is related very closely to an underlying slight ridge used by the route-way. At steeply sloping river sites, such as Drogheda Louth and New Ross, the line of the wall was a more individual or unique feature and so a more independent influence on the development of the street pattern. The same is true of the walled areas at basically flat sites or those with little topographic variation, such as Cashel, Castledermot and Athenry. Nonetheless, there is always the further possibility at any site that the line of the town wall has been directed to some extent by land-ownership considerations which preceded it. Church land, in particular, could have much influence and may account for some of the irregularity of the Cashel circuit in particular.

The intensity of the street pattern could be influenced by the extent and, sometimes, the shape of the walled area. On the whole this is likely only to have applied to the major cities and not to spacious walled towns like Ardee (25 ha.) and Athenry (28 ha.). Even in the mid-nineteenth century these were only partially used for urban developments, as were others with much smaller walled areas such as Youghal (19 ha.), Castledermot (15 ha.), Fethard and even Thomastown (7 ha. each). It is not possible to judge the 'high' medieval position accurately but, by the end of the sixteenth century, there was still much space within the walled areas of towns such as Youghal and Kilmallock, as their maps show. Nonetheless, extra-mural suburbs were not confined to the highly concentrated walled towns. They could be found at most to varying degrees, including such an apparently under-developed town as Ardee where there was a northern suburb which even had its own gate. Clearly, in these cases other factors, such as land ownership again, were probably more significant. At the other end of the scale the sheer intensity of street development within the walled areas of Cork (14 ha.), Dublin (20 ha.) and Waterford (23 ha.) must to some extent reflect the confinement of the circuit. At Waterford there is a discernible contrast in intensity between the earlier and later walled areas, which may also be a reflection of the change of shape and topography. The earlier had a triangular shape and a spur or ridge site, both of which must have contributed to a high density pattern, with some streets pinched out of existence towards the narrowest part. The later, at right angles to the only landward side of the former and simpler topographically, had a lower density and more flowing lines. Indeed it was not entirely built over even in the early eighteenth century. Limerick's two walled towns also had very different shapes within which the potential for street development was also different. The long narrow lozenge shape of the Englishtown on the ridge end of the island is reflected in a linear street pattern. In fact, the intensity was sufficient to turn this into a linear-based grid, despite the small area. The Irishtown had a simpler site topographically and a square shape, only touching the river at the connecting bridge point. A grid pattern developed there, too, but it was composed of generally square rather than rectangular blocks.

It is interesting to note that of the town plans produced by Speed in 1610—Dublin, Cork, Limerick and Galway—and even those by Moll in 1714—the same plus Waterford—it was only Dublin that had significant extra-mural suburbs. There were signs of such developments at Limerick Englishtown in 1714, and, even more so, at Cork, but only on the scale of those at Dublin a century before. In the early eighteenth century the walled area of Dublin was utterly dominated by extra-mural, suburban sprawl on all sides of its walls and across the river. This was so even before the walled area had been completely abandoned for the new commercial and political area then developing downstream.

Extra-mural areas around towns were dominated by the route-ways fanning out from the town gates or focussing in on them. They usually contained the town fields, the fair ground and often extensive church lands or those of manor houses and castles. Generally, expansiveness was the prevailing feature and it was probably most strongly felt if the walled area was small and tending to become more and more congested. Yet, it would be wrong to suggest that a once-walled area can be picked out now by a simple contrast in the intensity of its urban development. It is more complicated than that, depending in large measure on the stage of development. The reality is relatively complex—zones of intense building may lead away from the once main gates, as if seeping out, before becoming interrupted and more variable, with a mixture of open spaces and expansive development in between, such as recent housing estates, large-scale industrial plants, modern hospitals, eighteenth century garrison barracks and nineteenth century railway stations. But, within the walled areas market-places, church grounds and occasionally, too, castles and the lands around them, tend to reduce the intensity, even in highly developed towns such as Drogheda. Again, it depends on the site and the stage of development. The contrasts in the Middle Ages, and even later, may have often been stronger. Then the walls would have been present to emphasise the differences and the gates to intercept contact on a daily basis between the enclosed area and its suburban zone.

With such a diversity within the present urban scene, it seems unlikely that town walls at the macro scale can have had a profound effect on urban growth. While there was a choice—to remain within the relative safety of the walls or to risk building outside—it is not unreasonable to assume that there was an influence, the strength of which would vary with the prevailing defensive considerations and the stage of development that a particular town had reached. But, by now it is probably no more than coincidental that the present urban commercial core is still largely defined by the line of the walls at certain towns such as Kilkenny (3 parts), New Ross, Wexford, Carrickfergus or Coleraine. Occasionally the whole town is broadly coincident with the former walled town; for example, Castledermot, Kilmallock or Trim North, as it was in eighteenth century Carlow. What is, perhaps, more interesting is the space still unused for building purposes or for civic amenities, such as parks, within these and many other medieval circuits. Examples are Youghal and Thomastown, referred to earlier, and even small seventeenth century walled towns like Jamestown and Bandon North. This gives a measure both to the present level and nature of urbanisation in Ireland and to that of the past, particularly the medieval. It is true even without invoking the very large walled areas of Ardee and Athenry, which may stand in part as monuments to optimism and/or ambition. Idiosyncrasies of land ownership and topographic problems may, of course, have had an overriding influence, particularly in the case of Youghal where both these additional factors coincide just inside the long western wall, resulting in much 'open' space. Yet, the topographic factors, at least, could be overcome if the need to develop was strong enough, as other steeply sloping sites such as New Ross and Kinsale show.

To a certain extent the abandonment of the walled town(s) can be taken as an indicator of the strength of urban development at the medieval sites. At Dublin, Cork and Limerick new towns were built beyond the walls mostly in the eighteenth century. The walled towns were largely abandoned, becoming the preserve not only of small industries that had always been there but also, which was new, of a single class of population—the poor. In effect, the existing buildings, once merchants' shops/homes or professionals' offices/homes, became tenement dwellings, groups of which were often later acquired in order to allow an adjacent industrial concern to expand. In contrast, at other, lesser, regional centres such as Londonderry, Waterford and Galway, there was smaller scale development along more spacious lines beyond the walled area but no abandonment of it. Continuity of coincidence between the present commercial centre and the former walled town, therefore, still largely remains at these towns. Belfast is exceptional in most respects, being only latterly a provincial centre and a capital. In addition, its town walls lasted relatively briefly, enclosed a very large area and were contemporary with its development as a town, and so there is a considerable degree of coincidence.

The influence of elaborate mid or late seventeenth century defences at other towns such as medieval Sligo and Mullingar (list B), and within or around walled areas such as those possibly built at Dundalk and Clonmel, are difficult to assess.

Their relative ease of removal, if made mostly of earth, suggests that their influence would be slight. Yet, at Belfast the line of the largely earthen western wall is now marked by street developments and the same is true at Athlone West. Effects at the micro-scale will be discussed below but one aspect should be borne in mind. Where these defensive systems were introduced they may have resulted in much clearance of existing property, especially close to the circuit. When they in turn disappeared substantial areas could have been more readily available for development than they otherwise might have been. This may have happened at Dundalk, where short-lived Williamite period defences appeared, and at other places where more isolated structures such as citadels were built. Some of the eighteenth century expansion at Waterford took place south of the minor river that acted as a fosse to the earlier walled town, where a late-sixteenth century outer fort was built on the land of an extra-mural religious house. Likewise, the citadel built outside the main western gate became a barracks in the eighteenth century and, more recently, a substantial area for redevelopment.

The influence of the whole circuit, or parts of the curtain wall, as a boundary has been referred to briefly as an additional use. Apart from the possible impact of the whole system on the development of the street pattern, which will be discussed below, it is the most persistent, if often now indirect, influence. Although the line of the wall was not itself a legal boundary in the sense that it defined a town's lands, its use as a marker turned it into a boundary for land closeby. For this reason it acquired a legal status by being enshrined in property deeds. This boundary influence had, therefore, the capacity to be very persistent because to remove it required the revision of legal documents. Many have changed over the centuries but equally, where no change was made, the use of the wall or its line has remained. Where street or area development has been related to a property line, in turn related to the former wall, the impact has been doubled. Instances of this type of influence, however derived, can be found throughout Ireland and include places as diverse as Coleraine, Dundalk and Gowran. In these the town wall can be said to live on as an invisible but a real influence. At many towns, therefore, a careful study of property boundaries may be used to rediscover the line of the town wall if it is now unknown or disputed. This has been done for the north-east corner of Dublin with great skill (Burke 1974). It is probably too much to expect similar success at many other sites, given the general poverty of documentary evidence in Ireland, but land boundaries clearly aligned may now suggest likely areas for further study.

Turning now from the circuit as a whole to specialised parts of it, the degree of influence exerted by gates must be considered. On the face of it, this looks as if it might have been considerable but that may be the result of the prominence of gates as structures, and the visual concentration of routes on them which maps so easily portray. In fact, it may well be that main gates, at least, were often located in response to already established routes, with minor gates arising where local needs suggested within a framework so established. This was less likely to happen at new towns, such as Bandon and Londonderry, or their medieval equivalents, where the town and the wall were planned together. Yet, few sites, and certainly not seventeen century ones, were virgin ground and so local trackways, related to an existing church, castle or fort, and even parts of through-routes may have been available to exert an influence. This was true at Derry in respect as a church and forts and at Bandon it may explain the uneven distribution of gates, as well as some of the irregularities of the circuits. Moreover, the provision clearly made at medieval Waterford and Limerick for the later insertion of some gates could have been in response to the presence of existing but minor roads. Therefore, for some time a system of priority-building could have been in operation. Nonetheless, the lines of established routes may often have been altered in detail to allow for the use of a better location for a gate from a defensive point of view. Gates related to routes leading to bridges also seem to have responded frequently to circumstances, rather than to have been influencial themselves. It is striking how often there was a basically straight line between the original site of the bridge and the gate at the opposite end of the town. Cork, Galway, Dundalk and Ardee are cases in point. Yet, route lines, even with bridges, were not always as simple as at these. Clonmel, for example, was at a bridging point on the major River Suir but the dominant route there was probably usually the one alongside, rather than across, the river. The east and west gates there were aligned and connected by a straight street, but the street using the bridge was not so closely related to a northern gate. An even more staggered main street line is to be found at nearby Carrick-on-Suir. There, the bridge near the south-west corner did carry one of the main western routes from Waterford, but this then branched westwards towards Clonmel, using the West Gate of Carrick which was close to the bridge, and northwards towards Kilkenny, for which the only northern gate was towards the opposite north-east corner.

Perhaps the most complex situation, and one which shows clearly that the influence of a gate was but one of many, and possible not at all crucial, is illustrated by Dublin. There were really no straight lines from the river to the opposite south wall, although there were two 'flowing' lines to the two southern gates. Neither of these connected with the bridge or, indeed, with known fords. The original river crossings had eccentric positions at the east or west ends of the walls, and the only bridge was to the west, diametrically opposite to the castle although contemporary with it. As for east-west routes these, too, had complex lines. The oddities in the east were largely due to the local topography. The use of an island in the tributary River Poodle influenced the approach to the only medieval gate, and a zig-zag street line was required to rise up from it to the much higher level of the castle area. In the west there was from the thirteenth century at least the choice of streets—on the ridge or below—because of the positions of the two gates. The later, lower, west gate had the simpler approach from streets in the topographically simpler, reclaimed area. Its counterpart on the east wall was not made until the seventeenth century when reclamation took place in the Poddle estuary beyond it. Then the new streets required a new gate rather than being influenced by it. In the older, upper area of the west, streets do seem to focus on New Gate, leading to it from gates in the inner wall, as well as from the castle on the main street and from the nearest southern gate. This last street, Back Lane, looks like one that evolved in the classic manner as a sub-mural street, rather distant from the wall but providing, as its name suggests, access to the backs of properties facing onto the main street and a convenient direct link between two main gates, one to the south and one to the west.

The corn-market at Dublin was held at New Gate and this led to a widening of the street on either side of it. Such urban microfeatures were, however, subject to much change over the centuries; for example, market spaces were often reduced in area through in-fill development which was later removed at least in part to aid traffic flow. Consequently, very detailed site studies are required in each case to establish the major influences. To take the north side of Drogheda as an example, there is evidence to suggest that the pronounced narrowing of the main west street, as it approaches the gate site, was due to a line of buildings being squeezed in, as it were, between the street and monastic land. Consequently, it had little to do with the gate itself which may even have post-dated it, being built possibly as part of a later extension. Again, the deflection of the main street north from the Boyne bridge, which led to the eccentric position of the main north gate (Sunday's), may have been related to the presence of another religious house. In fact, the north gate may originally have had a more direct site relative to the bridge, on an earlier north wall to which the friary was extra-mural. At the surviving part of the east gate, the St. Lawrence barbican, there is now no noticeable difference in street width to the inside or outside. It is merely an interruption on a straight street line with nearby a set of side streets derived largely from sub-mural or post-mural developments, the latter along the line of the fosse. In a comparable position on the west side, a very broad street now exists outside the gates. Its origins may have been in a market or fair function, as at Dublin's New Gate, and/or as a stopping place for large wagons before entry into the town by smaller carts, or other forms of porterage.

Such a space exists at other towns too outside gates and seems to be the most common way in which a gate influenced a town. It can be seen still at Galway on the east, Cashel on the west and Kinsale at the north-west corner. It was a feature that could easily disappear through later building developments, although its outline might survive. At both Kinsale and Cashel, as at Trim (north) the focussing of routes towards a former gate is now clear but this could just as easily happen at some distance, as can be seen again at Trim on the east and south sides. Inner gates, such as those at Dundalk and Youghal, do not seem to have had a marked influence at the micro-level either. The one which survives at Youghal seems merely to interrupt physically the flowing street line. The main North Gate there had an outer defence by the late sixteenth century and its shadow does still seem visible in present property boundaries, and in a slight narrowing of the street. Yet, this was not so clear in the late-eighteenth century, to judge by the map evidence, and so the influence may be more apparent than real. The imprint of some seventeenth century bastions is clearer at sites such as Athlone. On the east side there the eccentric entrance to the bastion at the Dublin Gate survives in a minor street line set at an acute angle to the main street, and on the west side the shape of the central bastion remains clear in property boundaries. This is all the more surprising because its centre has been pierced by the main street. The south-east bastion nearby has left a similar imprint and, indeed, almost the whole earthen, but substantial, circuit can be traced in street lines or property boundaries.

The last service of a circuit may, therefore, have been to aid the modernisation of the street system by allowing both the widening of existing sub-mural streets, and the construction of new ones in its place as post-mural ring-roads at best. The constriction of gates, now so obvious at the few relics, was not perhaps always such a major problem when street widths were not great either. Nonetheless, few medieval gates would have provided two-way access for more than small carts and extensive barbicans would have been especially difficult to widen. There must, therefore, have been much waiting inside and outside the gates, which may have indirectly exerted some pressure on the width of the adjacent streets as well as leading ultimately to the removal of the gate structures.

In conclusion and summary, it may be useful to look in detail at the present street plan of a simple and largely intact, medieval walled town—Athenry. The main street lies between the north and south-west gates, possibly the original route from Roscommon to Galway. This is crossed, in the northern part of the town near the castle and parish church, by a street joining the east and west gates, now of very local significance and possible always so, at least on the west side. The main trunk road from Galway to Dublin via Athenry now skirts the southern edge of the town using an extra-mural road alongside the southern wall and fosse. It may, however, have originally gone into the town via the south-western gate and out via the eastern, using parts of the two main streets. The rest of the street system is subsidiary but, apart from a short street leading directly to the castle, it did for some time include an alternative system to the other southern gate. Apart from the stretch of wall no longer standing on the east side, there are only a few minor breaks in the circuit. One of these, on the west, has a curious, short, undeveloped street related to it. It may date from the period when there was a large garrison which may have used the extra-mural area there for parade purposes. Alternatively it may have developed in relation to the wall inserted in the sixteenth century to reduce the size of the town. This reduction ought to have required inner gate(s) but nothing is known of their locations. Throughout, the town wall acts as a property and townland boundary and entrance to Athenry from the north today is still through the arch of the partly ruined North Gate.

The visible presence of town walls is now, however, very limited in Ireland, confined largely in terms of actual circuits to the seventeenth century one at Londonderry and the more decayed, medieval ones at Athenry and Fethard. The many isolated stretches are so scattered throughout the land as to have little general impact. Occasionally, they are prominent morphological features when, as at Waterford, they are associated with fine towers or, as at Dublin and Carrickfergus, with modified gates and stone bastions. The best gates, whether intact, ruined or restored, are again few and far between, if impressive as entities. It is small wonder that being walled for long periods is not readily recognised as a common experience of many Irish towns. Yet it is an experience that has left some profound and persistent marks.

CHAPTER 5

Distribution

Discussion of the distribution of Irish walled towns, either in terms of time or area, is fraught with problems. This is basically because of the poverty of the record base. One major problem has already been considered in chapters 1 and 2, the identification of walled towns. It led to the formulation of two lists, A and B, of 'known' and 'proposed' walled towns respectively, and these will be used here again. Another major problem, specific to the topic of distribution, is the dating of the initial building of a town wall, generally in stone. This is a problem, not so much at the macro level of Hiberno-Norse, Anglo-Norman, Tudor or Stuart, as at the micro, particularly with regard to the medieval period to which the majority of walled towns belong. Quite precise dates are, of course, available for the Stuart period but relatively few towns were involved then. As regards the first period, recent archaeological work has produced a detailed evolution of the town wall at Hiberno-Norse Dublin, and the same may in time become possible for Waterford and the other few towns which had walls before 1169. Similar investigations could also help to date more precisely the large number of medieval towns walled later, but the scale of work required is of such an order that it is not likely to be embarked on except occasionally in the near future.

The following discussion, therefore, relies heavily on the murage evidence for the medieval towns. But, while murage charters or other grants are specific to town walls and individual towns, they do not often indicate the exact nature of the intended work—initial building in earth or stone, upgrading from earth to stone, repair or extension—or, except in rare instances, the sections involved within a particular circuit. This is even true of some of the early charters to Dublin which, it is clear form archaeological and other documentary evidence, already had a stone wall. Those for 1221 and 1233 simply read 'to inclose and fortify' and the 1295 'in aid of inclosing', as do the 1291 to Fethard or the 1286 to Tralee, Mallow and Ard(fert). Yet, the last two may have been initial grants and, as such, could be taken as marking the beginning of town wall construction at those sites. Fethard was the subject of a number of subsequent grants but no others are known for the three towns grouped together simply because they belonged to the one magnate. They are, therefore, on list B as 'proposed' walled towns because there is no corroborative evidence that the grant resulted in town walls. Fourteenth century grants are generally more informative, many indicate that a stone wall was involved and some even refer, in a general way, to 'amending' the town wall or, more specifically, to work on towers, gates and/or the quay area.

The murage records are also clearly residual, but to what extent it is difficult to judge. New Ross is a case in point. The poem of 1265, a rare document in the precision of its information, predates the earliest known murage evidence by about a century. So does evidence from a rental of 1279 in which reference is made to burgess holdings 'inside and outside the walls'. Two diagrams have been prepared partly in an effort to assess the reliability of any patterns based on murage evidence. Figure 5.1 illustrates the total number of murage grants known to have been active, and figure 5.2 the rate of initial murage funding to Irish medieval towns (from both lists A and B) for which there is evidence. Similar graphs have been prepared from data in Turner (1970, app.C) so that the situation in England and Wales can provide a means of evaluating the Irish.

Clearly, the levels of active grants were, on the face of it, of a quite different order in England and Wales until the fifteenth century when the Irish rate caught up. The number of towns involved, 78 out of a possible 108 in England and Wales, and 68 (45A + 23B) out of a possible total of 81 (49A + 32B) in Ireland, was not very different. Yet, there were rarely more than five grants operating during any two year period at Irish towns before 1375, while the number active at English and Welsh towns rarely fell below ten and often peaked above twenty. The scale of activity was much closer in the fifteenth century with Irish towns in time even receiving larger number of grants than English and Welsh. Also, for the Irish towns the rate was by then much higher, generally around ten and occasionally peaking around fifteen.

Initial murage funding, again during the early period, was also much more spectacular in England and Wales than apparently in Ireland—20 towns in the first fifteen years after 1220 as opposed to only 3 Irish, with the 20 mark not being reached in Ireland until 1300, by which time 50 towns had received first grants in England and Wales. Looked at another way, the peak came in Ireland in the period 1285–1315, when 20 towns were involved, while there had been two previous peaks in England and Wales, in 1220–30 and 1260–70, each of which involved 16 towns. Thereafter, from 1315 to 1450, apparently as many Irish as English and Welsh towns were receiving initial grants. On both islands the rate of initial murage grants was by then reduced and, to a certain extent, this was inevitable unless the proportion of walled to non-walled towns had remained low or the creation of new towns was very active. The former is just possible but the latter certainly peaked by *c*.1300. For both medieval England and Wales it had risen rapidly from *c*.1000 so that, in the period 1200–1300, 70 English and 42 new Welsh towns were founded but in the following period only about 10 each (Beresford 1967 app. I and II).

Given that the urbanisation of Ireland began later than that of England and Wales, a slow start to the granting of initial murage is not unexpected but, in view of the known security problems in the colony which developed post-1250, these two graphs do suggest that the picture may be partially distorted by a lack of evidence. It is noticeable that in the later fourteenth, and especially the fifteenth, century, when conditions remained difficult in Ireland but were more stable in England and Wales, the Irish trends tend to be the reverse of the English and Welsh. However, if the loss of thirteenth century records is not as great as the evidence suggests, then the graphs indicate a level of attention to urban defences during the Irish colony's development phase at least no greater than that prevailing

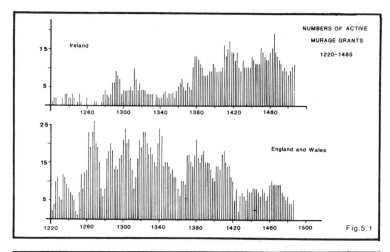

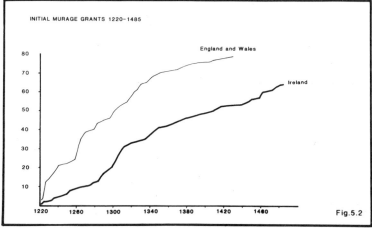

in contemporary England and Wales. In the later Middle Ages, the Irish Parliament took an active interest in the defence of towns and the survival of its records may be reflected too in the graphs. But this may also point to the greater efficiency of a funding system based within the colony rather than one dependent on a distant 'central' administration. In the earlier period, therefore, while fewer Irish towns may have applied for murage funding, the processing of applications would also have taken much longer for two reasons. Firstly, the documents—the request for murage from the town and the reply from the king—often had to travel considerable distances, even possibly to France on occasions when the king visited his lands there. Secondly, given such extensive interests Irish affairs often had a low priority for the medieval English Crown (Frame 1981, 68). Of course, the king was often absent from England too for long periods in the thirteenth and fourteenth centuries and, consequently, accessibility at least was not necessarily so very different for the two islands. In addition, like their English counterparts, major Irish magnates such as fitzMaurice were often with the king. It is known, for example, that he made such a visit in 1282, four years before the murage charter was granted to his towns of Tralee etc. (*CDI* II 1915). The thirteenth century records contain long lists of less prominent individuals who were granted permission to 'leave Ireland' to visit England, Wales or continental Europe and so it would be wrong to think of the Irish colonists as very 'cut-off'. Furthermore, the granting of the first murage charters, to Dublin and Waterford, followed closely on the first in England—to Shrewsbury and London. Undoubtedly, the processing of applications must have been delayed from time to time by the vicissitudes of sea-travel at least, but, if the king was at Bristol rather than London and the weather good, the whole business might have been carried out quite rapidly.

Problems with the surviving records must, therefore, reduce the extent to which the medieval walled towns of Ireland can be considered in their historical setting, and even used as an index of colonisation. Nonetheless, it is not unreasonable to view them as such. Towns were an important feature of both the Hiberno-Norse and the Anglo-Norman colonisations, despite the different scales of these undertakings, and they were also crucial to the later re-colonisations of the Tudor and Stuart periods. During these last there was much discussion at government level of the need for walled towns, in particular, and for towns generally, the former as a strategic base for a resettlement programme of which the latter was a key component. These ideas will be discussed later but it is possible that they were not new. Medieval defensive measures may have been more fragmented, both in the sense of being short-term and localised, but they could still be part of a strategic whole from the Crown's point of view. In England the development of urban defences seems to be closely related to specific internal or external threats. The interest shown during the tenth century English-Danish conflict was not sustained in the succeeding peace of the eleventh and twelfth centuries, but it was revived when invasion was a major fear in the years 1204–20 (Turner 1970, 13–14, but she also refers to a lack of documentary evidence possibly distorting the early English picture). Later, even when murage funding was most active relatively few towns were actually involved in England. Furthermore, only about 30% of English and Welsh walled towns were funded at any one time, even during peaks of funding such as the end of the thirteenth century when there was war with the Scots, Welsh and French. However, these small numbers could, and often did, represent a strong local concentration. For example, in 1280 thirteen out of eighteen murage grants were made to towns in South Wales and along the Welsh March, and work on Caernarvon and Conway in North Wales followed within a few years. Attention to a strategic, countrywide framework is less obvious in thirteenth-fifteenth century England but this was already well established in the earlier Danish period. London, Bristol and York continued to receive regular grants throughout the Middle Ages, but attention was generally concentrated on a few areas—East Anglia and the south coasts, to meet the threat of French invasion; Northern England towards the Scottish border; and Wales, especially the Welsh March. The last two were both areas of instability due to being adjacent to lordships or kingdoms independent of and often antagonistic to the English Crown. Even in the fifteenth century, when grants slowed down, these border areas remained prominent recipients of murage. For Ireland the available evidence suggests that not more than 25% of all possible walled towns received funds at any one time, or nearly 33% of those on list A. These figures give a means, however flawed, by which contemporary terms like 'Land of Peace' and 'Land of War' can be evaluated.

HIBERNO-NORSE:MAP 5.a

In Ireland the basis of a strategic framework also dated from the Scandinavian period. Dublin, Waterford, Wexford and Limerick all had Hiberno-Norse town walls. The form of their structures has only been established clearly at Dublin, on the riverside, where an evolution from an earthen bank, with wooden reinforcing and a topping of varying types, to a stone wall has been found in excavations carried out from 1969 to 1981. By 1169 walls at the other towns may have developed along a similar pattern, without being necessarily as sophisticated as that at Dublin, the strongest Hiberno-Norse settlement. It is known that settlements existed too at Cork, Arklow and Wicklow, but their form is not clear. More Hiberno-Norse settlements may yet be proved, for example at Youghal and Drogheda, or some site nearby in the Boyne estuary. Any of these, or even sites further north along the Irish Sea coast, could have been defended urban settle-

ments, ranging in scale from trading posts to small towns, but their defences would probably have been simple earthen structures with a relatively short life-span. Therefore, their impact on later town walls might have been less strong than that of the stone walls of the earlier Roman towns in England. On the other hand, there was continuity of settlement in Ireland between the towns of the Hiberno-Norse and the Anglo-Norman periods, whereas in England a considerable lacuna existed between the periods of Roman and Anglo-Saxon or Danish urban development.

Very little evidence exists for inland Scandinavian settlements in Ireland and, given the nature of their main interest in Ireland as a base for Atlantic seaboard trade, this is not surprising. It is, necessarily, reflected in the distribution of the Hiberno-Norse walled towns. This is unique in being entirely coastal. The small number involved, only four for certain, is also unique and reflects the apparently small scale of Scandinavian settlement operations in Ireland. Nonetheless, the pattern is both wide areally—from Limerick south and east to Dublin—and fairly evenly spread, especially if Cork is included, which seems feasible. The lesser known settlements would, if also included, tend to fill in the gaps in such a pattern (except in the south-west) and extend the distribution northwards along the Irish Sea coast. The defence of these settlements was probably a high priority given this isolation, the small numbers of settlers and the unenviable reputation that they had acquired amongst the Irish population, following the initial Hiberno-Norse raiding phase of the late eighth and early ninth centuries. As time went on and they forged alliances locally with Irish rulers, on the basis of different but essentially complementary economies, the threat to security may have changed. Then it probably became more external in source and was based on the attractiveness of the growing prosperity of major centres such as Dublin and Waterford. At Dublin, in particular, the defences were not only strengthened on a number of occasions but may have been extended by the time of the first stone town wall which has been dated to $c.1100$. Simms (1979, 34) notes the small size of even such an extended walled town ($c.12$ ha.) compared with contemporary continental trading posts such as Dorestadt in Holland (100 ha.). However, further north Haithabu on the German-Danish border was distinctly smaller (25 ha.) and so were Swedish walled towns both at home and in eastern Europe—Birka near the site of Stockholm was similar to Dublin while Gdansk and Poznan were less than half as large. None of the other Hiberno-Norse walled towns are likely to have been larger than Dublin but, as always, size can be misleading. The excavations at Dublin, at least, have indicated the social and economic nature of the settlement which is a more significant index. This was clearly sophisticated and was manifested on the ground in the form of a densely built urban area (Wallace 1985). Excavations of Hiberno-Norse Waterford, Wexford, Limerick and Cork are now urgently required to establish, not only the nature and extent of their defences, but their economic structure and urban status, relative to that of Dublin.

This period was so long, 1169–1485, and involved so many of the Irish walled towns that, for the sake of convenience, it is necessary to sub-divide it. This could have been done in a totally arbitrary fashion, for example three 100-year periods. But three unequal periods are suggested by the murage evidence—I the initial phase, 1170–1250 but effectively *c*.1200–1250; II the expansion phase, 1250–1350; and III the consolidation phase, 1350–1485. The dates, 1250 and 1350 should not be seen as exclusive or highly significant but rather as the approximate dates when trends were changing.

PHASE I, 1170–1250, MAP 5.b   Ireland in 1169 may have been one of the less developed regions of western Europe but it was not empty. The period, *c*.1050–1300, has been called the 'Age of Clearing' by the French historian Marc Bloch, a time of population expansion and movement into marginal areas both to the east and west (Smith 1967, 163). The nature of the existing settlement pattern in Ireland, its balance of dispersed rural and nucleated urban or proto-urban elements, is currently the subject of much research and some dispute. It is at least fair to say that, to the incoming Anglo-Normans, the potential for agricultural development and the already existing framework of well-established and defended Hiberno-Norse ports towns were probably equally important. Indeed, the general economic possibilities were greatly enhanced by the existence of the

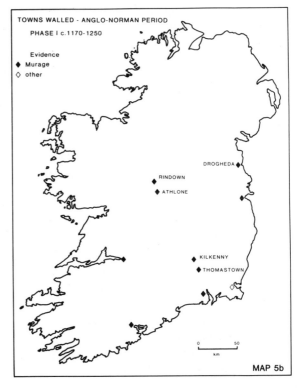

153

towns of Dublin, Wexford, Waterford, Cork and Limerick. This is indicated by the fact that the initial invaders acquired most of them with all possible speed, and that the king, also, was quick to gain control over them, directly or indirectly. They were, infact, considerable economic prizes in themselves. There is no evidence that the Anglo-Normans were in a hurry to extend the thin framework of walled towns that these provided. They seem to have just made use of the lesser Hiberno-Norse ports of Wicklow and Arklow without upgrading them, while they developed towns more rapidly at Drogheda and Youghal. They also apparently quickly infilled the urban system with the creations of new ports such as Dungarvan, Carlingford and Carrickfergus. How virgin these sites were it is impossible to tell without archaeological investigation but most of them acquired early castles, some royal. Attention may have been given also to defensive enclosures at each of these sites but there is little evidence for this yet, except at Drogheda.

Anglo-Norman attention to the Dublin town wall is known for at least three occasions prior to the introduction of murage charters—1204, 1206 and 1214 (*CDI* I 226, 315, 529). The wording of the earlier documents indicates that 'fortifying' Dublin was regarded as necessary, rather than advisable, at least on the part of the king. Certainly, the direct grant involved in the last gave substance to this view in that it would have involved a considerable short-term loss of revenue to the Crown. It is tempting to see this grant, in particular, as marking the upgrading of the Hiberno-Norse wall generally or just of its westward extension, including the building of St. Nicholas's Gate as a second opening to the south.

Apart from Dublin, it is only for Cork that there is murage evidence which predates the granting of murage charters from 1220. The Pipe Roll accounts for 1211–12 note the spending of £55.5s.6d. on 'the wall of Cork'. This, too, was a considerable sum of money because it was similar to the value of the fee-farm rent as set out some years later in the 1243 charter. One of the difficulties illustrated here once more lies in the terminology—should 'wall' be taken as meaning 'stone wall'? If so, it is possible that the town wall at Cork, known from the sixteenth century maps, was then being built, or a Hiberno-Norse structure improved and/or extended. Yet, a document, dated to 1218 (*CDI* I 842), states that the king had been informed 'that it would tend to the security of the king and of Ireland if the city of Cork were fortified'. This, taken also at its face value, seems to contradict the former but it may simply mean 'if Cork were better fortified.' As already indicated in the section on murage, many later charters used the words 'to enable them to inclose their town/city' when it is known from other sources that a wall existed, and so again, the words 'well' 'in stone', or perhaps 'completely', may be missing. No such difficulty exists with the first known murage charter to Cork, dated 1284, which does state that the customs were to 'improve their walls' and other facilities such as bridges and the port. Nonetheless, 'pre-1284' is clearly a very inadequate date for the beginning of the Anglo-Norman town wall at Cork, as is the comparable 'pre-1275' that still can only be assigned to nearby Youghal.

Drogheda appears in the records at this early stage only in regard to its bridge or castle. Indeed, the need to fortify lands generally by building manorial castles

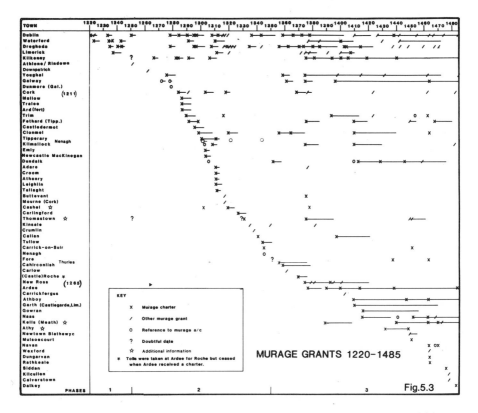

MURAGE GRANTS 1220–1485

Fig.5.3

was often emphasised at this early stage (*CDI* I 125, 574 for the years 1200 and 1215 respectively). It may well be that at Drogheda and other towns a castle was sufficient, either alone or in combination with a simple earthen enclosure, and/or a nightly watch system. As in the earlier Hiberno-Norse period, there was probably still space enough in Ireland for a reasonable *modus vivendi* to develop, given the different social and economic systems of the invaders and most Irish natives, although it is undoubtedly true that there were clashes too. As the 'stuff' of history they may well draw attention away form relations that often were generally friendlier, or at least more quietly resigned, so that by the mid-thirteenth century a *status quo* situation had been established with the Anglo-Normans concentrated in the valleys of the lordship and the gaelic Irish in the hill and bog country within and beyond its limits (Frame 1984, 34).

There are no specific references to early murage measures either for the already existing walls at Waterford, Wexford and Limerick. The accounts of the Anglo-Norman attacks on these towns leave no doubt that they were already substantial structures. It is possible that the chroniclers exaggerated the strength of the town walls, and so the task facing the attackers, but it is unlikely that they invented them entirely. It would have been natural to have kept such defences in repair or to have improved them. Early Anglo-Norman documents for both Waterford and Limerick use the wall as a marker for defining burgages either as 'within or without' or 'between the river and the city wall'. Both these towns were early subjects of murage charters but Wexford disappears from view until the fifteenth century. Nonetheless, there is other evidence which indicates that its wall was probably extended in the intervening centuries.

The first murage charters post-1220 (fig. 5.3), can be seen as providing for an Anglo-Norman consolidation of an essentially Hiberno-Norse distribution pattern because the only one new town was involved—Drogheda. Attention to the Dublin and Waterford walls was continued, both of which were possibly extended as well as repaired or considerably improved. The first of the Drogheda charters, 1234, may mark the beginning of the stone town wall there at least. It is unusually specific in stating 'to inclose their vill with walls' and it was addressed to both the Louth and Meath towns. Subsequent similar charters, spread over a ten-year period, may have been used to complete the two circuits as far as the river. Yet the Limerick charter of 1237 notes the desirability of the citizens also contributing directly to the financing of work on the wall. Possibly this was generally the case, especially with regard to details such as the style and number of gate houses and towers.

With the exception of a typically brief three-year charter to Dublin in 1250, neither Waterford, Drogheda or Limerick are known to have received grants for 40 years or more post-1245. In this first phase, therefore, unless many records are missing—Cork's probably and Youghal's possibly, at least—the emphasis was on improving the existing framework of walled towns and adding to it only slightly. The coastal emphasis of the Hiberno-Norse period remained unaltered and the concentration in the south-eastern half of the island. However, new inland settlements were springing up throughout the colony as the frontiers were pushed north and west from time to time, to reach east Ulster and east Limerick in the late twelfth century, and east Connacht by 1237 (*NHI* II 1986, 115–6, 129–30 and 160–5). This process involved both the development of rural manors and the founding of towns to service them, many on new sites but some at existing nuclei (Graham 1980, 17–18). While some failed, in Ireland as in Europe largely due to the over-optimistic use of urban status as a bait to encourage incoming settlers (Otway-Ruthven 1965, 77–9), there is no evidence that they were intended as walled towns from the start. Indeed, the evidence for New Ross, founded *c*.1207–11, makes no reference to any existing enclosure, only to a watch system. In such an overtly advertising document as the 1265 poem, it seems curious to have missed the opportunity to compare the new enclosure with an existing one, either in terms of structure or extent, and so it must be assumed that there was none of significance.

PHASE II, 1250–1350, MAP 5.c. The murage grant of 80 marks made in 1251 to the 'king's vills of Athlone and Rindown' points to a new trend (CDI I 1359). While it continued the pattern of a concentration on royal towns, it involved a change to inland sites—few could have been further from the sea—and reinforced the attention to new towns possibly started by the grants to Drogheda. Another aspect of Drogheda, its creation by local lords, was now to become a dominant

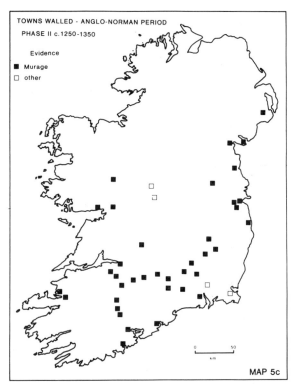

TOWNS WALLED - ANGLO-NORMAN PERIOD
PHASE II c.1250-1350

Evidence
■ Murage
□ other

0   50
km

MAP 5c

feature too. Indeed, direct Crown interest stopped with the original Hiberno-Norse towns and the occasional new venture such as Athlone, which had a special strategic value. The Shannon, which was bridged there and crossed easily by ferry from Rindown, marked the inner boundary of the late and thus weaker colonisation of Connaught. Therein problems might, and in fact did, later arise for the longer and more heavily settled Meath lands of the core area.

Generally, the towns which appeared now for the first time in the murage records were overwhelmingly new seignorial developments, sometimes at long established Irish centres of political or religious significance, and mostly inland. They included Kilkenny, Downpatrick, Trim, Castledermot, Clonmel, Mallow and Kilmallock amongst the earliest. What such a group, apparently walled c.1250–1300, represented was a fanning-out into the interior along the river route ways from the port towns walled during the earlier phase. These, too, were also attended to and increased in number. Both Galway and Youghal received grants and, in the last twenty years of the thirteenth century, murage was apparently renewed to the increasingly key towns of Dublin, Waterford and Drogheda. The majority of towns now had general charters of liberties from their lords, but they were clearly also seen by the Crown as entities capable of serving a wider strategic purpose by providing a network of refuges. The preambles to their murage charters emphasise this. The words of the 1291 Kilkenny charter was characteristic— 'in aid of inclosing their vill, for improvement thereof, and the security of the men of the parts adjacent'. It is possible, therefore, that whether or not a murage charter was granted may actually have depended on how well the town concerned fitted into the general political setting, as least at this stage.

The really strong period for initial murage granting in England and Wales was probably c.1260–1340. In Ireland too it may have begun to take off about 1260. The murage records (figs. 5.1–3) suggest c.1275 as the turning point but, for reasons outlined in the last chapter, this may well be too late. Evidence for this is available both for major centres, such as Youghal, Cork and Kilkenny, and for less prominent ones like Thomastown, including some rather remote examples such as Downpatrick and Dunmore. Yet, the apparent gap in murage funding to the most prominent towns, noted earlier as existing post-1250, was at least confirmed for Waterford in the 1290 request for renewed murage. Murage was restarted at Dublin and Drogheda apparently rather earlier but not at Limerick until 1310. Then the grant for walling the 'Irishtown' was essentially an extension project.

The New Ross poem of 1265 is quite specific about the reason for walling that town for the first time then. It was the fear of an attack arising out of a conflict being waged in the general area by two Anglo-Norman lords. At other towns a similarly based fear may now have been felt too from time to time. While the early thirteenth century was not always peaceful, the lordship was expanding generally successfully (Lydon 1967, 89), but after 1250 that ceased for the most part. In so doing the expansion ended before it completely encompassed the whole island, leaving about one third untouched directly. Troubles then began to develop because of this partial colonisation which interacted with others arising for different reasons within the colonised area, even within those parts settled earliest and most firmly. Significant dates include—1241, the break-up into two parts of the large Meath lordship; 1243, when problems in the Ulster lordship led to its being in Crown control and thus lacking a resident power for some time; 1245, the break-up into five parts of the vast Marshall lands in central and south Leinster. Like Meath, this was an early major grant and soon it suffered similarly from absenteeism because the succession was secured through the husbands of heiresses, who were often already based abroad (Otway-Ruthven 1969, 191). The importance of this has been noted by a number of historians, including Frame (1982, 54–8), who point to the essential feudal requirement of lords to defend their lands on behalf of the king. This requirement absentee lords could only fulfill by proxy, rarely a satisfactory situation. In addition Crown attention was increasingly focussed on developing Gascony, the only, but very valuable, continental possession left after 1259. Later, especially in the 1290s, Edward I was preoccupied by periodic wars against the Scots, Welsh and French, for all of which he expected and received substantial help from Ireland in the form of men, money and goods. In time this also added to the defensive problems in Ireland without altering its priority level in the eyes of the Crown. In addition, within Ireland but arising beyond the colony proper, the pressures of what has often been called the 'Gaelic Revival' were increasingly felt. As a development this is probably more obvious now at the distance of several centuries than it was at the time but it can be dated back to the arrival, and use, of Scots-Norse mercenaries by Gaelic lords in Ulster from c.1250 (*NHI* II 1986, 241). It manifested itself initially only here and there, as energetic Gaelic leaders arose and/or opportunities developed such as those provided by Anglo-Norman absenteeism, but it became particularly troublesome from the 1270s in Connacht and Wicklow. From the latter it was to become a running sore for the heavily colonised corridor formed by the Liffey and Barrow valleys between Dublin and Waterford, and for the city of Dublin itself, the very centre of the colony (Lydon 1972, 163).

The gathering clouds produced by these and related problems, for what was now, probably, a generally well-developed colony, can be seen in the preambles to many of the fourteenth century murage grants. From 1310 at the latest, it appears that the concepts of refuge and of a minimum security in emergencies gave way to specific instructions about constructing a 'stone wall' for many more towns, which suggest a 'holding' brief instead. By mid-century the nature of the danger was spelt out in the grants—being 'situated in the march' and subject to attack by 'Irish rebels and other enemies', meaning usually degenerate Anglo-Normans. The Adare grants of 1310 and 1376 illustrate this development, as do the Cashel of 1319 and Caherconlish of 1358, or Ardee's one acquired in 1376. Lydon (*NHI* II 1986, 240) notes the appearance in documents of 'March' meaning new frontier or disputed land, as early as 1215, first of all in connection with advancing colonisation in the Waterford and Cork areas. Later it had connotations of contraction, or a re-appearance of 'March' conditions which often became permanent. Other terms used frequently were 'Land of Peace', from 1248, and 'Land of War', from 1272, both of which indicate a general turn for the worst.

There are, therefore, at least two ways of viewing this second phase of town walling in the medieval lordship. Firstly, it can be regarded as an almost inevitable development within the growing urban settlement system, whereby second-order towns—caput centres or ports associated with major lands grants—sought to come up to the standard of the king's towns, which had been the main feature of Phase I. In this, one magnate might have been tempted to copy another so that a snow-balling reaction might have occurred. Certainly the local lord was mentioned in the murage charters to Youghal granted in 1275, Tralee, Mallow and Ard in 1286 and Trim in 1289, but not, apparently, in those to Fethard, 1291, or Castledermot, 1295. Yet, pride alone would hardly have been a sufficient motive except in isolated cases. Lydon (1972, 97) has suggested that the prosperity of this period is illustrated by much building activity, in particular that of town walls, but the connection may have been such a close one as to be difficult to separate in this way. A secure market centre would encourage trade, indeed in troubled times it might be essential for its continuance, but there may well have been a delicate balance to be struck, at least at this early stage, between enhanced security and market profits. Local trade was probably directed to the lord's market town anyway, and so had to pay whatever tolls were imposed, but foreign trade, either local produce acquired for export or imported goods, both essential and luxury, brought to the market from abroad, would not be so easily directed. The finance for town walling was derived largely from market tolls at this time and so the extra tolls charged under murage charters would have tended to lose particular towns an economic advantage that they might have already enjoyed over existing walled towns then operating such grants, and over other towns without walls. Moreover, the towns listed above were allowed to take tolls for periods of seven years each, which was generally longer than those of contemporary grants to Dublin, Drogheda or Waterford. The range of goods listed in these charters as liable to murage tolls was uniformly wide and often very similar, whether the place involved was the capital or a new settlement in the depths of rural Cork, such as Mallow. This may suggest a uniformly high level of economic activity, indeed a general level of affluence, but it may also indicate that a mere formula was being employed without reference to the nature of the trade involved at any particular centre.

However, while the danger of markets being by-passed might have been a real one in the early stages of urban development in Ireland, as security worsened generally it would have lost its force. In addition, by then a particular market centre might have built up a sufficiently firm trading structure that could survive the imposition of new tolls. To that extent the building of town walls may have reflected a level of prosperity but only in so far as it also reflected fear for the future of that prosperity. This leads to the second view of renewed town-wall building—that it was symptomatic of a greater need for security as lawlessness, and occasionally out-right rebellion, became a feature of life. The details of this are well known and the under-lying causes have been noted above. The murage evidence too points explicitly to the security factor, as does the New Ross poem. While some towns like New Ross may have got on with the job, unaided by the Crown at least initially, and irrespective of the local lord, then absentee there, the growing number of murage charters point to Crown approval. They were all issued, directly by the king or indirectly by his justiciar, apparently in response to local application in the first place by the town or the lord, but possibly only if they fitted into a wider strategic plan. The basis for this view is the frequent emphasis in the preambles to the charters on the security of the area as well as that of the town itself. The growing number of walled towns in late thirteenth and early fourteenth century Ireland and their areal distribution must, therefore, largely reflect the security situation. Phase II can be seen in effect as a fleshing out of the earlier, rather bare-bones type of policy by the addition of more coastal bridge-heads and especially their interior counterparts on the extensive navigable river systems of Leinster, Munster and east Connacht. As the map (5.c) shows the towns involved lay in a broad sweep from south-east Ulster to the plains of east Galway.

Over twenty towns probably received murage for the first time in the period 1260–1310. This implies an average rate of about one new town starting to build its town wall every two years. Put another way, it may have produced a trebling of the existing number of walled towns, some of whose origins went back centuries. A further ten towns were added during 1310–50 when the rate of activity slackened somewhat. A concentration in south Leinster and east Munster is clear, particularly in the major river valleys which linked those areas to the southern seas or to Dublin. Apart from Dundalk on the east coast (almost as far from Drogheda as the latter was from Dublin), the only towns involved there were the main caput centres, Downpatrick in Ulster and Trim in Eastmeath. Trim provided an interior base for the rich and early settled east central lowland, with river access to other inland towns on the extensive Boyne system and to the sea at Drogheda. Indeed, the later murage grant of 1393, in describing Trim as a place 'where all the *fideles* of county Meath congregate', summed up its centrality very well and its need to be a walled town. By 1260 the Ulster colony was shrinking fast and little is known about Downpatrick apart from a reference for this period to a grant of the fee-farm rent, worth only £5. It was the result of a letter from the mayor and the head of a local priory recounting how the community and the county had helped in the recent Battle of Down against the resurgent O'Neills. No murage references are known for this period for the northern Ulster port town of Carrick-fergus, where there was a royal castle, or the lesser settlement of Coleraine, which later disappeared virtually completely from the records. However, Carlingford, the ferry port for Ulster and also the site of a royal castle, did receive a grant in 1326.

In the Dublin area three minor settlements are known to have received murage grants at this time—Crumlin, Tallaght and Newcastle Mackinegan (all list B). The last two were both on the edges of the Dublin/Wicklow mountain mass and so their grants were clearly related to the defensive problems ensconced within its glens; Tallaght belonged to the archbishop and Newcastle had a royal castle. Crumlin's grant of 1337 was a little later than the others (1310 and 1303 respectively). It seems curious because the settlement was only 5km from Dublin but it, too, was a royal manor. Other isolated cases were Dunmore (list B), Athenry and Galway in the east Connacht lowland, all relatively new settlements following the colonisation of the area post-1237. The 'work of masons and the burning of lime', listed in the murage account for Dunmore, might have been deflected there to work on the lord's castle but equally it is possible that the foundations of a stone town wall were started then. A considerable amount of wall may have been built at any such obscure sites, which was later overwhelmed or allowed to decay away leaving no trace on the ground or in the later records. For a short while these may indeed have been 'walled towns'. The same may have been true of the three fitzMaurice towns, two of which, Tralee and Ardfert (list B), were close together in the coastal lowland of north Kerry. Nothing is known of the medieval murage history of Dingle, the main medieval Kerry port. Kinsale, in a similarly rather isolated position west of Cork, did receive murage late in this phase, in 1333, for the repair of its walls but it is not known when they were first built.

The majority of towns featuring in phase II were in the south-central area, in the short river valleys focussed on the Shannon estuary and the much longer, and more extensive, systems draining towards the south coast between Cork and Waterford. There were prominent towns, such as Kilmallock, Cashel, Clonmel and Castledermot, and lesser ones, such as Leighlin, Buttevant, Emly and Tipperary. Two pairs were located very close together and they each also had substantial castles—Mora and Mallow, Croom and Adare (all list B, except the last). The distribution pattern can be seen as one composed of a series of staging-posts on the routes from the phase I walled towns—Cork to Limerick via Mora, Mallow, Buttevant, Kilmallock, Croom and Adare; Limerick via the last three, or more directly via Emly and Tipperary, to Cashel and from there either south via Clonmel to Waterford, or northeast via Fethard and Kilkenny to pick up the Waterford/ Dublin route, which went via Leighlin and Castledermot. Kilkenny, like Trim a major caput centre, could have acted as a focus for its area, with Thomastown equidistant between it and New Ross, its port on the navigable River Nore. These towns give phase II its strong interior bias. Most are on major rivers, like Leighlin at a crossing point on the Barrow, Clonmel and Carrick on the Suir and Mallow on the Blackwater. With a couple of exceptions, the rest are on branch streams which in medieval times linked them into the major navigable river systems. Examples of these are Buttevant, from which a stream fed into the Blackwater, and Fethard and Tipperary, from which streams led to the Suir. Even the exceptions, Cashel and Castledermot, are within 10km of the nearest major river and thus generally within their valleys.

This distribution pattern would, of course, have been more marked if towns such as Carlow and Naas were in fact walled much earlier than their murage evidence suggests. Leaving aside the areas of west Connacht and west Ulster, which were not colonised to any extent except in the Sligo lowland between them, there were still a few areas within the lordship which apparently lacked walled towns and so must be considered. The bog lands around Athlone and the mountainous peninsulas of the south-west were extra-colonial to all intents and purposes, in the way that Wicklow and other isolated areas of highground were too. They may have been used by the colonists for hunting and summer grazing, or wood and peat cutting, but they were not settled with villages and farms to any considerable extent. Frame (1981, 71–2) emphasises the new settlers' interest in 'profitable' land which meant generally that capable of arable farming. Thus only areas below 120m OD, excluding bogland, were actually colonised. Other writers, such as McNeill (1980, 83) with reference to east Ulster and Orpen (1911, 261) more generally, opt for a 500 foot (150m) limit and Lydon (1972, 150) notes the prevalence of Irish settlement above 600 feet (180m). This leaves the lowlands of Clare focussing onto the Shannon estuary, the Sligo and north Shannon lowland and the south-east corner of concern for this study.

In fact, the south-east corner, an area early and heavily settled by colonists, was to some extent encircled by walled towns and contained Wexford as a walled bridge-head. From there the River Slaney could be used to supply it via Ferns, a pre-Anglo-Norman focus with a later castle but not known to have been walled. There was also New Ross to its western side; Clonmines to the south, a port then but later silted up and a little known walled town; and to the north the old Hiberno-Norse port of Arklow, about the defences of which even less is known. As today, this area had the easiest access to England and its long coastline meant that access to Dublin via the sea was also relatively easy. Consequently, it was exceptional for a number of reasons. Clare, in contrast, was one of the last areas settled from Limerick. Bunratty at its centre was a port and large borough at least in the late thirteenth century and it may have been walled (list B app.). Otherwise Limerick was the nearest walled town to that area. The north-west Leinster lowlands around the upper Shannon were really an extension of the Meath-Dublin plains and were settled earlier than Clare. However, the quality of the land falls westwards and northwards generally in Ireland, and this area was also always prey to attacks from both West Connacht and West Ulster. To that extent it would seem a prime area for a refuge town, as Athlone was further south, but there is no evidence that Longford or Sligo were walled in the Middle Ages. It is not impossible, especially for Sligo which is known to have had the basic ingredients of a medieval town, including the castle of a prominent lord and a friary. However, the intensity of settlement generally may have been slight there and may have been composed mostly of dispersed castles and associated hamlets.

The accumulated murage pattern shows a marked strengthening in the period 1275 to 1330. This results from very active murage at Dublin, in fact almost continuous, and moderately active murage at Waterford, Drogheda (both towns), Kilkenny and Cork. At Limerick only the walling of the Irishtown suburb is known for certain. This was exactly contemporary with what was probably initial walling at Adare, Croom and Emly in the hinterland, and additional measures at Kilmallock. The absence of murage grants post-1250 lasted apparently much longer at Limerick than it did at the other three main towns, and seems to have recurred post-1320. It may reinforce the 'loss of records' theory, although a long spell without murage is known to have existed at Waterford earlier. It could, of course, also indicate the presence of well-built walls that did not need attention. The flurry of activity known to have occurred at the Dublin and Drogheda walls during and after the Bruce emergency might be expected to show up elsewhere, especially in the area over which the Bruce forces rampaged, but it does not do so to any noticeable extent.

For those towns probably walled initially in phase II there is evidence of a repeat of murage funding at only eight—Trim, Kilkenny, Clonmel, Fethard, Cashel, Tipperary, Kilmallock and possibly Thomastown. Three others, Dundalk, Adare and Buttevant, received murage later in the fourteenth century but for thirteen, or more than half, no further records of murage are known. These include Castledermot, where town walls survive in part today and at which the parliament often met in the late fourteenth century, Crumlin and the old cathedral centres of Emly and Ardfert. The last, along with Tralee and Mallow, may be seen as an attempt by an energetic lord to enhance his settlements and area generally. Thomas fitzMaurice had acquired Mallow only in 1282 and so the murage of 1286, covering the three towns, may be a case of ambition although it could equally have been the only way in which such settlements, particularly the two in Kerry, could have hoped to survive in the march conditions then developing. In fact, the 1333 grant to Kinsale emphasised how that town was 'surrounded by Irish enemies and English rebels'. This was increasingly the experience of many Irish towns, whether walled or not, as the tide turned for the lordship.

PHASE III, 1350–1485, MAP 5.d.   The beginning of Phase III is marked by an apparent resumption of murage grants to established walled towns, slowly at first but gathering pace and occurring throughout the lordship in time, and a lessening in the rate of creation of new walled towns. The latter was inevitable and may

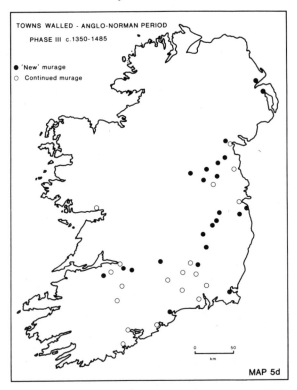

TOWNS WALLED - ANGLO-NORMAN PERIOD

PHASE III c.1350-1485

● 'New' murage
○ Continued murage

MAP 5d

have been more marked than the data suggest, if the earlier grants for some towns have been lost. In fact, semi-continuous murage, already a feature at Dublin, became apparently more widespread at major towns. To some extent, again, this may be due to the better preservation of records but also it resulted from the lengthening of the duration of grants. Only two granted in Phase II, to Clonmel in 1298 and Tipperary in 1300, reached double figures being for ten years each but, post-1350, charters below ten years were exceptional and above twenty years common. Kilkenny provides a good example for there was apparently a long interval between its early and late fourteenth century grants. Then they appear to have gathered momentum by ever more rapid re-issuing. The 1375 was granted for seven years (i.e. up to 1382), but it was reissued in 1381 for twenty years and again in 1394 for another 20 years (CPI 70, 79–80, 89). In the fifteenth century, especially, some apparent re-issuing may have resulted from the confirmation of charters following each of the many changes in the succession to the English Crown, but the effect was essentially the same, to re-affirm the right to take tolls for murage. The Galway charter of 1396 and Ardee's of 1437 appear to have been granted *in perpetuity,* which to some extent was the *de facto* situation at about twelve other towns already.

The steady granting of murage to Irish towns on an increased level in the century following 1375 is very striking. More varied measures increasingly joined murage charters at this time—grants of the cocket and local sources of revenue such as that of salmon weirs at Galway and Limerick; taxes on the local area sometimes also involving labour services, as at Dundalk in 1458; the use of fines for offences with regard to murage and possibly other matters; and the remission of the fee-farm rent. This last was actually a return to a pre-1220 device and similar trends became common in England and Wales too. Many of the changes can be seen in Ireland as resulting largely from a downturn in the economy. This would have reduced the returns for murage tolls at a time when both the structures were ageing and the need for them was growing.

Looking at the towns involved (fig. 5.3) there seem to be three groups, or four, if those which first appeared in phase II but fail to recur are included. They range from those receiving (a) semi-permanent or (b) frequent murage, to those that were only (c) occasional or (d) nil recipients. The first two groups consist of about ten each and could be regarded as an inner and an outer group. In fact they should possibly be considered together because the differences between semi-permanent and frequent murage funding may well be more apparent than real. However, separating them helps to emphasise the dominance of two distinct distribution patterns. Firstly, there was a wide scatter of prominent towns and, secondly, there was a concentration for the first time in eastern Ireland. This latter consisted of, in addition to Dublin and Drogheda, not only Dundalk and Trim, both walled earlier, but also Ardee, Athboy and Naas. Indeed, over a third of the twenty or so towns receiving frequent murage grants were located in the area between Dublin and Dundalk which, later in the fifteenth century, became known as the Pale. This was itself demarcated on the west by a defensive double-ditch and defended by many individual new castles or tower-houses in rural areas. Therefore, concern for the defence of the eastern heartland, the largest area of coastal lowland, was, perhaps, the most striking new feature of phase III. It illustrates most clearly the serious contraction of the colony, especially in the lowlands of central and north-central Ireland, which exposed increasingly to attack areas that had previously been more or less immune. But, attention to the Pale towns may be distorted to some extent by the relatively good preservation of records belonging to the Irish Parliament, which also now more often met close to Dublin and so was particularly concerned with this area.

Beyond this inner group, and so more widespread areally, a number of prominent towns continued to figure notably as before—Waterford, Kilkenny, Youghal, Galway and, apparently on a lesser scale but possibly not so, Limerick and Cork. These were all probably acting now more as major regional centres in the modern sense, that is as alternative foci to Dublin, with which access was increasingly difficult except by sea. This was due especially to attacks on the Barrow corridor from both east and west, that is from the Wicklow mountains and the bog areas of central Ireland. These walled towns became again to some extent refuges in the original sense, especially if other walled towns in their valley or coastal lowland hinterlands were not receiving murage actively and so were becoming weaker. Examples of this could be the walls of Galway being upgraded or kept in repair while those of Athenry and Dunmore were left un-touched, and the Limerick circuits similarly as opposed to those of Croom and Adare. Kilmallock remained apparently an alternative focus in the latter area, receiving occasional murage grants. The comparative fragility of the Galway area is particularly striking, both in terms of its isolated location and the absence of many other walled towns in its hinterland. Certainly, Athenry remained a walled town, and indeed may not have received aid because it did not require it, but it was the only known alternative to Galway. Other inland settlements did survive, including Loughrea known to have been walled in Tudor times but the evidence points generally to contractions in the west of the lordship. By contrast, in the south-east, in the Suir and Nore valleys leading to Waterford Harbour, Clonmel, New Ross and Fethard received quite frequent murage grants and Thomastown possibly only occasional ones.

Of those already mentioned, three of the Pale towns were apparently 'new' on the murage scene—Naas, Ardee and Athboy. Other places in that area which also may have appeared now for the first time were Fore, where the date of murage is uncertain; Navan, where murage came rather late, from the 1460s; Siddan and Roche. The settlement status of the last two may have been more modest. They feature only once in the murage records and so are on list B. Little is known of the Naas and Athboy walls beyond the fifteenth century murage records, but there is map evidence or material remains at Ardee and Navan. How many were actually receiving murage for the first time, indicating that their town walls were new, it is impossible to judge, either for the Pale or for other areas in south-central Ireland. The 1375 grant to Ardee, apparently its first, is also the only reference to the lesser manorial settlement of (Castle)Roche. This would seem to suggest that the grant was for repair and or extension at Ardee, rather than the initiation of town walling there, if Roche had a murage grant earlier. The Ardee grant was contemporary with one for New Ross, where the walls are known to have long pre-dated it. Perhaps, even more in this last phase apparently initial grants to established towns should be read merely as evidence of attention, for both New Ross and Ardee received fairly constant grants for some time after 1375. There is also only one murage reference known from this period for Wexford, where Hiberno-Norse walls had probably been developed by the first Anglo-Normans and frequently repaired. Stylistic evidence suggests so, but there is no known link with this single medieval murage record.

A couple of towns, Gowran near Kilkenny and Garth (list B) on the Tipperary/Limerick border, appear to figure fairly prominently by virtue of particularly long single grants, of forty and sixty years respectively. Others, like Carrickfergus, Carlow, Athy, Wexford and Dungarvan appear very fleetingly because the lengths of their grants are unknown. They, too, may have been long-lived, especially as they date from the fifteenth century when long grants were common. Still others had apparently only occasional renewal grants, for example Kinsale, Callan and Carrick-on-Suir.

Coastal sites figured again as they had in phase I and much more strongly than they did in phase II. They stretched from Carrickfergus southwards via Dungarvan to Galway, with the exception of the south-west corner. Attention in the Cork area was it seems entirely concentrated along the coast. Ports, which are known to have existed but did not apparently feature as recipients of murage grants, were those of north Kerry, Sligo and the north and south-east coasts of Ulster. In the last area Newtown Blathewyc (list B), presumably at the head of Strangford Lough, did receive a murage grant but the result is not known. Also apparently new to receiving murage was Dalkey, the out-port of Dublin, but all the others involved were long-established ports, most also long-walled. The central interior remained a largely negative area. There are no references for murage in phase III, as there were none in phase II, to sites in the Shannon lowlands above Limerick, including the vital crossing at Athlone. All attention there may have been concentrated on the royal castle and the settlement may have suffered from being under the control of many, often short-term and usually very pre-occupied, justiciars. To the south the main areas of attention, as in phase II, were the three major valleys focussed on Waterford Harbour and the south bank of the Shannon estuary. Effectively, this may have increased by about 50% the number of walled towns in the Limerick area, from five to eight, but only added marginally to the much larger concentration in the Waterford-based valley system, from thirteen to fifteen. But, as indicated earlier, there is only evidence that half the existing walled towns in the Limerick area received additional grants in phase III and of these, just two, Limerick and Kilmallock, did so at all frequently. In the Barrow/ Nore/Suir area a comparable situation may have existed—about half the walled towns there are known to have received additional grants but nearer a third did so frequently. In summary, phase III was apparently characterised by a continuation of frequent murage to major regional centres and more occasional murage to other important towns. In addition, a small number of new walled towns were apparently added to the system while others seem to have been forgotten. In the Kilkenny area these trends could be illustrated by Kilkenny, Thomastown, Gowran and Leighlin respectively.

The pattern generally for phase III does not look, therefore, like a reinforcing of the route-based aspect apparent in phase II, but more a regionalisation. This produced strengthened, but more restricted and so isolated, areas such as the Limerick lowlands, the Waterford valleys, the Liffey valley flanking the Dublin mountains and the northern Pale, especially in the Boyne valley and north of it. Phase II, consequently, illustrates quite well the concept that the period was characterised by the development of many unstable frontiers, producing new or reviving former marchlands as the colony faltered. Through them movement would often have been hazardous and from them attacks on towns could be expected from time to time. Lydon (1967) called this the 'frontier problem'. It has been taken up by a number of writers including Duffy (1982–3) and Frame (1982, 382), who described the late medieval lordship as a 'land of numerous frontiers'. Phase III in turn seems to point quite graphically to the change which the continuation of this instability brought—the development of clear regions based on a number of strong centres. This was, perhaps, an inevitable process but also a necessary one in terms of the use of scarce resources. It suggests that some towns may well have been 'swallowed up' or overwhelmed by expanding Gaelic areas, while others survived 'safe behind strong walls' as 'little islands in a Gaelic sea' (Lydon 1967, 15). In addition, Frame (1981, VIII, 71), in pointing to the 'highly regionalised' nature of medieval Ireland, emphasised that the geography of the island played a strong contributing part. This, too, is clear from the trends apparent in the development of walled towns.

Although once again the walled town was seen as a refuge for its area, the areas concerned being the richest in the island, less extensive areas of good lowland remained apparently unaffected. The most notable of these was the area of the Pale between the Liffey and Boyne. This could, of course, be defended easily from either Dublin and Naas or Drogheda and Trim. Besides, it was protected by the other defensive measures of the Pale and it was probably by now the most heavily settled area of the colony. Lowland south-east Wexford, heavily settled too originally was, as before, capable of being defended by New Ross and Wexford, and possibly Clonmines. Nonetheless, it was increasingly prey to attack from the mountains to the north, as was New Ross itself. Apart from one grant to Buttevant in 1375, the Blackwater valley seems to have been ignored, except its port of Youghal, and thus the land link with Cork looks very tenuous. The increasing number of murage measures based on the hinterland of a town, for example those for Thomastown and Fethard in 1449 and Naas in 1467–8, also points to the refuge role being dominant. It may, at the same time, indicate a low level of return on murage tolls due to the general lawlessness and consequently reduced economic life of the colony. Yet, there were times in the fifteenth century in particular when there was something of an economic revival. This was largely urban based, as the evidence of its fine architectural relics, both tower-houses and churches, shows (Quinn, *NHI* 1986 II 597). It is not clear to what extent this may have involved attention to town walls, but investigation leading to more precise dating of surviving structures might be revealing in this respect.

In a vain attempt earlier to halt the incipient fragmentation of the lordship, the Exchequer was moved from Dublin to Carlow because it was easier for access from the south. The only reference to murage for Carlow is related to this episode, 1361–94. Subsequently, the Barrow routeway from Dublin to Waterford was maintained, but only just, by a variety of additional means, including the paying of tribute to the Irish of Wicklow. This also happened in the north Pale area as a further defence for the most vulnerable walled town there, Dundalk. The role of walled towns generally may well have been crucial at this time. Few specific examples can be cited but it may be significant that the ecclesiastical centre of Irishtown at Kilkenny was probably walled, and certainly received murage, in the late fourteenth century, although it was located right beside the strongly walled Hightown. Unless both were very densely populated, as they may have been, it seems curious that the large Hightown could not have provided refuge for the small Irishtown in an emergency, despite their different administrations. On the other hand, this may have been a case of ambition or competition leading to the creation of town walls. Similarly, such factors may always have been instrumental at the twin, but likewise independent, towns of Drogheda on the Louth and Meath sides. Equally, if a settlement was to survive at this stage it may have needed town walls, or some less elaborate defence which would hold off an attack for a sufficient time to allow retreat to the main walled town of the area.

The fifteenth century parliamentary papers in particular indicate the extent of the danger to settlements generally and the varied response. In 1458 it was stated that villages and towns were 'being laid waste at night for want of enclosure, barring or trenching' (*SR* II 501). The problem seemed to be that there was a conflict between rights of passage along a highway and the defence of a settlement astride it. The barring referred to was presumably the closing of the main street by means of a gate. This would impede traffic, especially if the settlement was also 'enclosed', presumably with a fence and/or entrenched by a ditch without an extra-mural road. A specific instance cited was the town of Louth (list B), the original centre of the Crown lands in the county. It was claimed that 'if it were defensible and repaired it would cause all the county to be repaired and built, and to be in more quiet peace from the Irish'. Yet, the method recommended was just 'entrenching' by the labour of two men from each inhabited ploughland for two days a year during two years, or else a fine of four pence a day. Louth was in a rather exposed position, almost half way between Ardee and Dundalk on a westerly route, but there is no mention of it having a town wall. Considerably later, in 1475–6, Siddan (list B), a comparably situated Meath settlement and an equally old one in terms of the original Anglo-Norman colonisation, was stated to be 'not walled or enclosed, and the inhabitants not able to wall or enclose'. It did receive permission to gather tolls for that purpose, with the fines for impeding collection to go in equal parts to the Crown and to the town's murage fund. It is not known if these tolls resulted in a town wall, but the contrast with Louth seems to suggest a certain inconsistency in the approach to the defence of lower order settlements generally. Similarly diverse measures were suggested at this time for small settlements in the area south-west of Dublin, for example Kilcullen, Calverstown and Saggart (all list B or app.).

New settlement projects were also being contemplated at the end of the medieval period, perhaps also as a defensive measure. In 1450 permission was granted to Sir Edward Mulso 'to make a town called Mulsoecourt' (list B) in the lordship of Fercullen, the Powerscourt area of Dublin/Wicklow border on the mountain edge. It was described as 'in the frontiers of the Marches, a key and protection for the whole of counties Dublin and Kildare'. It was to have a portreeve and burgesses, a market and fair, and 'customs of all goods for sale in the said town, as does the Mayor of Dublin, for murage and pavage'. No accounting to the Crown was required and there was a ten-year exemption from Crown subsidies. At the same time, a more general request was lodged by the 'commons of County Kildare' to 'anyone who would build towns in the wasted borders' of the county, with the promise of freedom from customs for six years (*SR* II 240). The spread of urban settlement was apparently making a comeback in the life of the colony. To some extent this may have been based on a general desire to increase the numbers of 'reliable' colonists because the thicker settlements of all sorts were on the ground the less susceptible they would be to attack in the first place, and the better able they would be to aid each other. But it also possibly illustrates just how thinly stretched the colony had become through depopulation due to plague, war and emigration, if even such limited recolonisation was needed on the edges of its heartland—the Pale.

TUDOR 1485–1603: MAP 5.e

Mulsoecourt may be seen as the forerunner of a much more extensive recolonisation policy in which a very active role was envisaged for walled towns, if not always achieved. In the generally more stable conditions of Henry VIII's reign it was possible once again to take a more studied view of Ireland rather than simply to react to events. Various remedies were mooted which varied from all-out military reconquest, proposed in 1520, to local small-scale measures such as the earl of Ossory being required in 1553 to get his 'loyal' people to place their heirs in borough towns, where they would learn English etc. (*SP Hen* VIII 1520 XV; 1533 LXIV). Recolonisation provided, therefore, a policy mid-way between outright reconquest or total withdrawal, the former expensive and the latter unthinkable. It was one that arose naturally from the desire to increase the safety of the surviving colonised areas, which were in many places by then weak and much fragmented. Initially, it involved three main objectives but they can be seen as essential to a longer term aim, that of eradicating the Irish 'problem', an aim that could only be achieved by bringing all parts of the island into a stable

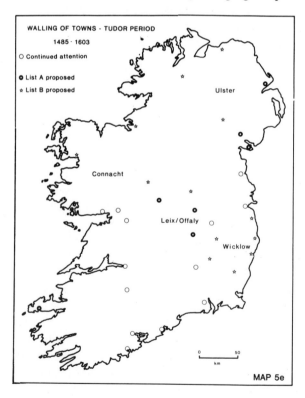

MAP 5e

relationship with the Crown. The first was to reclaim areas of lowland only tentatively held, if that, in south-east Ulster and around Sligo and Athlone. The second was to make safe the Barrow routeway which provided the best land link between the southern areas and Dublin, and the third was to eradicate the ever present danger to Dublin from the south. The problem underlying the last two aims lay essentially in the one area, the fastnesses of the Wicklow mountains. Thus, in 1536 it was proposed 'to plant Wicklow with eighty English and the rest from the Pale and to wall the town' (fig. 5.4). Similar efforts were to be made at Arklow, a 'good haven'; at 'the strong castle of Ferns', at Leighlin, and at Timolin in Co. Kildare (*SP Hen* VIII 1536, 323–7). In addition, a walled town was to be 'built and inhabited in the midst of the Fasagh of Bentree'. This was a revival of the Mulsoecourt project but as one set further east, possibly at Fassaroe near Bray. There is no firm evidence that early medieval enclosures were available for re-development at any of these sites, including Arklow and Wicklow, the Hiberno-Norse/Anglo-Norman ports. The implication in each case is that new town walls were to be built. Leighlin had figured once in the medieval murage records and so this new project may confirm that a town wall was not built then or had virtually disappeared.

As with the medieval evidence, the terminology can be taken at face value or interpreted in the light of other knowledge, sometimes with different results. It was also recommended in the 1536 document, for example, that the castle of Carlingford should be 'repaired' and the town 'walled' and inhabited. But, Carlingford is known to have received a murage grant in 1326 for six years and another in 1492. The surviving but now rather degraded town wall may, therefore, date from the fourteenth and/or sixteenth century. With Carrickfergus 'repair' is again the term used for the castle but 're-edify' for the walls. This process is known not to have been completed in stone even by the end of the century, when it was described as walled 'partly with stone and partly with sods'. Yet, in 1536 Carrickfergus was apparently considered 'walled' and Carlingford not. Armagh, an ecclesiastical centre from Celtic times, appears as a new base in Ulster. It also was 'to be walled', as was Sligo, possibly for the first time although it had an Anglo-Norman castle, and was prominent for a while in the fourteenth century as part of the extensive earldom of Ulster. For Athlone the stated object was 'to win the castle and town, repair and inhabit'. The town wall, for which finance was provided by the Crown in 1251, was not mentioned. Likewise, there are no references to town walls in extensions to this scheme envisaged for County Clare or the area around the castle and town of Nenagh. In all, a total of ten walled towns, new or revived, were projected, two-thirds of which were associated with the Dublin/Wicklow/Carlow areas, the southern approaches to the capital.

Nothing further is known of the 1536 proposals except the planting of garrisons, generally in existing castles at some of the sites mentioned. The Sligo proposal was revived and extended to other Connacht towns in 1579 (*CPCR* 18–21). Probably at towns such as Carrickfergus and Carlingford, where there were medieval walls, they were strengthened although even at them resources may have been concentrated chiefly on the castles. By the middle of the century,

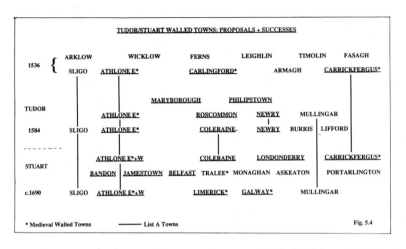

Fig. 5.4

attention was turning to the central area of Leix/Offaly which had long been 'beyond bounds' as far as the colony was concerned. Yet, for Maryborough and Philipstown, which were created as the shire towns and principal market and garrison centres, little is known of the town walls. A stone fort was built at each as a first stage, *c*.1550, and these survive to varying degrees. A map for Maryborough dated *c*.1560 shows the fort, the developing town and the surrounding wall, for which murage was provided at least by the end of the century, specifically for a stone structure with a fosse. Interestingly, the permission to build the wall stated that it was intended for 'the better defence of (the town) and of the fort'. This illustrates clearly the possible role of the walled town as an outer, additional defence for the garrison centre, reinforcing it both by its wall and its resident population. Such a role was suggested by the proximity of medieval town walls to large castles, such as those at Dungarvan, Carlingford and Carrickfergus, all of which were also the sites of royal castles, the medieval equivalents of these forts. Some documents dated to 1570–1 suggest that the town wall and fosse existed by then at Philipstown but, again, this may only have been on paper and progress may have been as slow as at Maryborough. Unfortunately no map is known for Philipstown and so comparison between the design of the walls intended for the two new walled towns is not possible.

In fact, the beginnings of a grand plan which can be seen in the 1536 project, failed to develop, although it reappeared in very similar form half a century later (fig. 5.4). In between, two trends can be recognised, the first involving limited and isolated re-colonisation projects such as Leix/Offaly and the second being the continuation of murage aid to many of the existing walled towns. The first trend also comprised private schemes for new towns or the re-development of an existing, and sometimes already walled, town. The individuals concerned were often Crown officials, military or civilian, serving in the area. One example was the proposed re-development of County Roscommon from 1578, by Sir Nicholas Malbie, who served in that area as a soldier and later as Lord President of Connaught. This project included the walling of the towns of Roscommon and

Athlone, either of which may already have had town walls, especially Athlone. The plan for Roscommon which resulted is dated *c*.1581 and is similar in style to the *c*.1560 for Maryborough, but apparently on a more ambitious scale. Nothing more is known of this wall, just as at the end of the thirteenth century there is a single reference to the 'north gate of the town', which may or may not mean that there was a medieval wall. Private and state projects met at Roscommon because it was the site of a major medieval royal castle beside which the new walled town was planned. It continued to be a garrison centre into modern times and so maybe, like Wicklow and other centres, this was where Tudor attention actually materialised on the ground. Also in Connaught, in 1580 a walled town was projected for Burris in County Mayo (list B) where there had been an early medieval borough and, later, a friary. Nothing seems to have come of this scheme but it is interesting in so far as it illustrates the development of a total island concept underlying apparently unconnected projects. This area had been touched only very lightly by the medieval colonisation, and so it had for long been both beyond the control of the Dublin Government and a source from which raids could be mounted on East Connacht and even beyond the Shannon. Another example, first suggested by Sir Nicholas Bagenal, Marshall of the English forces in Ireland, in 1557 and revived in 1579, was the walling of Newry. He already held the medieval walled town of Carlingford and he saw the lack of walls at his new town as breeding 'danger to his whole country'. This may be seen as a repeat of the medieval concept of 'tending to the security' of the area or the kingdom, stated so often in the murage charters.

The second trend, the continuation of aid to existing walled towns, sometimes involved concentrated attention. Athenry is a good example. Its 're-edifying' in 1576 involved the 'town, abbey, church and walls', and was paid for by a locally based tax. The town, walled probably by the fourteenth century, had been described in 1567 as 'large and well-walled' with 'three hundred good house-holders' once but by then reduced to just twenty. So, to all intents and purposes this too was a re-colonisation. Following a vicious attack by the local 'degenerate English', now barely distinguishable from the 'Irish', it was decided that the medieval walled area was too large and should be cut in half by the construction of a new inner wall. This, perhaps more than anything else, provides a measure for the extent of the thirteenth century colonisation in an area of good lowland close to the sea but far to the west of Dublin. In fact, the lord deputy, Sir Henry Sidney, compared an obviously decayed Athenry quite favourably with Calais, then recently lost and for so long the heavily defended and only surviving English foot-hold in France. At the same time and only a short distance away, Loughrea, originally the chief medieval caput in east Galway, was said to have 'fair walls begun'. It is not known whether this too was a case of the re-development of a medieval town wall but it is not unlikely. Further east but in the same central area, murage was requested for the town of Mullingar in 1583. Its medieval history is obscure beyond early thirteenth century beginnings, but in 1436 murage tolls were collected there for the town wall at Fore, not far away. In 1583 Mullingar was described as 'lying open to all attempts' and the citizens as 'willing to provide carriage for the proposed walling, as well as labour'. The constable of the castle sent the application and so this was another instance of military involvement in town defence. This was particularly characteristic of the Tudor and later periods but may have lain behind some of the medieval requests too.

These developments in the midland area, however unconnected, resulted in the establishment of a broad corridor from Dublin westwards to Galway. Earlier, in 1515, murage had been granted for Kildare, an old monastic and medieval centre situated just beyond the south-western tip of the Pale. This is its only known grant but it did specify a stone wall and a fosse. Within the Pale, Naas continued to receive murage throughout the sixteenth century, as did Dublin. But increasingly, the major regional walled towns, especially those that were ports, seem to have been picked out for attention, not only for continuous murage but also for a new development, the building or proposed building of citadels or forts. One was proposed for Galway in 1583 and the *c.*1590–1 maps of Waterford show fort-type features, large and small, both connected to the town wall and at a short distance from it. Again, at the end of the century when the fear of a Spanish invasion was strong, it was suggested that some gates or corners of certain towns should be further defended by the construction of citadels (*CSPI* 1596, 45). These, it was argued, would only require a few men to guard but could hold many if necessary and so could be used to prevent a revolt in the towns. This was a new fear; the loyalty of the towns, and especially of the walled towns, had never been doubted in medieval times. Indeed, many commentators have remarked on the special importance of towns to the survival of the medieval Irish lordship. Curtis (1938, 415) called them the 'sheet anchor of the state' and Watt the 'economic backbone of the Anglo-Irish' (*NHI* II 1986, 367). However, in the post-Reformation period it became possible to say that 'though most of the inhabitants are of English race, yet are they more Spanish in heart than the country people' (*CSPI* 1596, 45). By 1600 the bishop of Cork was even able to claim that towns were the 'nurses of rebellion for they furnish the traitors with munitions and victuals' (*CSPI* 475). The firm bridge-heads of the medieval lordship had become potential Achilles' heels for the Tudor principality.

The development of forts as additional but related structures was largely the result of two new factors. Firstly, there was the increasing use of semi-permanent professional garrisons in the towns, instead of a guard provided by the inhabitants or by occasional forces raised in the local area. The new garrisons required larger bases than were often available at town gates or towers, especially if there was no substantial castle. In 1589–9 it was proposed to have 4000 men 'in readiness', including some at Waterford, Limerick, Cork and Galway, where engineers were to provide earthen intrenched fortifications (without the said towns)' (*CSPI* 31). In a contemporary 'plot for the establishment of sound and severe government in Munster', made in the context of the plantation there, it was reckoned that 50 horsemen 'may be well maintained by the walled towns' as follows—16 in Waterford; 9 each in Cork and Limerick; 4 in Clonmel and 3 in Youghal; the rest being made up of 2 each in Kilmallock and Kinsale and one each in Fethard, Cashel, Dungarvan, Dingle and Rosse-in-Carbery (*CSPI* 1589, 80). The major regional centres stand out conspicuously in that list. Secondly, changes in warfare, particularly the use of cannon and gun-powder, made the medieval walls both less useful and more vulnerable. An additional, but not a new, factor was the increasing age of the older town walls. These, therefore, required ever more attention and this too must have encouraged alternative developments. Yet, the concept of a walled town was clearly not becoming redundant as the projects listed above show. In fact, it was very much to the fore in that walled towns were now seen often as a category, or as a significant group in any hierarchy of towns. An instance of this has already been quoted in chapter I for 1598 and there are others. In 1575 for example, the rebellious earl of Desmond was said to be 'afraid to come into any walled town', since his kinsman, the earl of Kildare, had been committed to the Tower of London much earlier (*CSPI* 74). Also, in a description of Ireland written in 1581, it was stated, probably for propaganda purposes and so with some exaggeration, that 'Irish men, except in the walled towns', were not 'christians, civil or humane creatures' (*CSPI* 318).

The return to a more obvious strategic plan came in 1584 from Lord Deputy Perrot, following a journey in the north (*CSPI* 533). He recommended 'seven towns to be walled' and, as if it were a magic number, seven bridges and seven castles to be built and garrisoned, at a total cost of £50,000. The towns included some already walled or proposed as such—Athlone, Sligo, Newry and Mayo, presumably Burris; Coleraine, an old medieval settlement at which a town was planned in 1575; Lifford on the River Foyle in west Ulster; and Dingle, the chief medieval port of north Kerry. A murage grant of £300 went to Dingle the following year. It had also been the object of a number of earlier proposals, including a request for £1000 for walling in 1569. Newry and Athlone were parts of private projects which aimed to produce walled towns, as Coleraine was to be in a slightly different context.

Between 1536 and 1584 a fanning out can, therefore, be detected at least at the planning level, involving the development of walled towns even in areas, such as west Ulster and west Connacht, previously barely touched by the Anglo-Norman colonisation. But, as always in Elizabethan Ireland, the costs were looked at carefully. Indeed, this was the chief problem in the delay over the improvement of the Carrickfergus wall. The Queen wrote to her deputy in 1566—'you require money for the fortifying of certain places in and towards Ulster, and expressly of the towns and castle of Carrickfergus and Dundalk . . . a very great sum . . . if there be not in the writing some mistaking . . . £4000 . . . our subjects should of their own charges fortify the towns upon the frontiers, for so they used to do hitherto' (*Sidney SP* 12). Medieval practices still had a distinct, if highly personal, appeal despite the more overtly centralised approach to the defence of the whole island. Again, in 1579, in orders for the 'better government' of Connacht, it was required that, where suitable assize towns did not exist, 'the county at their charges be induced by good persuasion and not by constraint, to circuit a convenient place, apt for a town, with a wall of lime and stone, which place we are content to incorporate with such liberties to draw inhabitants to it'(*CPCR* 18–21; *CCP* 124). The places suggested were Sligo, Burris, Roscommon and Ballinasloe, the latter only being unique to this proposal.

When the O'Neill-led wars against the Crown moved at the very end of the century to the then newly-planted area of Munster, the old role of the walled town as refuge was clearly manifested again. The 'wealthier sort [of English], leaving their castles and dwelling houses . . . made haste into the walled towns, where there was no enemy within ten miles', it was reported (*CSPI* 1598, 140). However, some were superior to others for the bishop of Cork showed little faith in the town walls of his own Rosscarbery, where he had a 'strong stone house'. He decamped to a house near Cork and finally into the walled town of Cork itself, despite his doubts regarding the loyalty of towns quoted earlier. The reason for this variability may have been in part a problem said to have been widespread— that munitions and fortifications had been neglected 'in the late time of peace', that is in the ten years or so following the recolonisation there known as the Munster Plantation (*CSPI* 1598, 140). This, too, must have been a constant problem in the medieval period, as it was also later. Admonitions were issued in 1662, noting that, as almost all the walled towns had murage rights, they should devote them to their proper use. Nonetheless, there may have been an important change since early medieval times because there was clearly an imbalance now between the size of the population and the area of some of the older walled towns, despite the presence of some new settlers. The reduction of Athenry's medieval walled area has been noted earlier but it was not entirely the result of a unique problem. In a survey of the main walled towns for the privy council in 1598 it was said that Youghal was 'weak' because the walls were 'too large' for the inhabitants to defend. Similarly, at Kinsale the walls were described as both 'spacious and decayed' and a garrison was needed there, too, to secure the town. Yet, the walled area planned for Roscommon seems to have been large, the map evidence suggests an area not much smaller than that of medieval Athenry, but it may be misleading in this respect.

The Munster plantation, the first state effort since the Leix/Offaly, was unique in that it did not produce directly any new walled towns. This is hardly surprising in that it was concerned essentially with reviving the agricultural economy of the former fitzGerald lands. In addition, the original medieval colonisation of the rich and extensive but interrupted lowlands of Munster had been substantial. The spread of walled towns there in the Middle Ages beyond the few pre-existing Hiberno-Norse centres was one of the strongest. The surviving walled towns, especially those that were ports, were used as bases for the plantation and strengthened, as noted above for 1589. Bandon was created in the early seventeenth century as a belated new walled town. It is not known what the medieval centres of Mallow, Tralee and Ardfert were like by the late sixteenth century but certainly they are not referred to as walled towns. However, Mallow did figure as a new centre for the administration of the area, and was incorporated in the early seventeenth century. Walls were later proposed for Tralee, following the developments at Bandon. New towns did also appear, usually at old nuclei such as Lismore or nearby Tallow. These, too, were incorporated under James I, as was Newry and the later Ulster foundations.

The Ulster plantation, which followed on from the defeat of O'Neill and his Spanish allies at Kinsale in 1601, was more clearly associated with the creation of walled towns, or re-creation in the case of Carrickfergus. But then, of course, it involved an area hardly penetrated by the Crown since the thirteenth century and only lightly settled then. Even so, while new towns were created throughout the counties of west and central Ulster—the 24 proposed in 1609 was reduced to 18 in 1611, and a slightly different list of 15 was incorporated between 1610 and 1615 (Hunter 1981 Table I)—only two were walled and they had peripheral or coastal locations. They were Londonderry and Coleraine, to which may be added the completion, finally, of the walling of Carrickfergus and the later walling of Belfast. The last two were both located outside the area of the plantation, as was Newry, by then presumably walled. Armagh (list B), proposed as a walled town in 1536, was within the planted area but it remained the archbishop's concern. It grew fast from this time but, apparently, it was not walled although the need for town walls was noted on a number of occasions in the early seventeenth century. The instructions in the plantation articles for Enniskillen required that the 'town should be built in streets and squares in such a manner and form as shall best suit the site and situation, and for defence and decency' (Hunter 1981, 58). Yet here, and elsewhere, only forts were established to the prevailing design and to varying

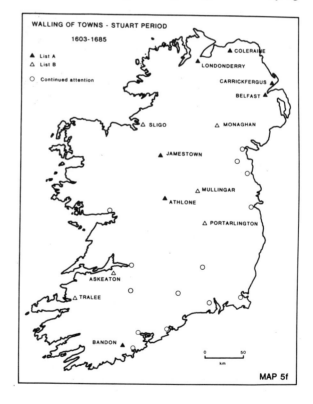

MAP 5f

177

degrees of complexity. A late seventeenth century map survives for Charlemont, County Armagh (list B app.), which seems to depict a walled town surrounding an elaborate central fort on a hill, but little is known of it. In the early seventeenth century the military fort was important and so excluded the town from the plantation proper, although it was one of those proposed and incorporated in 1613. A slightly different case is Lifford (list B), also within the plantation area and one of its designated and incorporated towns. Like nearby Derry, its origins as a fort and a proposed walled town were pre-Plantation, dating from 1607, but there is no evidence that the proposal was put into effect. A final Ulster town, again outside the seventeenth century planted counties but possibly walled at this time, is Monaghan (list B). Its area was planted privately in the late sixteenth century. There is an early seventeenth century map of the town which shows a central square fort surrounded by a square town wall, with streets on two sides that are slightly less geometrically regular. A 1606 description of the settlement at the old and new forts was not flattering but perhaps this map was the blue-print for the town. Again, it is not known if the walled circuit with its four corner and two side bastions and four gates was ever built.

As with the medieval towns, the towns of seventeenth century Ulster seem to have had a variety of enclosure structures. A few clearly were town walls but some were probably closer to informal ditch-and-bank fences. Maps of Londonderry and Omagh (list B app.), referred to in Chapter I, provide examples of the extremes. At Carrickfergus the long evolution of the elaborate seventeenth century stone town wall is well established. Briefly, a partial and simple earthen enclosure was developed into a complete circuit made of stone in at least two major stages. As an exercise in upgrading it may well point to what happened at some medieval towns too. The walls of Coleraine, and later of Belfast, were definitely intermediate in structure but they were also a long way beyond Omagh's enclosure in terms of design and scale. Once more, to distinguish between walled and not-walled towns may be partly artificial but murage funding was a specific right and, faced with a particular danger such as the 1641 rising, positive and often elaborate defensive structures were built at certain towns. Belfast had murage rights from 1612 but the evidence of activity—finishing the rampier and making dams for water to fill the trenches—comes from 1642–5. This may have involved rendering defensive the sort of boundary visible on the Omagh map, an upgrading exercise carried out at last in the face of actual danger. This particular course of development may reflect the fact that Belfast in the seventeenth century grew essentially as an offshoot of Carrickfergus and so, by 1641, it may have been more convenient to wall the new town than retreat to the old. Such a scenario would have been not unlikely in medieval times too, for example in the area around Limerick or Kilkenny. To that extent, specific instances of walls being made or proposed may in some cases be linked to periods of instability following considerable growth of population at individual settlements.

Nonetheless, even at the beginning of the seventeenth century, walled towns were still seen theoretically as having a strategic value. A 'Discourse of Ireland' recommended that the queen should build many walled towns in the districts near the rebels, 'placing a garrison of horse and foot in each . . . loyal subjects could retire into such towns in times of emergency; these towns might be supplied with tradesmen and handicraftsmen from England, which could easily spare them; these towns will not cost much' (*CSPI* 1601, 255). No figures were provided to support these assertions but they tie in with the concept of a strategic framework composed, probably economically, of individually developed walled towns, one of whose functions was to serve the national good.

A new factor on the Irish scene now was the fear of foreign invasion. This had kept the walls of the English south and east coast ports in repair in the Middle Ages, but it does not seem to have been a serious factor in Ireland until the sixteenth century, except for the occasional piratical attack such as that experienced by Waterford in 1377 (*MCI* 582). The building of forts or citadels at the main southern Irish ports from Galway round to Dublin has already been noted for the sixteenth century. It continued after the battle of Kinsale with renewed vigour, despite the fact that these towns all had town walls and sometimes castles too. Such ports were now seen in a very real sense as a defence for the country as a whole, as well as safe refuges for their particular interiors. Londonderry and Coleraine, at the opposite end of Ireland, were created as walled towns especially to allow the interior to be developed, but this also had a strategic value in helping to complete the colonisation of the island. The roles of bridge-head and refuge they both provided in 1641, but Londonderry alone did so in 1690 when the inadequacy of Coleraine's walls was proved all too correct, given the likelihood then of having to face a formidable besieging force.

Two other towns are known to have been walled in the early seventeenth century and only slightly later than those of the Ulster plantation. These were Jamestown, situated close to the south-western limits of Ulster on the upper Shannon, and Bandon, located upstream from Kinsale. Both of these inland towns were created to secure the settlement or recolonisation of their areas. The walling of Tralee was proposed on the same basis and funded similarly. The results there are not known but cannot have been very fruitful because Tralee surrendered following a siege in 1641, after which it was largely destroyed. At Bandon, in particular, the motivation may have involved an element of ambition or at least the desire to build a properly equipped town. However, that area was close to the mountainous parts of west Cork, which were as yet hardly penetrated, and so it was undoubtedly in an exposed position. Rosscarbery (list B) was the only town further west and it had a coastal location. Another inland town founded in the 1620s was Gorey (list B) in the south-east, half-way between Arklow and Ferns both of which were proposed for walling in 1536. It was originally called Newborough and provision was made for a local levy on landholders to finance the walling. This was also the arrangement at both Bandon and Jamestown initially. Ramparts are said to have been erected in 1641 at Gorey but there is no evidence of them on the slightly later Down Survey map of 1655–6. The same type of structure is recorded for Antrim (list B app.)—'dug an eight foot broad ditch and flankers'—and it was probably quite a widespread development but short-lived, except at Belfast. At Tallow (list B app.), one of the newly developed towns of the Munster Plantation and associated with Boyle who developed Bandon, a similar defensive system appeared, again briefly. Smith (1744, 39–40), who wrote the first histories of counties Kerry, Cork and Waterford in the eighteenth century, using original sources and a first-hand knowledge of the area, claimed that Tallow 'was never encompassed by a wall, nor was it a place of any defence; but in the rebellion of 1641, an entrenchment was cast up round it, having four gates'. Clearly, he felt that there had to be an element of permanence about urban defences, irrespective of the nature of the wall, before a town could be regarded as walled. Smith described in detail the town walls of Waterford and Cork and noted that Buttevant had once, and possibly twice, been walled. It would be interesting to have had his assessment of Belfast, or even closer to his base, of Callan, both possibly with less than conventional circuits.

There are maps from the end of the seventeenth century for Sligo and Mullingar (both list B) which show quite elaborate defensive circuits, not unlike those by then erected around the medieval walls at Limerick and, to a lesser extent, at Galway. Both Sligo and Mullingar featured in various sixteenth century schemes, as did Athlone, but it is only at the latter that steady progress is known to have resulted. There, the eastern, and originally possibly medieval, town wall was redeveloped over a long period as a sophisticated stone structure with bastions and gates. The western new wall, created in the mid-seventeenth century, was made basically of earth, but in a similar style. It enclosed the medieval royal castle and effectively provided a large bailey for it.

One final walled town was planned in the 1660s, again for the Leix/Offaly area as were the first of the plantation towns. It was Portarlington (list B), at a fresh site on the upper reaches of the River Barrow but, only a few kilometres from that of the late thirteenth century new town at the castle of Leys. Truly this was a recolonisation but there is no evidence that the walls planned for it, and shown on the 1678 map, were ever built. Property within the town was organised, *c*.1666, in relation to the town wall but nothing further is known of it. In style and as a town it was a natural successor to Londonderry, Bandon and Jamestown but on land surrendered after the 1641 rising which provided the first test of their walls. It was more of a civil undertaking than the later defences of Sligo and Athlone West may have been. The documentary evidence is thought to have been an advertisement for settlers and, perhaps, similar documents circulated in medieval times. At this distance it seems arguable that the continuing need for such urban defences in the seventeenth century so close to home might discourage rather than attract would-be settlers. Indeed, the slow growth of Londonderry and Coleraine, in terms of houses and people, may bear that out. Yet, as an alternative to crossing the Atlantic, this may not have seemed a major problem. Besides, even a few English towns still needed their walls, although Berwick alone received a new and elaborate circuit in Tudor times. In addition, the walls of at least one town probably still survived in most English and Welsh counties, as Speed's 1610 atlas shows, although the proportion of walled towns in England was not high. Certainly the government planners or theorists saw no such problems. In 1630, in the context of small scale plantations proposed again for counties Sligo, Mayo,

Roscommon and North Tipperary, it was stated—'if the King would allow the rents of the plantation to be allocated for a few years to wall the towns [proposed], that side of the kingdom would be much more secured . . . [because] where-soever they had walled towns [in the past] the country about them was kept by those towns, and the English families encouraged to keep upon their lands, having so sure a retreat if they were driven to the worse' (*CSPI* 151). The experience quoted seems to have been that of the later Middle Ages and it was clearly judged a success, however limited the colonisation it maintained may have been.

There were, therefore, trends which were common to both the Tudor and Stuart periods. Some were continuations from the medieval period and some were new but perhaps only apparently so. The granting of murage was a common theme throughout the centuries, but increasingly in the later periods it went apparently to the larger towns, especially to those that were or became major regional centres. In Tudor and Stuart times a few medieval sites were revived as walled settlements or as proposed new walled towns. For some the proposals were made on a number of occasions but apparently without much effect. This, too, may have been a feature of the medieval period and may be the explanation for the existence of murage grants but of no other wall evidence at some sites. The new trends were the strategically-based, almost countrywide schemes and the organised plantations. Yet, both of these may well have operated in medieval times, the former as part of a general Crown aim or even policy, and the latter in the guise of manorial-based development which, in some areas, involved extensive areas belonging to the major land grants.

Figure 5.4 is an attempt to identify the towns involved in Tudor and Stuart times and to judge their respective success rates in terms of town walls actually built. These later records are more satisfactory than the comparable medieval ones, at least as to the period and identity of those involved. There is also a good deal known about the background of the projects, but still many doubts exist as to the outcome at certain sites. However, when a town like Sligo keeps appearing in the lists it must indicate that progress was meagre, if it existed at all in the earlier years. Some towns, especially in south-eastern Ireland, only appear once, for example in the 1536 proposals, but it does seem clear from other evidence that town walling may have been dropped at them in favour of the creation of small garrisons. These were placed often in surviving medieval castles, some of which were strengthened. This too may have been the fate of some medieval 'proposals', the apparent instances of single murage grants. The long-running problems of the Barrow corridor and the back-drop to Dublin were solved, indeed, by these more limited measures in the sixteenth century but, of course, within a framework that contained some walled towns already.

The overtly strategic schemes did not produce the new walled towns proposed, for example Fasagh or Burris, and even the walls intended for existing towns were often built as a result of plantation type schemes, as happened at Newry and Coleraine, and to some extent at Athlone. Comparison of the Tudor and Stuart plantations shows that in fact they were very similar in terms of the small number of towns involved, about six and nine respectively, and the success rate was particularly close—about 60%. The net result was to extend effective colonisation back to the early medieval maximum and even beyond, at least in Ulster. The south-western peninsulas and the west Galway/Mayo areas remained untouched. In fact, no attempts were made at all in Galway and the Mayo project did not materialise. However, a few were built in the central bog lands, the other only faintly colonised section of the landscape. The general effect was to reverse the 'land of numerous frontiers' of the later Middle Ages for a solid area over which the Crown's writ could be more effectively enforced, if still not always without opposition. The remaining many small areas of bog and mountain were thus neutralised by the planting of adjacent garrisons, some in walled towns. The march was reduced and moved west to the most barren areas. With the important exception of central Ulster this was what was almost achieved at the height of the Anglo-Norman colony, *c*.1250, when the settlement may have been heaviest and its walled towns were possibly still largely coastal, as well as few and far between.

SUMMARY: MAP 5.g

Considered purely geographically the distribution of walled towns in Ireland was overwhelmingly non-coastal—only 20% had coastal situations. Of course, the picture was totally different for the earliest, the Hiberno-Norse period, when all the towns were directly on the coast or at the heads of estuaries. Estuarine loca-

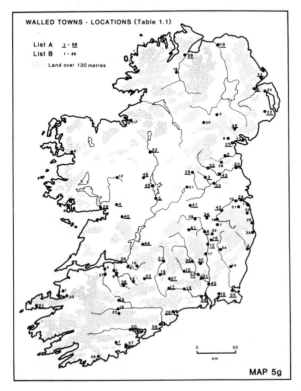

WALLED TOWNS - LOCATIONS (Table 1.1)

List A   1 - 56
List B   1 - 35

Land over 130 metres

MAP 5g

tions added almost another 10% to the coastal figure generally, and were a common feature of both the Anglo-Norman and the Stuart periods. Given the solid land-mass of Ireland, such distribution patterns are not surprising but, in fact, they were very clearly concentrated on certain sections of the coast line, particularly the south-eastern. Almost half of all the walled towns were situated on a major river and about a third on minor streams which were often part of these major river systems. Therefore, if not directly related to the coast, there was an indirect link for most by river transport which, only for a minority, meant re-transport more than once. Again, this meant a pattern with a strong south-eastern bias due to the extensive river systems flowing towards those coasts.

Looked at from the viewpoint of lists A and B, the proportions of inland, as opposed to coastal/estuarine sites, were basically the same, close to 70%. The main contrast lay in the relationship to major rivers which was significantly higher for list A towns, at about 50%, but only involved about 25% of list B. On the other hand only one sixth of list A towns were at minor rivers compared to one third of list B.

The later plantations never really altered the overwhelmingly south-easterly aspect to the distribution pattern, already established. This was itself largely a reflection of two factors which combined in that half of the island: firstly, the greater ease of access to western Europe, including England and Wales, via the adjacent east and south coasts and the estuaries of the south-west; and secondly, the generally higher fertility of lowland areas there as opposed to fertility levels which fall increasingly northwards and westwards, except occasionally in the major valleys of Ulster, the Foyle and the Bann. There, and in the more marginal lowlands of the west and centre, the later plantations aimed to develop walled towns where the earlier colonisation had often failed to take firm hold.

CHAPTER 6

Continuity amid Diversity

To identify walled towns in Ireland was something of a challenge, or at least an exercise in detection, because so much structural and documentary evidence has been lost. Indeed, at a first glance, a walled town appears to have been a rarity in terms of the Irish urban landscape. Londonderry springs readily to mind, but not necessarily as the best preserved of a common type. To those familiar with Irish towns generally isolated structures may easily be added—the medieval and massive St. Lawrence Gate barbican at Drogheda, the imposing but modernised gatehouses on the main streets of Youghal and Clonmel and, if familiarity extends to back streets, the considerable stretch of bastioned wall by the simpler North Gate at Carrickfergus or the six, isolated and varied, medieval mural towers scattered around Waterford. More modest towns such as Athenry, Kilmallock and Fethard are not necessarily part of everyone's experience, or even that of many historians or geographers, worthy though they are of close inspection. Yet, these too were walled towns and actually still have standing considerable remains of their circuits, Athenry's being almost as complete as Londonderry's if less well preserved. In fact, many well-known Irish towns, for example Cork, Galway and Kilkenny, were walled for most of their history, and so would have looked for long periods like present-day Conway, Chester or York, their centres marked off by a very visible town wall pierced by occasional, and sometimes formidable, gates. Indeed, it has even been suggested (Lydon 1973, 15) that 'most [Irish towns] were walled in the later Middle Ages'. The scene set thus by Webb (1918, 43–5)—'in the Middle Ages every Irish town of importance was surrounded by strong walls, pierced here and there with great gates, and fortified with towers overlooking the neighbouring countryside'—is but a verbal equivalent of the picture provided by a number of late sixteenth century map-views, particularly those for the towns of Munster. It remained true on a wide scale long into the eighteenth century as Ravell's map of Drogheda, dated 1749 (ill. 33), shows—a town enclosed by a sophisticated circuit, clearly of medieval origin and complete on both sides of the River Boyne as far as its banks.

Webb's book is an important review of municipal government in Ireland, which built on the earlier work of Gale (1834) and the various collections of town documents, also published mostly in the nineteenth century. The basis of Webb's statement is, as with Lydon's, the murage evidence. He goes on to say—'the upkeep of the walls and gates and towers involved a constant drain upon the civic purse. The proceeds of tolls and customs, which the citizens were permitted to levy, were often specifically allocated by charter for this purpose. Murage grants are of frequent occurrence in the records of Irish towns. To render aid in defence of one's town was an important civic duty. Military service on the part of the inhabitants of Irish cities and towns seems to have been obligatory . . .

Fortification of the city was the most important of public works. No payment appears to have been made for such services, they being regarded as part of the civic duty of the inhabitants'. This is a view that Elizabeth I would have concurred with wholeheartedly as her reaction to requests for aid with walling Carrickfergus show.

One of the post-medieval documents quoted by Webb (149) was the Act of 1665, known as the 'New Rules' for better regulating 'the cities, walled towns and corporations of Ireland'. This use of 'walled town' as a category in Ireland went back at least a century or even two. What is more important, Irish walled towns had a long active service by comparison with most of their counterparts in England and Wales. The reason for this contrast lay partly the troubled political state of late seventeenth century Ireland, which ended with a European-wide war being fought there often actually at Irish walled towns. But, it was also because towns were used generally as a tool of the successive colonisations attempted in Ireland, with walled towns often playing a key role. For this reason, again unlike English and Welsh examples, a significant number of Irish walled towns, perhaps as much as 20%, were late creations, sixteenth and seventeenth century new walled towns. Maryborough, Londonderry, Jamestown and Bandon are examples. In addition, numbers of medieval circuits were extensively modernised at the same time, particularly those of Limerick, Athlone and Carrickfergus. A closer parallel may be found with mainland Europe, where new post-medieval town walls were not so uncommon and where town walls generally remained more often in active use well into the eighteenth century because of continuing political instability. Many fine examples still survive there of both medieval circuits and of the more elaborate, later ones, such as those of Naarden in the Netherlands and Palma Nova in north-east Italy. Also many of the small towns of Spain, France, Germany and Italy have escaped radical redevelopment and so have particularly well preserved and sometimes multiple circuits. But, Irish walled towns, compared even with those in England and Wales, have survived less well. The reason for this is largely the prosaic one of apathy leading to neglect, rather than dogma based on opposition to such visible manifestations of colonialism or even destruction in war. Opposition to the collection of tolls, including those for murage purposes, was indeed active by the end of the eighteenth century, largely as part of a general anti-landlord movement, and ultimately led to their abolition. Yet, where town walls were actually removed, it was done by the authorities as part of improvement schemes typical of 'the age of enlightenment'.

This study, therefore, involved an element of discovery which led to a considerable increase—of over 30%—in the number of sites involved. Ninety sites now comprise lists A and B of Table 1.1. It could be argued that the scope should have been confined to the medieval walled towns of Ireland. That would have reduced the gazetteer by about 25%, while still providing a cohesive topic, but it would have made for an artificial break because it is clear that operating as a walled town was an increasingly common experience in Ireland from the late tenth century to the seventeenth century. It may have varied in intensity and longevity at individual sites, and in distribution throughout the island, but it was

185

33 Drogheda, 1749, from J. Ravell's map

nevertheless an unbroken experience. Indeed, an important consequence of taking a comprehensive approach has been the emergence of common trends, as well as contrasting, at walled towns from the Hiberno-Norse through to the Plantation period. In addition, because a basic characteristic of the documentary evidence, particularly for the medieval period, is its partial nature the extrapolation, which a study of walled towns *per se* allows, may help to overcome some of the resulting problems. For the same reason, towns with good records must act as models for others, less well endowed but contemporary, until archaeological investigation in towns becomes both more intensive and extensive. The recent excavations at

Dublin in particular, but also at Carrickfergus, Cork, Drogheda, Limerick, Waterford and Wexford, show just how much can be discovered for both the Hiberno-Norse and Anglo-Norman periods. The Tudor and Stuart periods are generally better provided for in terms of documents, because of the existence of maps and accounts contemporary with the construction of the town walls, and so the need for excavation there is not so great. Nonetheless, some problems remain even for 'recent' and well-documented sites such as Bandon, or for establishing the relationship between medieval and later circuits at sites such as Carrickfergus. Further intensive localised studies of the existing documentary evidence may also help to solve seemingly intractable problems for medieval walled towns. Burke's (1974) detailed elucidation of the north-eastern section of the Dublin wall is a case in point, and the present study indicates that a considerable potential may exist in broad-based estate collections such as the Ormond Deeds. Intensive study there could help to establish the history of waterfront wall development, and other matters of historical/morphological detail, at towns such as Kilkenny and Carrick-on-Suir.

The importance of walled towns historically in the Irish urban scene is quite clear. For a long time the top layers of the urban hierarchy were all walled towns. They were crucial to each of the slight, coastal Hiberno-Norse colonies and the towns involved were acquired and augmented in the early years of the Anglo-Norman colonisation. Later their number was much added to and many were used actively, with some additions, in the sixteenth and seventeenth century re-colonisations. Now no longer visibly walled, with the exception of Londonderry and a few degraded circuits, these towns are still, for the most part, prominent amongst Irish cities and towns, although they have been joined at the top of the urban hierarchy by others, principally nineteenth century 'industrial' and twentieth century 'resort/conurbation' towns. Therefore, the walled towns of Ireland are not just relics of a former system. Neither are they only the older of those that are currently prominent. Like towns generally, there have been successes and failures amongst those that were walled. Indeed, this is part of their interest, as is the reality of their shared experience.

Running through the comparative study of Irish walled towns are two strands which form a cross-weave. These are the repetition of trends throughout the different periods and the diversity found amongst walled towns as a whole or within any period. Such diversity is the result of each town being capable of a unique response to a range of different and variable factors—topographic, political and economic. Thus one town may be similar to another in some respects but distinct from it in others. To some extent this is so because the settlements involved were intended, and usually functioned, as towns. Defence was simply one of a series of specialist services that they could provide, given the existence of suitable infra-structural devices. The murage charters, which were designed to provide finance for walling towns by the imposition of tolls, actually emphasised the essential trading role of a town and so linked two distinct functions. In addition, the concentration of population implicit in urban settlements provided the nucleus of a garrison. In fact, the safety of numbers provided the initial defence.

This might be augmented by the stationing within the town of professional military forces, temporarily in a time of crisis or permanently at the castles or forts of certain key towns. To this extent the walled, town could act as an extended bailey area but one, nonetheless, in which 'normal' life was still focussed at the marketplace and the workshop, and in specialist social activities related particularly to the church in medieval times. There was, therefore, a much greater range of function involved in the case of a walled town as opposed to a castle, where the main role was clearly that of defence and the subsidiary that of providing a residence for the political power. At a town the balance was reversed. Defence was but one of a number of specialist functions, and so it was often subject to the force of compromise for, despite Ireland's rather turbulent history, peace, however limited, was a more common condition than war.

The need for compromise was a trend common to walled towns throughout the ages. It was one that varied considerably, largely as a result of how the danger of attack was perceived and what actions were considered desirable or necessary. Occasionally, as at Leighlin, it is clear that attention to an individual defensive structure, in that case a tower but elsewhere more usually a local castle or fort, was the result but not every town contained such an alternative. Even there it does not seem to have been the preferred option but one made necessary by the low return produced by the murage tolls. This may have been a common cause of town walls apparently not being built in medieval times, after specific financial provisions were organised, or perhaps of being inadequately constructed. Yet, in a time of crisis a walled town probably had to act with a single-ness of purpose, almost as if it were a military base. This must have led to the requisitioning of structures near the wall, to the creation of new ones and the rapid alteration of others. Thus, gates might be closed and become, in effect, towers; suburbs might be flattened or extensions built to the circuit to enclose them; waterfronts might be shut off by the strengthening or formalisation of b'ick-end defence; and, in the post-medieval period, additional earthen structures might be built to reinforce parts of an existing stone circuit. When the crisis was over, some of these changes might remain, some structures might be abandoned and soon disappear, and a return to a previous non-defensive usage might be allowed at others, particularly gates and towers. Again, the perception of what was desirable or necessary at any particular site could vary considerably. At the worst, if the walled circuit had failed to provide an effective defence the settlement itself might well disappear, largely or completely, and so the range of possibilities was very wide indeed. It is one of the sources of the inherent variety displayed by the Irish walled towns.

Each site was in a sense intrinsically unique too, with particular strengths and weaknesses for the function of defence as well as others. Yet, while some towns started off with naturally defensive sites, such as Cork with its islands or Dublin and Derry with their distinctive spurs, they were walled early and completely. The walls were used, therefore, to enhance the natural defensiveness of the site but they were still considered necessary. Perhaps inevitably, extensions to the initial circuit sometimes involved development onto areas with quite different topographic features, and often less useful ones from a defensive viewpoint. The medieval extensions at Waterford, as well as at Dublin, are cases in point. This in turn frequently led to the creation of enclosed areas with varied and complex shapes. Yet, sometimes it seems as if the need to enclose the settlement was of over-riding importance. At Coleraine, for example, the need to create quickly a secure refuge for the new plantation may have influenced the structural nature and extent of the circuit. An earthen wall was constructed rapidly on three sides and the large river was left to provide defence on the fourth side. At Drogheda two walled towns were developed contemporaneously, and possibly both extended, on quite different sites, one of which (the Meath) was naturally highly defensive and had a castle too. As distinct towns initially, an element of competition may have been involved and the separate circuits may even have been useful in times of inter-urban strife, a not-unknown condition until the two towns were joined administratively in 1412.

A close relationship with major bodies of water, especially with rivers, was a very common feature of Irish walled towns generally, but the nature of the response varied. Some, like Cork and Limerick, were walled along the waterfronts for long periods and had heavily defended harbours, within the circuit in the case of Cork and outside in that of Limerick. For others, such as Dublin in the fourteenth century, waterfront walls may have only been made in the face of real danger, although there the earlier Hiberno-Norse circuit is known to have been complete. Even the responses of the distinct group of contemporary twin-walled towns was apparently varied. In time at least, the two river frontages at Drogheda were both probably walled, but at Bandon in the seventeenth century in-river defence was the method to be employed, according to the map evidence. This allowed the two separate circuits to meet within the river and so form a single unit. Such a method, possibly also employed in medieval times, would have imposed limitations on normal port activities just as waterfront walls did.

The reasons for what seems like an ambivalent attitude must lie with economics at two distinct levels. The river or sea provided a natural defence by making access to the town more difficult along its line and so reduced the costs of enclosure. In addition, that area was the most economically active part of a town, particularly in the Middle Ages when water-transport was the most important form available. Therefore, a walled line, with the need for an access zone within, consisting of a rampart and/or a street, and with a limited number of exit points to the river or sea, could be a real hindrance to loading and unloading. In fact, a wide range of possibilities existed between a totally open waterfront and a fully enclosed one; a firm line of warehouses interrupted only by streets at which there were gates was a mid-stage. It provided the possibility of both a degree of defence by individual action and the use of the gates as a convenient control mechanism for port, and as well as for other, purposes. Because of the ever-present need for flexibility in this area it is not always possible to know now at many sites whether the circuit was once complete. The evidence generally seems to point in that direction for at least part of the middle period, perhaps from the fourteenth to the sixteenth century. At Clonmel and Carrick-on-Suir, for example, the waterfront seems to have been the last section to be walled and the first to have the wall removed. Either may have happened over a long period in stages. Certainly the walling of the sea fronts by the castle at Carrickfergus was a prolonged, stage-by-stage process, starting with individual responsibility and ending with a complete stone wall with only one or two openings.

The very distinctive forces operating against each other in the waterfront area over many centuries were an extreme case but similar factors could, and did, lead to variety elsewhere within a circuit. Time, allowing decay by weathering and/or attack, was perhaps the strongest motivator. The capacity for change at the medieval towns was therefore particularly great. Repair might become necessary in different parts of a circuit at different periods, unless the town was especially unfortunate and the whole circuit was destroyed at the one time. The medieval circuits, as displayed by the limited evidence of surviving structures and of the best but later maps, often show signs of being a hotch-potch of styles, especially with regard to their gates and towers. This is one area where a distinction can be drawn between the medieval and later walled towns but it is only valid up to a point. At Londonderry, the present reality and the original design is very close but even there changes were made to the gates and improvements proposed for the circuit but not put into effect. The two Bandon circuits, in contrast, had quite a different history, being largely demolished less than a century after they were built. To judge from the slight remains, the reality there was not so close to that planned. Such variety of experience between two towns built at the same time, and with knowledge of each other, must indicate the considerable potential for variety within the longer and less inter-connected medieval period. Yet, the excavation evidence from thirteenth century Waterford and fourteenth century Limerick points very clearly to walls being constructed to such a high degree of planning that provision was made for the later insertion of substantial but not main gates. Consequently, a small number of blue-prints may have been used even in medieval times originally, and peripatetic experts, perhaps military men in the sense of being castle-builders and/or strategists, may have been involved as they undoubtedly were in the seventeenth century.

The extremely detailed evidence provided by the 1585 verbal survey of the Dublin circuit illustrates the nature of the evolution possible, over a period of at least five centuries, at a site where the walls enclosed two areas with quite different topography—the spur walled initially by the Hiberno-Norse and the area below reclaimed from the river by the Anglo-Normans when the settlement grew rapidly as their chief town. The curtain wall, gates and towers were all most formidable on the landward south side, close to the castle. Elsewhere the width of the wall was fairly constant but its height varied considerably along the west side, being lowest towards the river and highest between the two gates. These were quite different in style, indeed at least three main gate styles were represented by the five gates described. The mural towers, too, varied throughout the circuit in style and in scale. By 1585 most bore the names of individuals and were probably used in part for non-defensive purposes. Of the fourteen listed one seems to have been replaced by a private house, another was largely in-filled with earth, and a third was described as 'ruined' with a house built against it. These were each located in different parts of the circuit. Two on the quay were very large, possibly modified for warehousing purposes. The internal rampart, which was particularly high towards the south, had possibly completely disappeared along half of the west side and houses had been built there, 'close to the wall'. Also along the whole of the west side buttresses from the fosse supported the wall externally. They, in particular, may have been recent and the result of ageing.

Dublin in 1585, like many other Irish medieval walled towns, had a stone curtain wall but the original one built by the Hiberno-Norse is known to have been an earthen rampart, reinforced with wood. Such structures were inherently weak and therefore very subject to weathering. The stages by which it was replaced by ever-stronger systems of mixed earth, wood and gravel, until the first stone wall was built are known from the excavations at Dublin. Small amounts of archaeological evidence from Waterford and Drogheda, and the written records for Carrickfergus, suggests that such transitions may have been quite common. The latter case also shows that they might take place over a very long period of time. On the other hand, similar upgrading may never have been completed in some cases. The eighteenth century map evidence for Gowran shows, for example, a circuit composed in part of a stone wall and in part of a 'rampart and trench'. While early property references for Gowran mention only the fosse the murage grant of 1414–15 did specify a stone wall. It is not known, therefore, whether this was a case of upgrading halted because of a lack of funds or because a stone wall was considered unnecessary on one side. Another possibility is that the stone circuit may have once been complete but that decay, for whatever reason, had been more marked on one side.

A single circuit, or a number of circuits in existence at a particular time, might, therefore, contain much structural variety. Perhaps surprisingly, this trend was common to both the medieval and the later walled towns. The Coleraine and Belfast walls look very like the Londonderry on paper but they were built essentially of earth, reinforced internally by wood and stone and surfaced with sods and hedging. At the same period at Athlone there was one circuit of stone and one of earth, although in style there was little to distinguish them. The continued use of earthen structures must still have owed something to expediency, but changes in warfare were also significant. Cannon-balls could be entrapped in earthen 'walls', whereas there was a tendency for a dangerous ricochet effect to occur at stone walls unless they were very high and/or wide. But the easier weathering of earthen structures remained a problem and produced its own costs, as the experience at Coleraine showed. It must always have been the main objection in medieval times, too, when there was no real advantage to using earth except that of short-term economy.

Considerable internal variety existed due to the nature of a 'conventional' stone circuit. The curtain wall provided a visible boundary and a barrier through which movement was restricted to a small number of points, the gates. As inherently weak points their number had to be limited but, like large mural towers, gates were often distinct buildings in their own right. They also varied considerably in style, some being just simple openings in the curtain wall while others were sophisticated double-towered structures with gate houses above a long passage way, in front of which there could be a barbican, in effect a second or foregate. Some of the medieval gates may have evolved into a complex form through much rebuilding, for example the New Gate at Dublin. Others may never have changed structurally, including perhaps the other, and later, western gate at Dublin which had a single-towered form in 1585. Still others varied in function over the centuries: sometimes acting as gates, sometimes as towers. One of the most interesting cases is that of St. Martin's Gate at Waterford. Provision was made for its later insertion when the wall was originally constructed but, subsequently, it was closed and then it changed in form from a double-towered gate to a massive mural tower-house. The internal earthen rampart was another quite different feature. It was made of earth and often had associated with it a sub-mural space or street. The external fosse, in contrast, was intended to hold water although it was often allowed to infill. All these different sections had many potential alternative uses which might also cause them to alter to different extents. There was a very natural tendency for other uses to develop when conditions were peaceful and the insurance value of the wall was in fact its dominant role.

Clearly, while these 'other uses' could to some extent also change through the centuries, most could be abandoned in the face of danger. The problem really lay in the extent of compromise involved. Indeed, there was an argument in favour of additional uses, of a limited nature at least, because the funds so raised could be used to offset the cost of maintaining the circuit as a defence mechanism. However, there must always have been a strong temptation both to over-develop the 'other uses' and/or to use the funds raised for other urban needs. Various malpractices were listed as prohibited at Dublin and other towns from the Tudor period. This must have been a constant problem but probably one in which only intermittent interest was taken. A slightly different problem, but sometimes consequent on misuse, was general neglect of a circuit's structure. This was not simply a common feature of the eighteenth century, when the need for defence was diminishing, but is recorded for Athlone in the middle of the previous turbulent century, which in fact ended with a major siege of that town. Some towns in the Middle Ages may have been taken by besieging forces for the same reason.

Despite the other advantages of such a system, defence was clearly its *raison d'etre*. There is no evidence that enclosing walls were built as a necessary ingredient of a town during the medieval period or later, except perhaps in the cases of Dublin and a few Hiberno-Norse port-towns. Some more primitive forms of enclosure may have been generally common but the murage charters indicated that the need for protection was paramount. The tone of the New Ross poem is even apologetic that a town wall was required, refers only to an existing 'watch' system and points to fear, arising out of deteriorating political conditions, as the cause. That particular circuit was large, perhaps to allow for expected growth, but then and earlier, a town wall did not set the bounds of the town's lands. This is quite clear from the charters. It did, however, provide a distinct area of maximum defence, either in the absence of a major castle or in close conjunction with it. Here, again, common practice and diversity went hand in hand; in the Tudor and Stuart periods forts took the place of medieval castles. Sometimes there was a close relationship, for example, at the new town of Maryborough but at Londonderry no fort at all was built. Earlier, Dublin's castle was built in a corner of the circuit and Limerick's along one side, while no castle was associated closely with either the Waterford or Galway circuits, although in the post-medieval period major citadels were placed beside each circuit.

A town wall provided defence in a number of ways. Firstly, it prevented attack by appearing to make it a hopeless or costly exploit on the part of an assailant. For this purpose the visibility and the structural quality of the wall were very important. Nonetheless, the evidence from Cork and Wexford shows that what might look strong from the outside might be less so within. Such 'economic' repair was probably very common. It was not unsuitable either because, as a town's population grew, its density of buildings within increased and these could to a large extent obscure such potentially weak points. Thus the deterrent value of a town wall might be, to varying extents, a bluff. On the other hand the strongest possible wall was only as good as its management allowed and as its garrison served it. A single act of treachery was enough to breach the best wall, while myriad acts of carelessness, such as poor supervision of postern gates, buildings placed against the wall, rotten stairs or floors within towers or filled-in fosses, could singly or together provide the opportunity that an assiduous assailant needed.

Secondly, a town wall defended by protecting both the area within and the garrison manning it. It had thus a passive and an active role in this respect. It provided a barrier to besiegers and a platform from which the garrison could attack them. The fosse made close access difficult and a high wall made over-riding it by missiles less likely. A range of detailed structural features helped, especially the battlemented wall-walk at the top. This gave a degree of protection to the defenders and the gates or towers provided them with assembly points and stores. The covered access within them could be disconnected if one was breached, and so assailants could be contained and prevented from having free access throughout the system. These structures also provided the means of both an internal signalling system and a lookout. Ideally they were located not just at openings or other especially vulnerable points but at frequent intervals. There is some evidence that they were less frequent on Irish circuits than on English and Welsh by the early seventeenth century. On the other hand, the Irish circuits then showed much more evidence of additional walls, usually extensions to the original circuits, and these too helped to sectionalise a walled area and to strengthen it. Indeed, internal gates and suburban ones seem to have been a particular feature of Irish towns, adding to the general level of defence. Either or both may have been quite common, particularly as gates could be used for all sorts of regulatory purposes within densely built-up areas. Bastions took the place of towers in the later periods but served the same purpose, to defend inherently weak points such as corners and to strengthen physically long stretches of straight wall. The introduction of cannon induced the change but it was limited largely to details of style and structure. There is also much evidence of towers being strengthened in post-medieval times to take the weight of guns, and of towers or gates acquiring bastion-type structures as additional, forward defences. Examples of both can be seen from the evidence for Waterford, Limerick and Clonmel in particular.

Thirdly, the town wall provided a base from which it was possible for a besieged town to mount offensive operations. The security it provided allowed armed forces to be gathered and watch kept for suitable opportunities for such forces to make sallies in order to attack the besiegers. This happened at Dublin in the earliest days of the Anglo-Norman period, when it resulted in raising the siege. It was a tactic employed less successfully at Londonderry five centuries later and, doubtless, on many occasions in the intervening period.

The 1690 Londonderry siege was, of course, raised only just in time by relief from outside. Consequently, it was a clear illustration of the double-bind nature of the protection that a town wall could provide. As a refuge for the area, Derry and its medieval counterparts were intended to take an influx of refugees but it then provided a single target within the region it served. Many casualties occurred inside Londonderry because it proved possible to project missiles within the walled area from cannon positioned at various high points around the town. At the same time, while some of the refugees could be useful as a means of swelling the garrison, they all—men and women, old and young—put a strain on its food resources. Indeed, this problem may account in part for the large walled area of some of the later medieval towns for a long siege meant starvation in the end, unless supplies could be built up or obtained by periodic sallies. The latter required a less than efficient besieging force. The only other sources of salvation were relief from outside or the onset of winter which usually curtailed sieges, at least temporarily. At Limerick in 1690 the walls of Irishtown had actually been breached and the end was in sight, but substantial repairs became possible once winter set in. Despite that, the town surrendered the following year because the political climate was judged to have changed. A town wall was, therefore, in essence a delaying tactic, a very useful insurance during times of difficulty but, for its success, subject to factors ultimately beyond its control.

Nonetheless, total security was not really what was generally required of a walled town. Its extensive use in Ireland during colonisations points to slightly different priorities. Colonisation or plantation projects were based on a presumption of ultimate success. Consequently, secure settlements that could act in a temporary emergency were important as a means of 'fixing' the colonisation by providing the necessary breathing space to deal with opposition, after which development could go forward in peace. The use of existing, and the creation of new, walled towns by the Anglo-Normans seems to point very clearly to this, as does the approach of the Tudors and Stuarts later. In each case only a few new towns were walled in order to increase the number of bridge-heads, and so both maintain the link with the colonial base and provide refuges if needed. To a large extent the Anglo-Normans found that the existing Hiberno-Norse walled towns were sufficient for this role, following improvement. The later colonists, too, had available an existing framework of walled towns. Some, like Carrickfergus and Athlone, needed extensive upgrading but, while walled towns continued to play an important role, their numbers, relative to that of new town creations generally, were again low. This was as true for Ulster in the early seventeenth century as it seems to have been throughout much of the island four centuries previously. The Leix/Offaly plantation was apparently an exception. Only two towns were developed, both possibly walled and certainly intended to be. In the periods before and after it, some walled towns were proposed for development but abandoned in favour of other, generally less expensive, defensive measures. Perhaps the main distinction lies in the apparent extension of the system as the Anglo-Norman colony faltered. Then, it seems, walls were built at existing well-established towns such as New Ross, Trim and Kilmallock. The documents available, especially the murage charters, emphasise the dual purpose of the defence they financed—for the particular town and for its hinterland, which was often described as suffering from 'march' conditions. The results, even allowing for those sites where their precise nature is unknown, were spectacular. For some decades at the turn of the fourteenth century, an average of possibly one new town wall every three years may have been started in Ireland, in addition to the maintenance or improvement of already existing circuits. In view of this it may not be too biassed to regard walled towns as having made a vital contribution to the survival of the medieval colony, albeit as a much weakened lordship.

Clearly, it is not possible to make simple correlations on the basis of period or area with regard to characteristics of walled towns such as size, shape, structure, funding or use. Perhaps not surprisingly a complex phenomenon has resulted in complex relationships with much variability and repetition of trends. One unexpected discovery of this study has been the degree to which circuits were extended in the medieval period. It was a phenomenon unique to that period and it has been proved for nearly half of the towns involved. At some, of course, the process was repeated. This incidentally provides a vivid illustration of the intensity of the Anglo-Norman colonisation. Post-medieval walled towns appear unique in a different respect—the speed of construction of their circuits. The evidence is generally for under ten years and sometimes for considerably less, even in the case of the sophisticated Londonderry stone circuit. This, however, may not really be so unique. Comparable evidence for the medieval period is not available, although constant attention to the town wall is clear from the records for some towns. Moreover, in terms of creating an effective defence mechanism, an incomplete circuit, as opposed to one of mixed quality carefully disguised, would be virtually useless if the threat to the settlement was a serious one. Consequently, rapid initial enclosure, followed by prolonged strengthening and embellishment, may have been characteristic of the medieval period.

The psychological effect on a town's inhabitants of such enclosure is difficult to assess now. It may have contributed something to the sense of independence that was characteristic of Irish towns in the late Middle Ages, and it may have fostered feelings of exclusivity. On the other hand, then and later, peace of mind may have been the over-riding effect. What seems indisputable is the sense of liberation felt much later when the walls were removed or the town was extended beyond them. The comments from towns such as Galway and Limerick focus on liberation from antique and unhealthy conditions. They were probably also under-laid, however subconsciously, by a sense of relief that such security was no longer necessary.

Now, and for the most part too late, a town's structural heritage is seen by a new generation of 'modernists' to be not only of intrinsic interest but also of economic value. Sadly this study shows just how much has been lost and how relatively little remains of real worth. To cite just one example, out of a total of ten or twelve gates at Drogheda four were still standing in 1820, but today only the barbican of one and a mere fragment of another exists. The circuit itself now survives just here and there in small sections while it was 'intact' then too. Nonetheless, its influence lives on through its use as a boundary to properties and as the source of a circulatory road system. Except at Londonderry, it is now no longer possible to perambulate the walls of an Irish town for pleasure, as inhabi-tants liked to do in the eighteenth century, or as a means of beginning a visit. It is from the vantage point of such encircling high walls that casual visitors, or earnest study groups, normally approach Chester, Dubrovnik, Valencia or a host of other European towns. Short of viewing a town from the air, such an approach gives the best insights into the street pattern and the variable intensity associated with its different land uses, not just along the streets but in the spaces between, even in the backyards. This might still be possible in Ireland, partially and occa-sionally, with the reconstruction of a wooden wall-walk or of an inner earthen rampart. It could be achieved at Athenry most realistically where a ruined gate house survives and the curtain wall with a number of mural towers forms a largely intact circuit still. Fethard, because of its smaller size and greater coherence as an urban unit, could give an even better sense of what a walled town meant in terms of an enclosed space, even though the fabric survivals are less distinguished there. Likewise, much of Waterford's west wall with its varied towers could be restored as a unit. But, the extent of the loss can, perhaps, best be measured by the fact that no gates survive at all at Waterford and the lone surviving gate at either Athenry or Fethard would have to act as a model for the three or four main gates each has lost. This might, or might not, be realistic conceptually but it would be an impossibly expensive task. However, it is not intended to criticise the removal of town walls *per se*. Towns are complex units with a number of important functions of which defence was but one. Local decisions have to be made within that context but it is well to recognise that, while uses and values may change considerably in the long term, sometimes they do so in an unimagin-able way. The sheer variety of uses to which a town wall or its parts have been put through the centuries itself illustrates this. The modern need for wide, inner ring-roads is a particular instance of unforeseen requirements that can be satisfied by the re-use of a relic system. Ironically, Ireland has been more enriched in this regard by a 'neglectful' rather than a 'modernising' attitude. With so little now sur-viving an informed and careful approach is urgently needed, both with regard to standing structures and to their foundations, which lie below so many Irish towns.

Sophisticated or simple, the town wall was a visible expression of a former urban function, just as the parish church, market house or town hall are still of others. At certain times the town wall must have literally enclosed the town, the church towers alone rising above it. At other times, however, the walled circuit must have been largely hidden by the suburbs, a defensive system 'in waiting', except on the main streets where gates, large or small, would still make its presence felt. A few of these gates remain as entrances to the centres of their respective towns, causing the visitor to halt briefly and be impressed—or irritated. The even fewer circuits that survive more or less intact also impress by the scale of their development. But, for the most part, the walled circuits of Irish towns now represent a mere phase in the long history of settlement evolution. All the same, it was a phase common to many and one whose shadow remains strong in some. At others it may well await discovery.

Bibliography

I. MANUSCRIPT AND PRINTED MAPS

Details are given in the text or gazetteer. The abbreviations used are as follows:

Bod Lib	Bodleian Library, Oxford.
BL/BM	British Library/Museum.
DS	Down Survey: photocopies in NLI; catalogue *PRIA*, XXXV, 1920, 396–407.
Hayes-McCoy	*Ulster and other Irish maps c.1600*: ed. G. A. Hayes-McCoy, Dublin, 1964.
Lamb Pal Lib	Lambeth Palace Library.
NLI	National Library of Ireland.
NMM	National Maritime Museum, Greenwich.
OPW	Office of Public Works.
OS	Ordnance Survey, Dublin: maps printed; letters—mss or published.
Pac Hib	*Pacata Hibernia*: ed. T. Stafford, London, 1633; O'Grady, S., 1896.
PRO	Public Record Office, London: catalogue of maps, 1967.
PROI	Public Record Office of Ireland, Dublin; now National Archive.
PRONI	Public Record Office of Northern Ireland, Belfast.
RIA	Royal Irish Academy
TCD	Trinity College, Dublin; printed catalogue of library.

II(A). PRINTED PRIMARY SOURCES: STATE PAPER AND CHARTER COLLECTIONS

CCP	*Calendar of the Carew manuscripts, 1515–1616*: eds. J.S. Brewer and W. Bullen, London, 1867.
CCR	*Calendar of Charter Rolls*, London, 1903–27.
CDI	*Calendar of Documents relating to Ireland*: ed. H.S. Sweetman *et al.*, 4 vols., London, 1875–86.
CJR	*Calendar of Justiciary Rolls*, Ireland: ed. J.Mills, vols. 1 and 2, Dublin, 1905–14; ed. M.C. Griffith, vol.3, Dublin, 1956.
CPI	*Chartae, priviligia et immunitates*: Irish Record Commission, Dublin, 1829–30.
CP+CR	*Rotulorum patentium et clausorum cancellariae Hiberniae calendarium*: ed. E. Tresham, Dublin, 1828.
CPCR	*Calendar of the Patent and Close Rolls of Chancery in Ireland . . . Henry VIII–Elizabeth*: ed. J. Morrin, 2 vols., Dublin, 1861–3.
CPR	*Calendar of Patent Rolls*, London, 1891.
CSPI	*Calendar of State Papers relating to Ireland . . . Henry VIII–Charles II*: ed. H.C. Hamilton, 12 vols., London, 1860–1912.
Haliday MSS	*Haliday manuscripts*: ed. J.T. Gilbert, London, 1897.
Orrery Letters	*A Collection of the State Letters of the first Earl of Orrery, 1660–68*: ed. T. Morrice, 2 vols., Dublin, 1743.
PR	*Pipe Rolls*: 'The Irish Pipe Roll, 14 John, 1211–12': ed. O. Davies and D.B. Quinn, *UJA*, IV, 1941 supplement, 1–73.
Sheriff's a/cs.	'Sheriff's accounts for Co. Tipperary, 1275–6': ed. E. Curtis, *PRIA*, XLII, 1934, 65–94.
Rep DK	various pipe rolls, fiants and other collections of documents in *Reports of the Deputy Keeper of the Public Records of Ireland*, Dublin, 1869–1961.
Sidney SP	*Sidney State Papers, 1565–70*: ed. T. O'Laidhin, Dublin, 1962.
SP Hen VIII	*State Papers Henry VIII*: Record Commission, London, 1830–52.
SR	*I: Statutes and Ordinances, and Acts of the Parliament of Ireland, John–Henry V*: ed. H.F. Berry, Dublin, 1907;

SR   *II-IV: Statute Rolls of the Parliament of Ireland, Henry VI–Edward IV*: ed. H.F. Berry and J.F. Morrissey, Dublin, 1910–14 / 1939.

II (B). PRINTED PRIMARY SOURCES: COLLECTIONS OF TOWN AND ESTATE DOCUMENTS

Alen's Reg   *Calendar of Archbishop Alen's Register*: ed. C. McNeill, Dublin, 1950.
CARD   *Calendar of the Ancient Records of Dublin*: ed. J.T. Gilbert *et al.*, I-XVIII, Dublin, 1889–1944.
COD   *Calendar of the Ormond Deeds, 1172–1603*: ed. E. Curtis, 6 vols., Dublin, 1932–43.
COM   *Calendar of Ormonde Manuscripts, 1572–1688,* Historic Manuscripts Commission, London, 1895–1909.
CS   *The Civil Survey, 1654–6*: ed. R.C. Simington, Dublin, 10 vols., 1931–61.
C. St. Mary's   *Chartularies of St. Mary's Abbey, Dublin*: ed. J.T. Gilbert, London, 1884.
Extents   *Extents of Irish Monastic Possessions, 1540–1*: ed. N.B.White, Dublin, 1943.
HMD   *Historical and Municipal Documents of Ireland, 1172–1320* : ed. J.T.Gilbert, London, 1870.
IHD   *Irish Historical Documents*: eds. E. Curtis and R.B. McDowell, Dublin, 1943.
IRC   Irish Record Commission, III (*Lands involved in Acts of Settlement and Explanation, 1666–84*), appendix to Report XV, 1825, Dublin and London.
Llanthony C   *The Irish Cartularies of Llanthony Prima and Secunda*: ed. E. St. J. Brooks, Dublin, 1953.
LMPH   *Liber Munerum Publicorum Hiberniae, 1152–1827*: ed. R. Lascelles, I, London, 1824.
LPK   *Liber Primus Kilkenniensis:* ed. C. McNeill, Dublin, 1931; trans. A.J. Otway-Ruthven, Kilkenny, 1961.
MCI   *Municipal Corporations in Ireland, report and appendix in Parliamentary Papers,* 1835 XXVII-XXVIII, and 1836 XXIV.
Na Buirgéisí   *Na Buirgéisí, XII-XV Aoisi*: ed. G. MacNiocaill, 2 vols., Dublin, 1964.
RBK   *The Red Book of the Earls of Kildare*: ed. G. MacNiocaill, Dublin, 1964.
RBO   *The Red Book of Ormond*: ed. N.B. White, Dublin, 1932.

(The records of specific towns are listed in full in the gazetteer.)

III. SECONDARY SOURCES: JOURNALS AND BOOKS.

Abbreviations used for journals:

Anal Hib   *Analecta Hibernica.*
BGSIHS   *Bulletin of the group for the study of Irish historic settlement.*
CLA(H)J   *County Louth Archaeological (and Historical) Journal.*
Decies   *Journal of the Old Waterford Society.*
Dinnseanchas   *Journal of the Irish Place-name Society.*
D of S   *Dictionary of Land Surveyors and local cartographers of Great Britain and Ireland, 1550–1850,* ed. P.M.G. Eden, 3 vols., Folkestone, 1975–76.
DHR   *Dublin Historical Record* (Journal of the Old Dublin Society)
Geog   *Geography.*
Hist Stud   *Historical Studies.*
I. Geog   *Irish Geography.*
IHS   *Irish Historical Studies.*
IHTA   *Irish Historic Towns Atlas,* eds. J.H. Andrews and A. Simms, Dublin, 1986–.
I. Sword   *Irish Sword.*
JBS   *Journal of the Butler Society.*
JCHAS   *Journal of the Cork Historical and Archaeological Society.*
JGAHS   *Journal of the Galway Archaeological and Historical Society.*
J Hist Geog   *Journal of Historical Geography.*

J Kerry AHS	*Journal of the Kerry Archaeological and Historical Society.*
JKAS	*Journal of the Kildare Archaeological Society.*
JOAS	*Journal of the Old Athlone Society.*
JOCS	*Journal of the Old Carlow Society (Carloviana).*
JODS	*Journal of the Old Drogheda Society.*
JOWS	*Journal of the Old Wexford Society.*
JRSAI	*Journal of the Royal Society of Antiquarians of Ireland.*
Lecale Misc.	Lecale Miscellany
Long Room	TCD Library journal.
Med Arch	*Medieval Archaeology.*
NMAJ	*North Munster Antiquarian Journal.*
OKR	*Old Kilkenny Review.*
PRIA	*Proceedings of the Royal Irish Academy.*
RDS	Royal Dublin Society: *Statistical Surveys* of counties (various authors), Dublin, 1801–24.
R na M	*Ríocht na Midhe.*
Stud Hib	*Studia Hibernia.*
TIBG	*Transactions of the Institute of British Geographers.*
Univ Rev	*University Review.*
UJA	*Ulster Journal of Archaeology.*
World Arch	*World Archaeology.*

Articles from the above journals are listed in the gazetteer for each town or are cited in the text. Books specific to particular towns are likewise listed in the gazetteer; works of more general interest are detailed below.

The basic historical text for Ireland now is the *New History of Ireland* (NHI), edited by T.W. Moody, F.X. Martin and F.J. Byrne, of which the relevant volumes are:

II *Medieval Ireland, 1169–1534*, ed. A.Cosgrove, Oxford, 1986
III *Early Modern Ireland, 1534–1691*, ed. T.W. Moody, Oxford, 1984
IX *Maps,* Oxford, 1984.

The work of many authors is involved and is cited in the text thus—Andrews: NHI, III, 476.

AA, *Automobile Association: Illustrated Road Book of Ireland,* Dublin, 1963.
Adams, I.H., *The Making of Urban Scotland,* London, 1978.
Almqvist, B. and Greene, D. eds., *Proceedings of the Seventh Viking Congress, 1973,* Dublin, 1976.
Andrews, J.H., 'Ireland in maps', *I. Geog* IV, 1962, 234–43.
——, 'Geography and government in Elizabethan Ireland', in Stephens and Glasscock eds., 1970, 178–90.
——, *History of the Ordnance Map,* Dublin, 1974.
——, *A Paper Landscape,* Oxford, 1975.
——, *Irish Maps,* Dublin, 1978.
——, 'The oldest map of Dublin', *PRIA,* LXXXIII C, 1983, 205–37.
——, 'Kildare', *IHTA,* fascicle I, 1986.
Anon. (? Dimmock), *A Description of Ireland, 1598,* ed. E. Hogan, Dublin, 1878.
Archdall, M., *Monasticon Hibernicum,* Dublin, 1786.
Arbman, H., *The Vikings,* London, 1961.
Armstrong, E.C.R., *Some Irish Seal-matrices and Seals,* Dublin, 1913.
Atlas of Ireland: ed. J.P. Haughton *et al.,* Dublin, 1979.
Bagley, J.J., *Historical Interpretation,* Harmondsworth, 1965.
Baker, A.R.H. and Billinge, M. eds., *Period and Place,* Cambridge, 1982.
Ball, F.E., *A History of the County of Dublin,* 6 vols., Dublin, 1902–20.
Ballard, A., Tait, J.J. and Weinbaum, M., *British Borough Charters,* II/III, Cambridge, 1932/1943.
Barley, M. ed., *European Towns—their archaeology and early history,* London, 1977.
Barry, T.B., *The Archaeology of Medieval Ireland,* London, 1987.
Bartlett, W.H. *et al., The Scenery and Antiquities of Ireland,* I, London, 1842.
Bassett, G.H., *County Directories* (Down, Kilkenny, Louth and Wexford), Dublin, 1884–6.
Bateson, M., 'The laws of Breteuil', *EHR,* XV, 1900, 73–8; and XVI, 1901, 92–110.
Belling, R., *War in Ireland, 1642–7,* ed. J. Lodge, *Desiderata Curiosa Hibernica,* II, Dublin, 1772.
Benton, J.F., *Town Origins,* Boston (Mass.), 1968.
Beresford, M.W., *New Towns of the Middle Ages,* London, 1967.

—— and St. Joseph, J.K.S., *Medieval England - an aerial survey*, Cambridge, 1958.

—— and Hurst, J.G. eds., *Deserted Medieval Villages*, London, 1971.

Biddle, M., 'Archaeology and the history of British towns', *Antiquity*, XLII, 1968, 109–116.

Boate, G., *A Natural History of Ireland*, (no place), 1652.

Bonnivert, G., 'Diary 1690', ed. R.H.Murray PRIA, XXX,1913, 338–40.

de la Boullaye le Gouz, *The Tour of a French Traveller in Ireland, 1644,* ed. T.C. Croker, (no place), 1837.

Bradley, J., 'The town wall of Kilkenny', *OKR* (ns), I, 1975–6, 85–103 and 209–19.

——, 'The topography and layout of medieval Drogheda', *CLAHJ*, XIX, 1978, 98–127.

——, 'The medieval towns of Tipperary', in Nolan ed, 1985, 34–59.

——, 'Planned Anglo-Norman towns in Ireland', in Clarke and Simms eds., 1985, II, 411–67.

——, 'Recent archaeological research on the Irish town', in H. Jager, ed., *Stadtkernforschung,* Koln and Wien, 1987, 321–370.

Brady, C. and Gillespie, R. eds., *Natives and Newcomers: essays on the making of Irish colonial society, 1534–1641,* Dublin, 1986.

Brady, C., 'Court, castle and country', in Brady and Gillespie eds., 1986, 22–49.

Brannon, N.F., 'Recent archaeological excavations in Downpatrick', *Lecale Misc.*, I, 1983, 27–9.

Brereton, W., *Travels in Ireland, 1635*, ed. Falkiner 1904, IV, 368–419.

Brewer, J.N., *The Beauties of Ireland*, 2 vols., London, 1825.

Buckley, M.J.C., 'The town wall of Youghal', *JCHAS,* VI, 1900, 156–61.

——, 'Notes for a visit' (Youghal), *JRSAI,* XXXIII, 1903, 307–32.

Burke, G.L, *The Making of Dutch Towns*, London, 1956.

Burke, N.T., 'Dublin's north-eastern city wall', *PRIA,* LXXIV C, 1974, 113–32.

Butler, L., 'Planned Anglo-Norman towns in Wales', in Clarke and Simms eds., II, 1985, 469–76.

Butler, W.F.T., 'Town life in medieval Ireland', *JCHAS,* VII, 1901, 17–27, 80–90 and 205–15.

Butlin, R.A. ed., *The Development of the Irish Town*, London, 1977.

——, 'Urban and proto-urban settlements', in Butlin ed., 1977, 1 1–25.

——, 'Irish towns in the 16th and 17th centuries', in Butlin ed., 1977, 62–97.

——, 'Urban genesis in Ireland, 1556–1641', in Steel and Lawton eds., 1967, 211–25.

Cahill, M. and Ryan, M., 'An investigation of the town wall at Abbey St., Wexford', *JOWS,* VIII, 1980–1, 56–61.

Camblin, G., *The Town in Ulster*, Belfast, 1951.

Camden, W., *Britannia,* London, 1587; revised ed. 1753.

Campbell, T., *A Philosophical Survey of the South of Ireland*, Dublin, 1778.

Canny, P., *The Elizabethan Conquest of Ireland*, Hassocks, 1976.

——, *From Reformation to Restoration . . . ,* Dublin, 1981.

Carrigan, W., *The History and Antiquities of the Diocese of Ossory*, 4 vols., Dublin, 1905.

Carroll, J.S., 'Some notes on Waterford's maps and plans', *Decies,* XX, 1982, 29–38.

——, 'Aspects of 18th and early l9th century Waterford city', *Decies,* XXVII, 1984, 13–21.

——, 'A century of change, 1764–1871', *Decies,* XXXI, 1986, 17–27.

Carter, H., *The Towns of Wales,* Cardiff, 1965.

——, *The Study of Urban Geography*, London, 1972.

——, 'Phases of town growth', in Dyos ed., 1968, 231–52.

Caulfield, R. ed., *The Council Book of the Corporation of the City of Cork*, Guildford, 1876.

——, *The Council Book of . . . Youghal*, Guildford, 1878.

——, *The Council Book of . . . Kinsale,* Guildford, 1879.

Clark, P. ed., *The Early Modern Town*, London, 1976.

Clarke, M., *The Book of Maps of the Dublin City Surveyors, 1695–1827,* Dublin, 1983.

Clarke, H.B., 'The topographical development of early Norman Dublin', *JRSAI,* CVIII, 1977, 29–51.

——, *Dublin c. 840–1540* (map), Dublin, 1978.

——, and Simms, A. eds., *The Comparative History of Urban Origins in Non-Roman Europe*, 2 vols., Oxford, 1985.

——, 'The mapping of medieval Dublin', in Clarke and Simms eds. 1985, II, 617–40.

Colvin, H.M. ed., *The History of the King's Works*, London, 1963.

Comerford, M., *Collections relating to the Diocese of Kildare and Leighlin*, 3 vols., Dublin, 1883–6.

Cooper, A., *An 18th century Antiquary—sketches and notes*, ed. Price, L., Dublin, 1942.

Cosgrove, A., *Late Medieval Ireland*, Dublin, 1981.

——, and McCartney, D. eds., *Studies in Irish History*, Dublin, 1979.

——, 'Hiberniores ipsis Hibernis', in Cosgrove and McCartney eds., 1979, 1–14.

Croker, T.C., *Researches in the South of Ireland*, London, 1824.

Cromwell. 0., *Writings and speeches*, ed. W.C. Abbott, Harvard, 1947.

Cromwell, T., *Excursions through Ireland*, 2 vols., London, 1820.

Cullen, L., *Life in Ireland*, London, 1968.

——, *Irish Towns and Villages*, Dublin, 1979.

Cunningham, G., *The Anglo-Norman Advance into the South-west Midlands of Ireland, 1185–1221.* Roscrea, 1987.

Curtis, E., *A History of Medieval Ireland*, London, 1938.

——, 'Norse Dublin', DHR, IV, 1942, 96–108.

D'Alton, J., *History of Dublin*, Dublin, 1838.

——, *The History of Drogheda . . .* , Dublin, 1844.

——, and O'Flanagan, J.R., *The History of Dundalk . . .* Dublin, 1864.

Davies & Quinn eds., *Pipe rolls* (section II(A) above).

Delaney, T.G., 'The archaeology of the Irish town', in Barley ed., 1977, 47–64.

Dickinson, R.E., *The West European City*, London, 1961.

Dineley, T., 'Journal of a visit, 1681' (NLI ms 392), ed. E.P. Shirley, JRSAI, IV, 1856; VII, 1862; and F.E. Ball, VIII, 1865, serialised.

Doherty, C., 'The monastic town in early medieval Ireland', in Clarke and Simms eds., 1985, I, 45–69.

Dolley, M., *Anglo-Norman Ireland*, Dublin, 1973.

Duffy, P.J., 'The nature of the medieval frontier in Ireland', *Stud Hib,* XXII-XXIII, 1982-3, 21–37.

Dunlop, R., 'Sixteenth century maps of Ireland', *EHR,* XX, 1905, 309–37.

——, *Ireland under the Commonwealth*, Manchester, 1913.

——, 'An unpublished survey of the plantation of Munster, 1622', *JRSAI,* LIV, 1924, 128–46.

Dunton, J., *Letters,* ed. MacLysaght 1939, app. 2.

Dutton, H., *Statistical Survey of the County of Galway,* Dublin, 1824.

Dyos, H.J., *The Study of Urban History*, London, 1968.

Eachard, L., *An Exact Description of Ireland*, London, 1691.

Edwards, R.D., *An Atlas of Irish History*, London, 1973.

Ellis, S.G., 'Irish customs under the early Tudors', *IHS,* XXII, 1981, 271–4.

——, *Tudor Ireland, 1470–1603*, London, 1985.

Empey, C.A., 'The manor of Carrick-on-Suir in the middle ages', *JBS,* II, 1982, 206–8.

——, 'Sacred and secular . . . Kells-in-Ossory', *IHS, XXIV,* 1984, 131–49.

——, 'The Norman period, 1185–1500', in Nolan ed.,1985, 71–91.

Ennen, E., 'The early history of the European town, a retrospective view (dated 1977), in Clarke and Simms eds., 1985, I, 4–11.

Falkiner, C.L. ed., *Illustrations of Irish History and Topography*, London, 1904.

Falkus, M. and Gillingham, J. eds., *Historical Atlas of Britain,* London, 1981.

Ferrar, J., *The History of Limerick, Ecclesiastical, Civil, and Military,* Limerick, 1787.

Fleming, J. S., *The Town Wall Fortifications of Ireland*, Paisley, 1914.

Fitzgerald, P. and M' Gregor, J.J., *The History, Topography and Antiquities of the County and City of Limerick*, 2 vols., Dublin, 1826–27.

Fitzgerald, W., 'The castle and manor of Carlow', *JKAS,* VI, 1909–11, 311–38 and 365–97.

Frame, R., *Colonial Ireland, 1169–1369*, Dublin,1981.

——, *English Lordship in Ireland*, 1318–61, Oxford, 1982.

——, 'War and peace in the medieval lordship of Ireland', in Lydon ed., 1984, 119–142.

Gale, P., *An Inquiry into the Ancient Corporate System of Ireland*, London, 1834.

Garstin, J.R. ed., 'County Louth OS letters', *CLAJ,* IV,1916, 93.

Gernon, L., 'A discourse on Ireland, c. 1620', in Falkiner ed., 1904, III, 352–5.

Gilbert, J.T., *A History of the City of Dublin*, 3 vols., Dublin, 1854–59.

——, *A Contemporary History of Affairs in Ireland from 1641–1652*, 3 vols., Dublin, 1879–80.

——, *A Jacobite Narrative of the War in Ireland*, Dublin, 1892.

Gillespie, E. ed., *The Liberties of Dublin*, Dublin, 1973.

Gillingham, J. and Holt, J.C. eds., *War and Government in the Middle Ages,* Cambridge, 1984.

Giraldus Cambrensis, *Expugnatio Hibernica, 1187,* ed./trans. A.B. Scott and F.X. Martin, Dublin, 1978; T. Forester and T. Wright, London, 1863.

Glasscock, R.E., 'Moated sites and deserted boroughs and villages', in Stephens and Glasscock eds., 1970,163–173.

——, 'Deserted medieval settlements (Ireland)', in Beresford and Hurst eds.,1971, IV, 289–296.

Gosling, P., *A Survey and Report on the Archaeology of Dundalk Town and District*, Dundalk, 1982.

Gowen, M., 'A bibliography of contemporary plans of late 16th and 17th century artillery fortifications in Ireland', *I. Sword,* XIV, 1980–81, 230–235.

Graham, B.J., 'Anglo-Norman settlement in Co. Meath, PRIA, LXXV C, 1975, 224–247.

——, 'The documentation of medieval Irish boroughs', *BGSIHS,* IV, 1977, 9–20, and V, 1978, 41–45.

——, 'The towns of medieval Ireland', in Butlin ed., 1977, 28–60, app.I.

——, 'The evolution of urbanisation in Ireland', *J Hist Geog,* V,1979, 111–125.

——, *Medieval Irish Settlement: a review*, Norwich, 1980.

Graham, B.J., 'Anglo-Norman settlement in Ireland', *GSIHS*, I, 1985,

——, 'Urban genesis in early medieval Ireland', *J Hist Geog*, XIII, 1987, 3–16 and 61–3.

——, 'Medieval settlement in Co. Roscommon', *PRIA*, LXXXVIII C, 1988, 19–38.

——, 'The definition and classification of medieval Irish towns', *I. Geog*, XXI, 1988, 20–32.

Graves, J. and Prim, J.G.A., 'The history, architecture and antiquities of the aity of Kilkenny', *JRSAI*, III, 1859, 322–31.

Grose, F., *Antiquities of Ireland*, ed. J. Ledwich, 2 vols., London, 1791–1797.

Gross, C., *A Bibliography of British (and Irish) Municipal History*, New York, 1897 (reprint ed. G.H. Martin and S. MacIntyre, Leicester, 1972.).

Gutkind, E.A., *International History of City Development*, 4 vols., London, 1964–69.

Gwynn, A. and Hadcock, R.N., *Medieval Religous Houses: Ireland*, London, 1970; reprint Dublin, 1988.

Haliday, C., *The Scandinavian Kingdom of Dublin*, Dublin, 1884.

Hall, Mr and Mrs S.C., *Ireland and its Scenery*, 3 vols., London, 1841–3.

Hamlin, A. and Lynn, C. eds., *Pieces of the Past*, Belfast, 1988.

Hanmer, M., ed., 'The Chronicle of Ireland, 1571', in Theiner, A. ed., *Vetera Monumenta Hibernorum et Scotorum Historiam Illustrantia*, Rome, 1864; reprint Osnabruck, 1969.

Hardiman, J., *The History of the Town of . . . Galway*, Dublin, 1820.

Harkness, D. and O'Dowd, M. eds., *The Town in Ireland*, Belfast, 1981.

Harris, W. ed., *Hibernica*, Dublin, 1747.

Harvey, A., *The Castles and Walled Towns of England*, London, 1911.

Hayes, R.J. ed., *Manuscript Sources for the History of Irish Civilisation*, 11 vols., Boston (Mass), 1966.

Hayman, S., *Memorials of Youghal*, Youghal, 1879.

Healy, P., 'The town walls of Dublin', in Gillespie ed., 1973,16–23.

Healy, W., *History and Antiquities of Kilkenny*, Kilkenny, 1893.

Heighway, C.M. ed., *The Erosion of History: archaeology and planning in towns*, London, 1972.

Hensel, W., 'The origin of western and eastern Slav towns', *World Arch*, I, 1969–70, 51–59.

Hinton, E.M., *Ireland through Tudor eyes*, Philadelphia, 1935.

Historic monuments of Northern Ireland: Guide, Belfast, 1963; revised 1983.

Hogan, E. ed., *A Description of Ireland, 1598*, Dublin, 1878.

Holinshed, R., *The Chronicles of England, Scotlande and Irelande*, 1577; reprint ed. J. Hooker, London, 1807–08.

Hore, H.F. ed., 'A description of Ulster, 1586', *UJA*, II, 1854, 137–151.

Hore, H.F. and Graves, J. eds., *The Social State of the Southern and Eastern Counties of Ireland in the 16th Century*, Dublin, 1870.

Hore, P.H., ed., *History of the Town and County of Wexford*, 6 vols., London, 1900–11.

Hughes, T. Jones, 'The origin and growth of Irish towns', *Univ Rev*, II, 1960, 8–15.

Hunter, R.J., 'Towns in the Ulster plantation', *Stud Hib*, XI, 1971, 40–79.

——, 'Ulster plantation towns', in Harkness and O'Dowd eds., 1981, 55–80.

Hurley, M. and Power, D., 'The medieval town wall of Cork', *JCHAS*, LXXXVI, 1981, 1–20.

Hurley, M.F., 'Excavations in medieval Cork', *JCHAS*, XCI, 1986, 1–25.

'Irish Society', *A Concise View of the Origins . . . of the Honourable Society . . . of London*, London, 1842.

Jones, S.J., 'The growth of Bristol', *TIBG*, XI, 1946, 55–83.

Jope, E.M., 'Excavations at Carrickfergus', *UJA*, XIII, 1950, 61–5.

——, 'Fortification to architecture in the north of Ireland', *UJA*, XXIII, 1960, 97–123.

——, ed., *Archaeological Survey of County Down*, Belfast, 1966.

Joyce, P.W., *Irish Names of Places*, 3 vols., Dublin, 1873–1913.

Kelly, E.P., 'Recent investigations at Navan', *R na M*, VII, 1982–83, 76–85.

Kenyon, K., *Digging up Jericho*, London, 1957.

Kerrigan, P.M., 'Seventeenth century fortifications, forts and garrisons in Ireland', *I. Sword*, XIV, 1980–81, 3–24 and 135–154.

——, 'The fortifications of Waterford, 1495–1690', *Decies*, XXIX, 1985, 13–23.

Killanin, Lord, and Duignan, M.V., *Shell Guide to Ireland*, London, 1967.

King, J., *History of Kerry*, Liverpool, 1908.

Leask, H.G., 'The ancient walls of Limerick', NMAJ, II, 1941, 95–108.

——, *Irish Castles and Castellated Houses*, Dundalk, 1944.

——, *St. Patrick's Rock and Cashel*, Dublin, n.d.

Lee, J. ed., *Ireland - Towards a Sense of Place*, Cork, 1985.

Lenihan, M., *Limerick, its History and Antiquities*, Dublin, 1866.

Lennon, C., *Richard Stanyhurst, the Dubliner*, Dublin, 1981.

Lewis, S., *A Topographical Dictionary of Ireland*, 2 vols., London,

Little, G.A., *Dublin before the Vikings*, Dublin, 1957.

Lobel, M.D. ed., *Historic Towns*, I, London and Oxford, 1969.
Loeber, R., 'A biographical dictionary of engineers in Ireland, 1600–1730', *I. Sword*, XIII, 1977–79, 32–313.
Luckombe, P., *A Tour through Ireland, 1779*, London, 1780.
Lydon, J., 'Richard II's expeditions to Ireland', *JRSAI*, XCIII, 1963, 135–70.
——, 'The Bruce invasion', *Hist Stud*, IV, 1963, 111–121.
——, 'The problem of the frontier in medieval Ireland', *Topic*, XIII, 1967, 5–22.
——, *The Lordship of Ireland in the Middle Ages*, Dublin, 1972.
——, *Ireland in the Later Middle Ages*, Dublin, 1973.
——, 'The city of Waterford in the later middle ages', *Decies*, XII, 1979, 5–15.
——, ed., *England and Ireland in the Later Middle Ages*, Dublin, 1981.
——, ed., *The English in Medieval Ireland*, Dublin,1984.
Lynch, A., 'Excavations of the medieval town defences at Charlotte's Quay, Limerick', *PRIA*, LXXXIV C, 1984, 281–320.
——, 'Dublin castle', *Med Arch*, XXXI, 1987, 266.
Lynch, W., *A View on Legal Institutions . . . during the Reign of Henry II*, London, 1830.
McCraith, L. M., *The Suir from Source to Sea*, Clonmel, 1912.
McCurtain, M., *Tudor and Stuart Ireland*, Dublin, 1972.
McEneaney, E., 'Waterford and New Ross trade competition c. 1300', *Decies*, XII, 1979, 16–24.
MacLysaght, E., *Irish Life in the Seventeenth Century*, Dublin, 1969.
McNeill, T. E., *Anglo-Norman Ulster*, Edinburgh,1980.
MacNiocaill, G. ed., *Na Buirgéisí*, (section II(B) above).
——, G., *Ireland before the Vikings*, Dublin, 1972.
——, 'Socio-economic problems of the late medieval Irish town', in Harkness and O'Dowd eds., 1981, 9–20.
——, 'The colonial town in Irish documents', in Clarke and Simms eds.,1985, II, 373–78.
Maher, J., 'Francis Place in Drogheda . . . ', *JRSAI*, LXIV, 1934, 41–53.
Maitland, F. W., *Township and Borough*, Cambridge, 1897.
Martin, G. H., 'New beginnings in north-west Europe', in Barley ed., 1977, 405–13.
——, 'Plantation boroughs in medieval Ireland', in Harkness and O'Dowd eds., 1981, 23–31.
Maxwell, C., *Irish History from Contemporary Sources, 1509–1610*, London, 1923.
——, *Country and Town in Ireland under the Georges*, London, 1940.
——, *The Stranger in Ireland*, London, 1954.
Maxwell, N. ed., *Digging up Dublin*, Dublin, 1980.
Milligan, C. D., *The Walls of Derry*, 2 vols., Londonderry, 1948–50.
Moody, T.W., 'Sir Thomas Phillips', IHS, I, 1938–39, 254–62.
——, *The Londonderry Plantation, 1609–41*, Belfast, 1939.
——, and F.X. Martin eds., *The Course of Irish History*, Cork, 1967.
——, and Simms, J.G. eds., *The Bishopric of Derry and the Irish Society of London*, 2 vols., Dublin, 1968–82.
Moore, M., 'City walls and gateway at St. Martin's Castle, Waterford', *Decies*, XXIII, 1983, 49–62.
Moryson, F., *Travels 1617*, ed. Falkiner, 1904, 156–9.
Mulloy, S., 'French engineers with the Jacobite army in Ireland, 1689–91', *I. Sword*, XV, 1983, 222–32.
Mumford, L., *The City in History*, London, 1961.
Murphy, D., *Cromwell in Ireland*, Dublin, 1883.
Murray, R.H., *Revolutionary Ireland and its Settlement*, London, 1911.
Murtagh, B., 'The castles of Naas', *JKAS*, XVI, 1983–84, 355–8.
Murtagh, H. ed., *Irish Midland Studies*, Athlone, 1980.
——, 'The town wall fortifications of Athlone', in Murtagh ed., 1980, 89–106.
Musgrave, R., *Memoirs of Rebellions in Ireland*, London, 1801.
National Gallery of Ireland: de Courcy, C. and Maher, A., *Fifty Views of Ireland*, Dublin, 1985.
National Monuments of Ireland, Dublin, 1964.
National Museum of Ireland, *Viking and Medieval Dublin: excavations 1962–73*, Dublin, 1973.
Nicholls, K.W., *Gaelic and Gaelicised Ireland in the Middle Ages*, Dublin, 1972.
——, 'Anglo-French Ireland and after', *Peritia*, I, 1982, 370–402.
Nolan, W. ed., *Tipperary: History and Society,* Dublin, 1985.
O'Brien, B., *Munster at War*, Cork, 1971.
O'Connor, G.B., *Elizabethan Ireland, Native and Irish,* Dublin, 1906.
O'Connor, P.J., *Exploring Limerick's Past*, Newcastle West, 1987.
O'Flanagan, P., 'Bandon', *IHTA*, fascicle III,1988.
O'Riordain, B., 'Excavations at High and Winetavern streets, Dublin', *Med Arch*, XV, 1971, 73–85; XVI, 1972, 168.

O'Riordain, B., 'High Street excavation', in Almqvist and Greene eds., 1976, 135–41.

Orpen, G.H., 'Mote and bretesche building in Ireland', *EHR*, XXI, 1906, 417–44.

——, Motes and Norman castles in Ireland, EHR, XXII, 1907, 228–54.

——, *Ireland under the Normans, 1169–1333*, 4 vols., Oxford, 1911–20.

——, 'The Earldom of Ulster', *JRSAI*, XLIII, 1913, 30–46 and 133–43.

O'Sullivan, M.D., 'The fortification of Galway in the 16th and 17th centuries', *JGAHS*, XVI, 1934, 3–46.

——, Barnaby Gooche, *JGAHS*, XVIII, 1938, 7–32.

——, *Old Galway: the history of a Norman colony in Ireland*, Cambridge, 1942.

——, *Italian Merchant Bankers in Ireland in the 13th Century*, Dublin, 1962.

O'Sullivan, T. F., *Goodly Barrow*, Dublin, 1983.

O'Sullivan, W., *The Economic History of Cork City*, Dublin, 1937.

Otway-Ruthven, A.J., 'The character of Norman settlement in Ireland', *Hist Stud*, V, 1965, 75–84.

——, *A History of Medieval Ireland*, London, 1968.

de Paor, L., 'Viking towns in Ireland', in Almqvist and Greene eds., 1976, 29–37.

Pender, S. ed., *Census of Ireland c. 1659*, Dublin, 1939.

——, *Waterford Merchants Abroad*, Cork, 1964.

Petty, W., *The Political Anatomy of Ireland, 1672*, ed C.H. Hull, Cambridge, 1899.

——, *Hiberniae Deliniatio* (Atlas of Ireland), (no place), 1685,

Phillips, J.R.S., 'Anglo-Norman nobility', in Lydon ed.,1984, 88–104.

Phillips,T., *Londonderry and the London Companies*, ed. D.A. Chart, Belfast, 1928.

Pirenne, H., *Medieval Cities*, Princeton, 1925.

Platt, C., *The English Medieval Town*, London, 1979.

Pococke, R., *Pococke's tour in Ireland in 1752*, ed. G.T. Stokes, Dublin, 1891.

Quinn, D.B., 'Ireland and 16th century European expansion', *Hist Stud*, I, 1958, 20–30.

——, *The Elizabethans and the Irish*, Ithaca (NY), 1966.

Regan, M., *History of Ireland, a fragment*, ed Harris, 1747, 4–21.

Richardson, H.G. and Sayles, G.O. eds., *Parliaments and Councils of Medieval Ireland*, Dublin, 1947.

Richter, M., 'The interpretation of medieval Irish society', *IHS*, XXIV, 1985, 290–8.

Robertson, J.G., *The Antiquities and Scenery of the County of Kilkenny*, 1851, Clifden, 1983.

Robinson, P.S., *The Plantation of Ulster*, Dublin, 1984.

——, 'Carrickfergus', *IHTA*, fascicle II, 1986.

de Rochford, J. A., 'A Description of Ireland after the Restoration', ed. Falkiner, 1904.

Rogers, R., 'Aspects of the military history of the Anglo-Norman invasion of Ireland', *I. Sword*, XVI, 1986,135–44.

Rowan, A., *North West Ulster*, Harmondsworth, 1979.

Russell, J.C., *Medieval Regions and their Cities*, Newton Abbot, 1972.

Rynne, E. ed., *North Munster Studies*, Limerick, 1967.

Sawyer, P., *The Age of the Vikings*, London, 1962.

——, 'The Vikings in Ireland', in Whitelock et al., 1982, 345–61.

Scott, B.G. ed., *Studies in Early Ireland*, Belfast, 1982.

Seward, W.W., *Topographia Hibernica*, Dublin, 1795.

Shaffrey, P., *The Irish Town*, Dublin, 1975.

Sheehan, A.J., 'The Munster rebellion, 1598', *I. Sword*, XV, 1982, 11–20.

Shell Guide to Ireland, ed. Lord Killanin and M.V. Duignan, London, 1967.

Shields, H., 'The walling of New Ross', *Long Room*, XII-XIII, 1975–76, 24–33.

Sieveking, G., Longworth, I. and Wilson, K. eds., *Problems in Economic and Social Archaeology*, London, 1976.

Simpson, M.L. and Dickson, A., 'Excavations in Carrickfergus, 1972–9', *Med Arch*, XXV, 1981,78–89.

Simms, A., 'Geographical implications of Wood Quay', *I. Geog Newsletter*, 2, 1978, 7–11.

——, 'Medieval Dublin', *I. Geog*, XII, 1979, 25–41.

——, 'Cartographic representation of diachronic analysis: the example of the origin of towns', in Baker and Billinge eds., 1982, 289–98.

Simms, J.G., 'Civil Survey, 1654–6', *IHS*, IX, 1954–5, 253–61.

——, *Jacobite Ireland*, London,1969.

Smith, C., *The Ancient and Present State of the County and City of Waterford*, Dublin, 1745.

——, *The Ancient and Present State of the County and City of Cork*, Dublin,1750; revised ed. 1774.

——., *The Ancient and Present State of the County of Kerry*, Dublin, 1756.

Smith, C.T., *An Historical Geography of Western Europe before 1800*, London, 1967.

Smith, A.P., *Celtic Leinster*, Dublin, 1982.

Smith, W.J. and Whelan, K. eds., *Common Ground: essays on the historical geography of Ireland*, Cork, 1988.

Soulsby, I., *The Towns of Medieval Wales*, Chichester, 1983.

Speed, J., *Theatre of the Empire of Great Britain*, London, 1611–12.

Spenser, E., *A View of the Present State of Ireland, 1596*, ed. Ware, Dublin, 1633; W.L. Renwick, Oxford, 1970.

Stanyhurst, R., *Chronicles of Ireland*, ed. Holinshed 1586.

Steel, R.W. and Lawton, R. eds., *Liverpool Essays in Georaphy*, London, 1967.

Stenton, D.M., *English Society in the Early Middle Ages*, Harmondsworth, 1967.

Stephens, N. and Glasscock, R.E. eds., *Irish Geographical Studies*, Belfast, 1970.

Stevens, J., *Journal 1688–91*, ed. R.H. Murray, Oxford, 1912.

Story, G., *A True and Impartial History . . .* , London, 1691.

Swan, L., 'Monastic proto-towns in early medieval Ireland', in Clarke and Simms eds.,1985, I, 77–99.

Tait, J., *The Medieval English Borough*, Manchester, 1936.

Taylor, A.J., *Caernarvon Castle and Town Walls*, London, 1953.

——, *Conway Castle and Town Walls*, London, 1957.

——, 'The King's works in Wales, 1277–1330', in Colvin ed., 1963.

Thomas, A., 'Drogheda, 1574', *CLAHS*, XVIII, 1975, 179–86.

——, 'Financing town walls in medieval Ireland', in C. Thomas ed. , 1986, 65–91.

Thomas, C. ed., *Rural Landscapes and Communities*, Dublin, 1986.

Tichborne, H., 'A letter . . . Siege of Tredagh (Drogheda) 1641', in J. Temple ed., *The Irish Rebellion of 1641*, Dublin, 1724, 173–99.

Tikhomirov, M.N., *The Towns of Ancient Rus*, Moscow, 1959.

Tout, T.F., *Medieval Town Planning*, Manchester, 1948.

Treadwell, V.W., 'Irish customs administration in the 16th century', *IHS*, XX, 1977, 386–416.

Turner, H., *Town Defences in England and Wales*, London, 1970.

Twohig, D.C., 'Cork city excavations, 1974–7', *BGSIHS*, V, 1978,19–22.

Vallancey, C. ed, *Collectanea de Rebus Hibernicis*, 6 vols., Dublin, 1770–1804.

Victoria County History of the Counties of England, London and Oxford, 1907-.

Wallace, P.F., 'Anglo-Norman Dublin', in O'Corrain ed., 1981, 247–68.

——, 'The origins of Dublin', in Scott ed., 1982,129–39.

——, 'The archaeology of Viking and Anglo-Norman Dublin', in Clarke and Simms eds., 1985, I, 103–40 and II, 379–407.

Walsh, A., *Scandinavian Relations with Ireland during the Viking Period*, Dublin, 1922.

Ware. J., *The Antiquities and History of Ireland, 1633*, Dublin, 1705.

Warren, W.L., 'The interpretation of 12th century Irish history', *Hist Stud*, VII, 1969, 1–19.

Waterman, D.M., 'Somersetshire and other foreign building stone in medieval Ireland', *UJA*, XII, 1970, 63–76.

Webb, J.J., *Municipal Government in Ireland*, Dublin, 1918.

Westropp, T.J., 'Early Italian maps of Ireland, 1300–1600', *PRIA*, CXXX, 1912–13, 361–428.

——, *The Antiquities of Limerick and its Neighbourhood*, Dublin, 1916.

Whitelock, D., McKitterick, R. and Dumville, D. eds., *Ireland in Early Medieval Europe*, Cambridge, 1982.

Wilde, W.R., *The Beauties of the Boyne*, Dublin, 1849.

Wilson, D., 'Defence in the Viking age', in Sieveking et al. eds. 1976, 439–43.

Wood, P.D., 'Frontier relics in the Welsh border towns', *Geog*, XLVII, 1962, 54–62.

Woods, C., 'Notes on the town wall of Cork', *JRSAI*, VII, 1882, 636–7; and VII, 1883, 61.

Wright, T., *Louthiana, or an introduction to the antiquities of Ireland*, (no place), 1748.

Young, J.I., 'A note on the Norse occupation of Ireland', *History*, XXXV, 1950, 11–32.

Index